Change(d) Agents

New Teachers of Color
in Urban Schools

Change(d) Agents

New Teachers of Color
in Urban Schools

BETTY ACHINSTEIN
RODNEY T. OGAWA
Foreword by Ana María Villegas

Teachers College, Columbia University
New York and London

Published by Teachers College Press, 1234 Amsterdam Avenue, New York, NY 10027

Library of Congress Cataloging-in-Publication Data

Achinstein, Betty.
   Change(d) agents : new teachers of color in urban schools / Betty Achinstein, Rodney T. Ogawa; foreword by Ana Maria Villegas.
      p. cm.
   Includes bibliographical references and index.
   ISBN 978-0-8077-5218-0 (pbk. : alk. paper)
   ISBN 978-0-8077-5219-7 (hardcover : alk. paper)
     1. English language—Study and teaching (Secondary)—United States. 2. Language arts (Secondary)—United States. 3. Urban youth—Education (Secondary)—United States. 4. Urban schools—United States. 5. Minorities—Education—United States. I. Ogawa, Rodney T. II. Title.
   LC5119.8.A34 2011
   371.820973—dc22   2011001959

ISBN 978-0-8077-5218-0 (paper)
ISBN 978-0-8077-5219-7 (hardcover)

Printed on acid-free paper
Manufactured in the United States of America

18   17   16   15   14   13   12   11   8   7   6   5   4   3   2   1

This book is dedicated to the extraordinary new teachers of color who participated in this study and are working to improve educational opportunities for students of color.

We also dedicate this book to Chad and Adin, for their exceptional support of Betty, and to Chris for her superb support of Rod.

Contents

Foreword

An expanding body of research suggests that students of color benefit academically from exposure to teachers of color. It is not surprising, then, that 31 states currently have policies aimed at increasing the racial/ethnic diversity of the teaching force. While much is now known about strategies for recruiting people of color into teaching, little empirical work has been devoted to understanding the experiences of new teachers of color in the profession. *Change(d) Agents: New Teachers of Color in Urban Schools*, by Betty Achinstein and Rodney Ogawa, expertly addresses this glaring gap in the literature.

This thoughtful book draws on a 5-year study of 21 teachers of color committed to using their cultural and linguistic knowledge to transform school practices to improve the education of students of color enrolled in high-poverty urban schools. Skillfully building on the teacher diversity and teacher socialization literatures, the authors propose a framework for understanding the cultural/professional roles of teachers of color as well as the personal and school-related experiences that shape the teachers' development. While the book conveys the strong commitment the new teachers of color brought to their chosen profession, it also captures the palpable frustration most of them experienced as they struggled to maintain their focus on improving education for students who have been left behind in the face of the powerful reproductive forces of schools.

The book masterfully depicts many ways these reproductive forces are enacted in schools daily. We see with great clarity how intense pressure to raise students' scores on state-mandated tests leads low-performing urban schools to adopt standardized instructional programs that focus on teaching to tests, using tightly prescribed and non-inclusive curricula, and maintaining a predetermined pace. Such conditions severely constrained the teachers' use of their own and their students' cultural and linguistic resources in the teaching/learning process and profoundly complicated the teachers' ability to establish trusting relationships with students.

A unique contribution of this book is the insight it offers into the internal struggles of the new teachers of color as they tried to use their cultural expertise to change schools from within. Finding themselves in settings that undermined the cultural/professional roles that brought them to teaching, the teachers were overcome by a sense of unresolvable tension that ultimately led them to make accommodations to the system. The intense pain the teachers experienced in letting go of the vision that originally inspired them to become teachers is powerfully illuminated in a set of moving vignettes.

Change(d) Agents: New Teachers of Color in Urban Schools raises critical questions about current policies that seek to diversify the racial/ethnic makeup of the teaching profession by focusing on recruitment while ignoring the conditions of the schools in which the new recruits must work. Achinstein and Ogawa make a convincing case that to maximize the promise of a diverse teaching force, schools must acknowledge the cultural capital teachers of color bring to the profession and actively support them in enacting culturally/linguistically responsive practices. Everyone concerned with improving the learning opportunities and outcomes of students of color should read this book.

—Ana María Villegas

Acknowledgments

We wish to express our gratitude to the participating teachers and educators in this study who shared so generously. We acknowledge the support for this research provided by the Flora Family Foundation. We appreciate Sally Hewlett for her undying commitment to this work. We recognize the significant contributions of the entire research team on the broader study on new teachers of color, including Michael Strong, Julia Aguirre, Lisa Johnson, Candice Tigerman, Anthony Villar, Sally Hewlett, Iris Weaver, Dena Sexton, Carrie Cifka Herrera, Casia Freitas, and Anthony Kuan. Thanks to Maura Furness, Ruchi Agarwal, Victoria Mata, Victoria Lee, Jennifer Wegner, and Kim Anderson for their support in this project. We thank the New Teacher Center, University of California, Santa Cruz; Ellen Moir, its executive director; and the staff at the center. Thank you to the Collaborative on Diversifying Teaching and Schooling group, who moved this work forward, including Gloria Ladson-Billings, Linda Darling-Hammond, Richard Ingersoll, Ana María Villegas, Jacqueline Jordan Irvine, Jeannie Oakes, Susan Moore Johnson, Ellen Moir, and Michael Strong. We especially want to acknowledge Ana María Villegas, Steven Z. Athanases, Geert Kelchtermans, Ken Zeichner, Ricardo Stanton-Salazar, and Victoria Lee for providing invaluable feedback on the manuscript. A final thanks goes to Brian Ellerbeck and the team at Teachers College Press.

CHAPTER 1

The Promise and Challenge of Diversifying the Teaching Profession

Because educators and policymakers have called for diversifying the teaching profession, this book examines the lives of new teachers of color who are committed to working in urban, high-needs schools that serve students of color. The experiences of these teachers reveal the promises and tensions they encountered in the schools where they work. Carmen's[1] tale illustrates the kinds of challenges that novice teachers of color who are strongly committed to serving students from non-dominant cultural communities may encounter in their schools.

CARMEN'S TALE

Carmen identifies as a Chicana, a first-generation Mexican American and native Spanish speaker. As a student in a public high school, she became president of the Latino organization. Carmen attended a state university, where she majored in Chicano studies and participated in community activities tutoring youth, teaching English language learners (ELLs) in a "newcomers" program, and working with inmates to prepare them for college. She co-chaired Moviementos Estudiantil Chicano de Aztlan (MEChA) and played a central role in organizing voters against Proposition 227, the English-only ballot initiative in California.

Carmen became a teacher to serve Chicano/a students: "There's such a need for Chicana educators, and there's not many of us. . . . I really want to become a teacher to promote that philosophy of social justice." She attended a highly regarded teacher education program focused on promoting culturally responsive and socially just teachers who work in urban, "hard to staff" schools. She was committed to teaching in culturally responsive ways, connecting her content and pedagogy to her students' cultures and lives, and teaching for change.

The school where Carmen chose to teach, like many large, urban high schools in California, was underresourced and categorized as a "program improvement school," ranking at the lowest level of the state's accountability scale. Large percentages of the school's students lived in poverty and were members of non-dominant cultural and linguistic communities. The school generally lacked a supportive professional culture, particularly for novices. This was marked by the lack of teacher involvement in decisionmaking, the absence of collaboration among teachers, their lack of control over curriculum and pedagogy, and the school's weak relations with its students' parents and community. The school did not support culturally and linguistically responsive teaching or dialogue about issues of race or equity. Carmen felt that the school did not create conditions that tapped her or her students' cultural and linguistic knowledge or lived experiences. The English language learners, with whom Carmen particularly chose to work, experienced marginalization and fewer resources in the "ELL track." The school had high turnover rates among both teachers and administrators.

Carmen continued to teach at her school and was entering her 5th year (beating the turnover odds of most new teachers in urban schools) even though she faced enormous challenges. Yet in many ways Carmen's tale marks a pyrrhic victory, because while she remained in teaching and at her school, she lost her vision:

> I've lost my vision by being at this school, . . . The socially just and culturally relevant teaching we talked about in preservice—I don't even know what that is anymore. That's not talked about at all, cultural relevance and social justice. . . . In fact I feel like we just go to teach and that's it, not connect with the students or anything. This is growing on me and it's suffocating.

As a new teacher, Carmen's cultural and linguistic backgrounds were marginalized and suppressed. While she chose to work with students who were English language learners in hopes of engaging in culturally and linguistically responsive teaching, conditions in her school resulted in her losing her voice and vision. Carmen's tale highlights the destructive dilemma that teachers of color confront. People of color may enter teaching with a vision of utilizing their cultural resources to contribute to transforming the educational system and may have even experienced a teacher education program that fostered such approaches. However, novice teachers of color, such as Carmen, often work in schools that do not support their efforts to be culturally and linguistically responsive teachers or agents of change for students of color. This underscores the need to examine more closely the impact of school conditions on the induction of new teachers of color who enter the profession bearing a critical frame. As Carmen's tale demonstrates, new teachers of color may not be supported in ways that acknowledge, value, and develop their cultural practices in support of students of color. Thus, they experience a form of "culturally subtractive schooling," where becoming a professional can mean leaving one's cultural assets at the schoolhouse door. We build on

Valenzuela's (1999) term *subtractive schooling*, which she identifies for Mexican-descent youth who experience cultural de-capitalization as they enter U.S. schools.

We wrote this book so that educators, policymakers, researchers, and community members would take heed of Carmen's tale as they seek to diversify America's teaching workforce. The experiences of the new teachers of color from the 5-year research study highlighted in this book call for us to make good on our commitment to address both the demographic *and* democratic imperatives for diversifying teaching and schooling.

DEMOGRAPHIC AND DEMOCRATIC IMPERATIVES

Educators and policymakers cite both demographic and democratic imperatives to argue for increasing the racial and cultural diversity of the teacher workforce. The *demographic* imperative notes the disparity between the racial and cultural backgrounds of students and teachers. Nationally, people of color represent 45% of the student population, while only 17% of teachers are people of color (National Center for Education Statistics [NCES], 2010). In California (where cases in this book occurred), 71% of students and just 30% of teachers are people of color (California Department of Education [CDE], 2010a, 2010b). Heightening the demographic imperative is a retention challenge. Analyses of the two most recently reported national Teacher Follow-Up Surveys (2004–2005, 2008–2009) revealed that teachers of color experienced higher rates of turnover than did White teachers (Ingersoll & Connor, 2009; Ingersoll & May, 2010; Marvel, Lyter, Peltola, Strizek, & Morton, 2007).

An underlying assumption of the demographic imperative is that in a pluralistic society it is problematic that public school students (students of color and White students alike) experience a primarily White teaching population (Carnegie Forum on Education and the Economy, 1986; Villegas & Irvine, 2010). Such an argument is sometimes linked to equity of professional opportunities for people of color to remedy the ethnic/racial gap within a labor market. Furthermore, new teachers of color are more likely to seek positions in urban settings with high proportions of low-income, non-dominant communities, thus addressing a workforce challenge in "high-needs" schools (Achinstein, Ogawa, Sexton & Freitas, 2010; Villegas & Geist, 2008).

The *democratic* imperative highlights the failure of schools to serve the educational needs of students of color, as reflected in their disproportionately high dropout rates and the widely documented gap between the test scores of students of color and White students (Haycock, 2001). This imperative underscores the need to improve learning opportunities and achievement for students of color in part by employing teachers of color who may foster culturally and linguistically responsive practices that draw on their own and their students' cultural re sources. Some studies report that teachers of color, when compared to White teachers, positively impact the following outcomes for students of color: standardized test scores, attendance, retention, advanced-level course enrollment, and college-going rates (Clewell, Puma, & McKay, 2005; Dee, 2004; Ehrenberg & Brewer, 1995; England & Meier, 1986; Evans, 1992; Hanushek, 1992; Hanushek, Kain, & Rivkin, 2004; Hanushek, Kain, O'Brien, & Rivkin, 2005; Haycock, 2001; Klopfenstein, 2005; Villegas & Davis, 2008; Villegas & Irvine, 2010). A growing body of research suggests that teachers of color may be particularly capable of meeting the needs of students of color by engaging in culturally responsive practices, serving as role models, and transforming education as change agents to prepare all students to engage in a multicultural democracy (Basit & McNamara, 2004; Beauboeuf-Lafontant, 1999; Foster, 1997; Galindo & Olguin, 1996; Gándara & Maxwell-Jolley, 2000; Irvine, 1989; Ladson-Billings, 1994, 1995, 2001; Quiocho & Rios, 2000; Su, 1997; Villegas & Lucas, 2004; Zeichner, 1996).

A critical element of the democratic imperative is that teachers of color make a significant difference in the school success of students of color. Villegas and Davis's (2008) recent review of research reveals that five of six studies reviewed found a significant relationship between teacher race/ethnicity and the academic performance of students of color, as measured by standardized test scores. The five studies are reported by Clewell and colleagues (2005); Dee (2004); Ehrenberg and Brewer (1995); Evans (1992); and Hanushek (1992), with Ehrenberg, Goldhaber, and Brewer (1995) not finding race-match impacting student achievement. A number of other studies showed that teachers of color had more positive results on students of color than White teachers on measures of academic performance other than standardized test scores, including absenteeism, high school dropout rates, college-going rates, and enrollment rates in advanced-level high school courses (England & Meier, 1986; Farkas, Grobe, Sheehan, & Shuan, 1990; Fraga, Meier, & England, 1986; Hess & Leal, 1997; Klopfenstein, 2005; McIntyre & Pernell, 1983 Meier, Stewart, & England, 1989). However, these studies do not examine how teachers of color produce positive learning outcomes for students of color. To address this issue, another body of literature identifies how learning occurs in a cultural context and reports upon the practices of effective teachers of color for students of color. Research identifies the importance of establishing cultural links between home and school cultures for student learning to occur (Heath 1983; Moll, Amanti, Neff, & Gonzalez, 1992; Tharp & Gallimore 1988) and that teachers of color may understand and bridge such cultural experiences, fostering cultural congruence or cultural synchronicity (Au, 1980; Irvine, 1988). In another recent review, Villegas and Irvine (2010) examine the literature on the potential of teachers of color to improve the academic outcomes and school experiences of students of color. The authors identify five practices that characterize the orientations and pedagogy of effective teachers of color: "(a) having high expectations of students; (b) using culturally relevant teaching; (c) developing caring and trusting relationships with students; (d) confronting issues of racism through teaching; and (e) serving as advocates and cultural brokers" (p. 180).

It is important to note that advocates of increasing diversity in the teacher workforce who cite the demographic and democratic imperatives do not claim White teachers cannot be effective teachers of students of color, that employment segregation should be promoted, or that all teachers of color are effective with students of color. Yet, proponents claim the demographic discrepancy between the racial and cultural backgrounds of teachers and students may contribute to the democratic failure to provide students of color with opportunities to learn (Banks, 1995; Cochran-Smith, 2004a; Dilworth, 1992).

It is also argued that teachers of color serve a democratic imperative in supporting all students, not just those from non-dominant communities. Advocates explain that the presence of teachers of color can provide role models of people of color in positions of authority that can benefit all students, prepare all students for a multicultural society, and promote the values of equality and representation of our democracy (Banks, 2003; Carnegie Forum on Education and the Economy, 1986; Cochran-Smith, 1997; Irvine, 1988, 2003; Villegas & Irvine, 2010). Moreover, the racial makeup of the teacher workforce can send messages to youth about how power is distributed in society (Mercer & Mercer, 1986; Villegas & Lucas, 2004). It is thus not surprising that by 2003 at least 30 states in the United States had adopted minority teacher recruitment policies (Education Commission of the States, 2003).

Employing more new teachers of color will address the numerical challenge of the demographic imperative. However, merely increasing the number and proportion of teachers of color will not address the democratic imperative, which will require that schools increase opportunities to learn for students from low-income and racially and culturally non-dominant communities. While research suggests that teachers of color may have a particular ability to address the educational needs of students of color by performing as role models, teaching in culturally and linguistically responsive ways, and thereby acting as agents of change, this book reveals that the presence of teachers of color is not sufficient. The organization of schools and responses to the policy environment can pose daunting challenges to teachers of color who seek to perform these cultural/professional roles aimed at improving educational opportunities for students of color.

Given the demographic and democratic imperatives, it is critical to understand the factors and contexts that not only attract people of color into the teaching profession but also can sustain these teachers by supporting the development of practices that serve the needs of youth from diverse racial, cultural, and linguistic communities. Ultimately, teachers must be supported by communities, schools, and educational policies that encourage their development as teachers who "'stay the course' of work for social justice across multiple roles and responsibilities" (Cochran-Smith, 2004b, p. 391).

ABOUT THIS BOOK

In this book, we examine the complexities of racially and culturally diversifying the teaching profession by drawing on a 5-year study of the lives of 21 new teachers of color, who are Latina/o, African American, Asian, Filipina/o, and mixed race. These teachers all sought out and attended well-regarded credential- and master's-granting teacher education programs at research universities that explicitly focused on preparing them to teach in culturally/linguistically responsive and socially just ways to improve learning opportunities for urban youth. The teachers all chose to work in urban public schools in northern and southern California that serve low-income and culturally and linguistically non-dominant communities. California was an important site for this study because its large size, racial/ ethnic and linguistically diversity, and active educational reform agenda make it a state that both represents and influences policies on key educational issues. In addition, California is home to a large and growing population of students from non-dominant cultural and linguistic communities, who fare poorly in the state's K–12 education system. A news report documents a 30% dropout rate for Latina/o students, who make up nearly half of California's public school enrollment, and a 42% dropout rate for African American students (Hull & Noguchi, 2008).

This book uncovers a paradox that the new teachers of color who participated in our research confronted: (1) They are deeply committed to improving educational opportunities for students from low-income and culturally and linguistically non-dominant backgrounds by acting as role models, engaging in culturally and linguistically responsive teaching, and thus serving as agents of change in schools. (2) These teachers worked in schools that profoundly limit opportunities and thus challenge their ability to perform these cultural and professional roles.

The chapters of this book unfold to reveal that this paradox has its origins in a "double bind," which occurs when a social system makes contradictory demands on its members—demands that individuals cannot confront, comment on, opt out of, or resolve. People often internalize the contradictions, which contributes to their experiencing personal and interpersonal tensions and turmoil (Bateson, 1972). The paradox that confronted the new teachers of color who participated in our study was rooted in the *systemic contradiction* of the transformational versus reproductive functions of schooling in the United States. The personal and professional commitments of the teachers to improve educational opportunities for students from low-income and culturally/linguistically non-dominant communities reflects the transformational view of schooling and was supported systemically by the teachers' families and cultural communities and by the education profession.

The challenges that teachers faced in attempting to act on their commitments reflect the reproductive purpose of schooling as embedded in the "subtractive" structures of schools and reinforced by schools' responses to state and federal accountability policies. The teachers internalized this systemic contradiction, which was reflected in their shifting personal and professional identities, issues concerning their cultural match with students, and their involvement in pursuing the mainstream goals of the educational system. They were change(d) agents: They were changed by the educational system that they are committed to changing.

The book details two related sets of conditions in schools that limit the ability of teachers of color to be role models to students of color, engage in culturally and linguistically responsive teaching, and act as agents of change. The first is strikingly similar to the structural qualities of schools that Angela Valenzuela (1999) characterizes as "culturally subtractive." She chronicles how schools divested U.S.–Mexican youth of social and cultural resources and thus relegated them to academic failure by subtracting, or dismissing, their cultural and linguistic resources and limiting the presence of social capital in their peer networks. Without social capital, Mexican-descent students lacked access to human capital, such as academic knowledge and information about how to succeed in school. Our book suggests that subtractive schooling may similarly inhibit teachers of color by silencing a dialogue about issues of race in schools, limiting their access to supportive colleagues, constricting their roles and access to learning, making them adhere to restrictive curricula and pedagogical practices, and thus inhibiting their ability to enact the cultural/professional roles that may have drawn them into the profession.

A second set of conditions that challenged the ability of the new teachers of color to engage in culturally and linguistically responsive teaching arose from their schools' responses to state and federal accountability policies. Educational reform in the United States focuses on holding schools and districts accountable for the performance of their students on standardized tests as part of the "No Child Left Behind Act" of 2001 and state accountability policies. The new teachers of color were motivated by their commitments to improve educational opportunities for students from low-income and culturally non-dominant communities to work in urban schools that served these communities. Many of these schools were deemed "underperforming" by accountability measures. It is well documented that such schools are the focus of accountability policies in the United States aimed at improving the academic performance of schools and reducing differences in the achievement levels of students from different racial and cultural backgrounds (Darling-Hammond, 2004; Diamond & Spillane, 2004; Haycock, 2006; Mintrop, 2004). Many of the schools in which the new teachers of color in our study sought to teach thus faced great pressure to raise scores on state-mandated, standardized tests. These schools responded by adopting standardized instructional programs, instructional pacing guides, and test-driven teaching that greatly restricted the ability of the new teachers of color to engage their own and their students' cultural and linguistic resources. Moreover, it resulted in many of the new teachers of color having to leave certain students behind in order to meet accountability pressures (e.g., having to adopt prescriptive standardized curricula tied to a predetermined pace and focus on teaching to a test disconnected from the cultural and linguistic resources of students of color). Thus, new teachers of color seeking to redress inequitable access to learning for students of color were inadvertently inhibited by the very accountability policies meant to promote greater equity for underserved students.

The book offers five critical contributions. First, it provides a rationale for diversifying the workforce that goes beyond issues of numerical parity for students of color to address the fundamental democratic values of changing educational opportunities for diverse youth. Second, the book focuses on new teachers of color who represent critical cases because they stand at a transition point that reveals the disjuncture between the promise that motivated them to enter teaching and the reality of schools. Third, the book offers a framework for understanding socialization of new teachers of color in their organizational contexts, highlighting personal background and multiple forms of school capital (including financial, human, social, and multicultural capital), and power relations within the school organizations that shape the capacity of new teachers of color to enact cultural/professional roles. Fourth, the book presents a critical analysis of the promises and challenges of supporting new teachers of color, as drawn from intensive case studies that provide richly textured vignettes of 21 new teachers of color working in urban, "hard to staff" schools serving culturally and linguistically diverse youth. Fifth, the book reveals an understanding of a systemic double bind that the novices of color faced—their commitments to their communities and profession versus culturally subtractive schooling contexts and restrictive accountability policies—with implications for practice, policy, and research. The book also exposes how many of the teachers internalized the contradiction of the bind, resulting in their becoming changed agents within the educational system they sought to change.

The book speaks to several audiences. First, school leaders and other educators who are interested in diversifying their teaching staff will find this book useful because it identifies school conditions that support or inhibit enactment of cultural/professional roles of teachers of color. The second audience for the book is new teachers of color themselves, who will deepen their understanding of the challenges they confront and the possibilities for practices that support students of color by learning from the experiences of other new teachers of color. Third, teacher educators and induction leaders will learn about the deep commitment of some new teachers of color and the preparation and supports needed for the democratic imperative to be addressed. Our fourth audience is policymakers, who will find the book useful in terms of exploring policies to enable schools to support teachers of color and also understanding how reform policies can have the unintended consequence of putting new teachers of color in a double bind. Fifth, the book targets educational researchers and graduate students by highlighting a conceptual framework, providing a literature review, reporting empirical findings from a longitudinal study, and offering future areas for investigation. Finally, the book speaks to community members who care about the diversity of public schools and wish to uphold a commitment to the democratic imperative to make both teaching and schooling more equitable.

AUTHORS' PERSPECTIVES

As authors of this book, we felt it important to identify our own subjectivities. One author is a White woman who is a former middle and high school social studies teacher in urban settings, school reformer, researcher, and teacher educator. The other author is an Asian American man who taught middle and high school social studies, developed multicultural curricula in the mid-1970s, and is a professor of education who, for the past 27 years, has studied the impact of educational reform on the organization of schools. We are both scholars and educators concerned with diversifying the teaching profession and achieving educational equity. In researching and writing together and in collaborating with a culturally and linguistically diverse research team, we identified subjectivities, debated different interpretations of the data, and examined how our backgrounds and perspectives influenced the work. We acknowledge complexities and limitations that our positions create in researching the lives of teachers of color. Our lack of membership in some of the specific groups under study may present problems. Further, the fact that one researcher is White, with the associated privileges of the dominant culture, and the other is a member of a minority group raises questions of bias, which we needed to address in our deliberations with our research team, with the participants, and with outsiders. Our aim is to acknowledge that our own sociocultural and professional positions influence this book. We continually reflected on the challenges and sought to address our outsider status, by soliciting feedback from the participating teachers about how we reflected their experiences, from collaborating researchers, from other scholars of color, from researchers on teachers of color, and from new teacher educators.

THE CHAPTERS AHEAD

Chapter 2, "Examining the Cultural/Professional Roles and Socialization of New Teachers of Color," introduces the framework and existing research about socialization of new teachers of color to enact cultural/professional roles that inform this book. It begins by discussing issues involved in defining constructs of race and ethnicity. The chapter introduces a framework built on conceptions of the cultural/professional roles of teachers of color to which the new teachers in our study were committed. The framework also incorporates teacher socialization theory to understand factors that influence development of cultural/professional roles for teachers of color. It highlights the influence of teacher background and organizational context. The chapter concludes with a brief overview of our 5-year study of the early careers of teachers of color in urban "hard to staff" schools as the cases informing the book.

Chapter 3, "Meet the Teachers: Commitments and Backgrounds of New Teachers of Color," introduces the teachers in the study. Through use of teachers' own voices and vignettes from cases, this chapter highlights the factors that shaped their commitment to teaching in their communities and to enacting cultural/professional roles as role models, culturally and linguistically responsive teachers, and agents of change. In particular, it explores the influences of their family backgrounds, schooling experiences, and teacher preparation on their commitments. Furthermore, we relate the new teachers' community commitments to other studies that have identified teachers of color having an advocacy or social justice stance, as well as to a view of teaching as community and cultural work (Beaubeoef-Lafontant, 1999; Dixson, 2003; Dixson & Dingus, 2008). The chapter concludes by raising the question: Given the messages that they received and adopted about their responsibilities to the community, how might new teachers of color be set up for an extra burden and challenge, and, ultimately, how might they be underprepared to address the complexities of enacting such cultural/professional roles given the schooling contexts they are about to enter?

Chapter 4, "Where Do the Teachers Go and Why?," follows the teachers from their initial commitments to the context in which they began their careers. The chapter explores the schools to which the new teachers of color were attracted and reports on teacher retention and turnover patterns and influences for the cohort under study. The teachers were drawn to schools with high proportions of low-income youth and communities of color and tended to stay in these schools over time at higher rates than the general teaching population. Those teachers who switched schools identified a lack of support in their initial school context and moved to other schools supporting low-income students and communities of color. Those few who left teaching noted a deep struggle with leaving behind students of color. The chapter also situates our cohort within a larger research literature base on the retention and turnover influences of teachers of color, highlighting humanistic commitments that draw teachers of color to work and remain in urban, high-needs schools serving non-dominant communities. Finally, it raises social justice questions about the problematic school conditions of the contexts where new teachers of color work.

Chapter 5, "Subtractive or Additive Schooling of New Teachers of Color: The Impact of Organizational Contexts on Cultural/Professional Roles," examines the school contexts that support or inhibit new teachers of color in enacting their cultural/professional roles. While examining cross-case themes about school conditions from the larger set of teachers in the study, this chapter also reports in depth from two contrasting cases of Mexican-descent teachers working with Mexican-descent English language learners in two different schools. Drawing on observations of their teaching practice and interviews with the teachers and administrators, the chapter illustrates the school contexts that are subtractive or additive of teachers' cultural resources. The chapter concludes with the forms of organizational capital and power relations that mattered in supporting new teachers of color to enact cultural/professional roles as culturally and linguistically responsive teachers, role models, and agents of change.

Chapter 6, "New Teachers of Color and Culturally Responsive Teaching in an Era of Educational Accountability," examines the policy contexts and how schools address accountability measures in ways that support or inhibit new teachers of color in enacting culturally responsive teaching. This chapter addresses how new teachers of color, who are drawn to working in urban, high-minority, low-performing schools that are most deeply affected by accountability measures, face competing tensions. Drawing from the cases, the chapter highlights three principal tensions, which correspond to the three dimensions of culturally responsive teaching: (1) Whose knowledge counts—cultural and linguistic relevance or standardization? (2) What type of classroom climate should be created—community of learners or teacher transmission? (3) What gets left behind—social justice or enhanced test scores? The chapter also identifies enforcement mechanisms: fear of monitoring and internalizing the link between testing and educational opportunity. The chapter concludes by examining how rhetoric often links accountability to equity, invoking language such as "No Child Left Behind" and calling for the elimination of the "achievement gap" as a principal goal. By specifically focusing on the impact of accountability measures on teachers of color and the pedagogical practices they employ in working with their students of color, this chapter highlights how policies inhibit the efforts of teachers of color to draw on their own and their students' cultural resources to engage in culturally responsive teaching and promote equity, thus exposing an unintended consequence of the reform policy.

Chapter 7, "Change(d) Agents: New Teachers of Color in a Double Bind," explores the uneasy state of new teachers of color trying to change the system from within and facing the systemic nature of a double bind. Having investigated teacher background issues in Chapter 3 and examined organizational and institutional influences in Chapters 5 and 6, Chapter 7 looks at the intersection of individuals and organizations as teachers seek to engage in change. This chapter explores how new teachers of color, who are drawn to working in urban, high-minority, low-performing schools that are most deeply affected by accountability measures, are caught in a double bind in their efforts to work with low-income students of color. *Double bind* was a term coined by Gregory Bateson (1972), an anthropologist, to capture conflicting demands, neither of which can be ignored. Ultimately this leaves the person torn between the two contradictory forces. We use *double-bind* as a metaphor for the professional, cultural, and personal principles that inspire and the organizational pulls that challenge new teachers of color who attempt to engage in cultural/professional roles. This chapter reveals the systemic origins of the contradiction among family, community, early schooling, and professional supports for teachers' commitments, on the one hand, and subtractive schooling and responses to accountability policies that undermine teachers' commitments, on the other hand. The chapter goes on to identify how the novices internalize the systemic contradictions and thus experience being both agents of change and changed agents within the system they hope to transform.

Chapter 8, "Supporting New Teachers of Color: A Call to Collective Action," includes a collective call to action for communities, educators, policymakers, and researchers to build schools that provide conditions that support teachers of color like those in the book who serve as reminders of a vision of the possible and to support such novices as they negotiate a double bind. This chapter returns to the democratic imperative described in the introduction of the book, drawing from lessons learned from the lives of new teachers of color.

CHAPTER 2

Examining the Cultural/Professional Roles and Socialization of New Teachers of Color

The demographic and democratic imperatives to diversify the teacher workforce underscore the critical need to understand supports and challenges for new teachers of color who work in schools serving students of color. In this chapter we introduce the conceptual framework, which is based on previous research and initially informed our study of the cultural/professional roles and socialization of new teachers of color. We begin by addressing issues concerning the definition of constructs of race and ethnicity, which were central to our study. We then turn to the framework, which builds on conceptions of the cultural/professional roles of teachers of color to which the new teachers in our study were committed. The framework also incorporates teacher socialization theory, which highlights the influence of teacher background and organizational contexts on new teachers of color. We close with an overview of the design and procedures we employed in the 5-year study that informs this book.

DEFINITIONAL ISSUES

The language of naming group identification is highly contested. In this book we often use the term *teachers of color* because it is a more contemporary description than the term *minority*, given the shifting demographics of the nation. As Nieto (2000) noted, the term *people of color* describes groups such as African Americans, Asian Americans, Native Americans, and Latina/os; emerged from the communities themselves; and "implies important connections among the groups and underlines some common experiences" (p. 30) in the United States. However, a mutual history does not equate to a uniform experience. We recognize the limitations of these terms and our intention is not to homogenize the groups. We further recognize that even within subgroups, such as *Latino*, such a term also reflects an enormously diverse group. It refers to people of Latin American and Caribbean heritage, while including the African and indigenous heritage as well as the Spanish heritage (Nieto, 2000). Yet the term does not capture distinct differences of national origin, immigration status, gender, socioeconomic status, language, political consciousness, and so on. At times we reference subgroup identifications of teachers in our study, such as teachers of Mexican descent, while the teachers in this study self-identify in many other ways in addition to being of Mexican descent (e.g., Chicano/a, Mexican, Mexican American, person of color, Latino/a).

CULTURAL/PROFESSIONAL ROLES AND SOCIALIZATION OF NEW TEACHERS OF COLOR: A FRAMEWORK

This book is informed by related literature on two topics. First, we draw on conceptions of the cultural/professional roles of teachers of color to which the new teachers in our study were committed. Second, to understand what supported or inhibited enactment of such roles, we turn to the influence of teachers' backgrounds and school context on the socialization of new teachers of color.

Cultural/Professional Roles of Teachers of Color

Scholars identify three cultural/professional roles through which teachers of color can enhance educational opportunities for students of color: (1) providing positive role models, (2) engaging in culturally and linguistically responsive teaching, and (3) working as agents of change whose critical perspective on schooling may contribute to transforming education (Gándara & Maxwell-Jolley, 2000; Moll, Amanti, Neff, & Gonzalez, 1992; Nieto, 1999; Quiocho & Rios, 2000; Valencia, 2002; Villegas & Irvine, 2010; Villegas & Lucas, 2002, 2004). Roles are sets of negotiated expectations, behaviors, and norms as conceptualized by actors in a social situation. Cultural/professional roles are sets of norms and expectations negotiated at the nexus of teachers' ethnic/cultural affiliations and occupational/organizational contexts. Thus, the three roles are situated in professional and cultural conceptions about being teachers of color working with students of color in particular school contexts. It is also important to note that the cultural/professional roles identified by the new teachers of color in our study were inextricably linked to their commitments to fostering educational opportunity, academic achievement, and equitable schooling for youth of color.

A potential limitation of conceptions of cultural/professional roles of teachers of color occurs when they become essentializing, thereby ignoring the variability of individuals. When one overlooks such variability, it can support stereotyping that can work to disadvantage some groups (Tabachnick & Bloch, 1995). We do not view such roles as static labels that are deterministic and simplistic; rather, we highlight the dynamic nature of cultural practices within communities (Guitiérrez & Rogoff, 2003). Nor do we suggest that White teachers cannot be effective teachers of students of color or adopt culturally and linguistically responsive practices, that teachers of color cannot teach effectively outside of their own group, or that all teachers of color are effective with students of color. We also challenge the assumption that teachers of color will easily be able to tap their cultural resources in practice with students of color. Just being a person of color does not guarantee effectiveness in teaching students of color, nor do new teachers of color necessarily have knowledge of pedagogy for diverse students (Quiocho & Rios, 2000; Sleeter, 2001). We also recognize that experiences of teachers of color vary according to their own and students' experiences of intersecting racial, ethnic, linguistic, generation, gender, religious, socioeconomic, and various other memberships.

Role Model

A *role model* is defined in the *American Heritage Dictionary of the English Language* (4th ed.) as "a person who serves as an example of the values, attitudes, and behaviors associated with a role." Research suggests that teachers of color can provide positive role models for students sharing the teachers' racial, cultural, linguistic, or class backgrounds (Valencia, 2002; Villegas & Lucas, 2004). Role models can promote high expectations, achievement, and college-going; challenge stereotype threat and racism; offer mentoring relationships that reflect home cultures and familial-like ties; and provide multicultural navigation and cross-cultural translation in helping youth to transition between dominant and non-dominant cultural settings (Carter, 2005; Dee, 2004; Ferguson, 2003; Steele, 1997; Yosso, 2006). For example, Basit and McNamara (2004) and Su (1997) indicate that teachers of color perceive themselves as role models who motivate students to higher academic achievement, broaden students' career aspirations, and challenge society's and students' stereotypes. Ochoa (2007) reports that Latino teachers identify the centrality of serving as a role model for Latino youth. Solomon (1997) notes that minority teachers of color are inspired by role models and committed to making a difference for the next generation, as evidenced in their relationships with minority children and parents of color as well as in their roles as multicultural/antiracist education experts. The role model rationale is used widely in the literature as part of the reason for diversifying the teaching profession (Villegas & Geist, 2008). The participants in our study identified being a role model for students of color as a critical motivator in wanting to become teachers, and they reported that being a role model to students of color was one way in which their cultural identifications influenced their teaching and interaction with students of color.

Research also identifies limitations of the role model hypothesis. In their review of research on the rationale for racially and culturally diversifying the teacher workforce, Villegas and Irvine (2010) find that no studies document the effects of role modeling on teachers of color or their students. Nor does research reveal how the role model function works in classrooms and schools. A study by Solomon (1997) suggests the complexity of role modeling, finding that teachers of color with role model commitments faced expectations by students, parents, and colleagues that resulted in unforeseen social, cultural, and psychological pressures. The experiences of the teachers in our study also complicate conceptions of role model, as new teachers of color who initially assumed a cultural match found that students of color, at times, questioned teachers' sociocultural identifications and connectedness (see also Achinstein & Aguirre, 2008). Irvine (1989) suggests looking beyond the role model concept to examine the pedagogies of teachers of color that support student learning.

Culturally and Linguistically Responsive Teachers[1]

Researchers have reported that teachers of color who share racial, cultural, and/or linguistic backgrounds with students may tap cultural resources in themselves and their students to engage in culturally and linguistically responsive teaching, support cultural boundary crossing, and provide a cultural bridge to learning (Carter, 2005; Foster, 1994; Irvine, 1989; Ladson-Billings, 1995; Villegas & Irvine, 2010; Villegas & Lucas, 2004). Galindo and Olguin (1996) describe how bilingual Chicana educators tap their own cultural resources to support Latina/o youths' identities, parents, and communities. Garcia-Nevarez, Stafford, and Arias (2005) note that Latino teachers were more affirming of Latino youths' use of Spanish than non-Latino teachers. Cabello, Eckmier, and Baghieri (1995) report that Latina/o teachers want to foster curricula that respond to and reflect Latina/o experiences. Dixson and Dingus (2008) identify a form of "other mothering" by African American teachers, and Lynn (2006) similarly describes "other fathering" by African American male teachers to foster academic success among African American students. Based on investigating successful teachers of African American and other culturally diverse children, Ladson-Billings (1994, 1995, 2001) proposes a culturally relevant theory of education. She highlights how teachers use student culture as a basis for learning, build on community and prior knowledge, and see themselves as members of the community.

We highlight three dimensions of culturally and linguistically responsive teaching identified in the literature as promoting academic access and success: It

(1) engages communities of learners that socially construct knowledge; (2) demonstrates cultural competence and connects pedagogy and curriculum to students' cultural and linguistic backgrounds; and (3) reflects a critical social justice perspective that reveals the "hidden curriculum," names inequities, supports students in questioning, and challenges the status quo (Anyon, 1994; Apple, 1990; Banks, 1991, 2003; Banks et al., 2005; Cochran-Smith, 2004b; Gay, 2000; Ladson-Billings, 1994, 1995, 2001; Nieto, 2000, 2002; Sleeter & Grant, 1999; Villegas & Lucas, 2004). However, we cannot assume that new teachers of color will know how to enact culturally and linguistically responsive teaching. While they may possess valuable cultural and linguistic resources, these resources would need to be acknowledged and developed for teachers to enact such practices (Sheets, 2004). Further, Tabachnick and Bloch (1995) warn that when cultural compatibility theories, generally, and culturally responsive teaching, specifically, essentialize culture, they can support stereotyping that disadvantages some groups.

Agents of Change

Research suggests that teachers who enhance educational opportunities for students from non-dominant communities can act as "agents of change" (Villegas & Lucas, 2002). These teachers recognize that schools reproduce inequalities and, thus, see themselves not as isolated educators but as participants in a broader struggle to change society and the education system (Cochran-Smith, 1991, 1997). Some teachers of color are particularly likely to view themselves as agents of change if they have experienced injustice in schools (Beauboeuf-Lafontant, 1999; Gordon, 1993; Michie, 2005; Murrell, 1991; Nieto, 1999; Quiocho & Rios, 2000; Toppin & Levine, 1992) and marginalization as teachers (Nieto, 1999). Foster (1991) notes that African American teachers are informed by their understandings of the historical conditions of Black, urban communities. Weisman (2001) similarly concludes that Latina teachers pursue social change because they have developed a "bicultural identity" to function in two worlds (home culture and dominant culture) and thus hold a critical perspective on the histories of non-dominant groups.

Researchers have documented that teachers of color can act as agents of change through their teaching. The new teachers of color, who are characterized as "teaching for change" in Michie's (2005) study, engage students of color in working for a socially just community and confronting racism in texts and in their local environments. Studies document that teachers of color are more supportive of antiracist education than are White teachers (Carr & Klassen, 1997b), engage students in "color talk" (Thompson, 2004), and attempt to alter the education system by incorporating "politically relevant teaching" (Beaubouef-Lafontant, 1999), which highlights the significance of teachers' political convictions that schools can be vehicles for social change. King (1991) attributes much of the success of African American teachers who work with students from low-income, predominantly African American communities to their use of "emancipatory pedagogy," which links mastery of basic skills and school knowledge with critical thinking about "liberating, antiracist, and antielitist content" (p. 255). Koerner and Hulsebosch (1995) identify teachers of color as "gate openers" for access to success rather than "gate keepers." Teachers of color can also act as agents of change in arenas beyond their classrooms, effecting schoolwide and district change as well as engaging parents as partners in transforming schools (King, 1991; Villegas & Lucas, 2002). Alternatively, teachers of color can carry the burden of internalized oppression or face institutional forces that may reproduce, rather than transform, the status quo in schools.

Socialization of New Teachers of Color[2]

Understanding the socialization of new teachers of color will help identify factors that support or inhibit the development of cultural/professional roles. Socialization involves the means by which people are enculturated into a profession. We draw from the interpretive and interactionist traditions of research on teacher socialization, which hold that both individuals and their social contexts shape socialization (Lacey, 1977; Lawson, 1992; Zeichner & Gore, 1990). Thus, the framework that guided this study highlights the influence of teacher background and the organizational context of schools on the ability of new teachers to act on principles and commitments about appropriate ways to teach.

Teacher Personal and Professional Backgrounds

We focus on the teachers' personal backgrounds and histories, which influence teachers' professional socialization by shaping their worldviews (Weick, 1995) and professional commitments or beliefs. Teachers' personal backgrounds also affect their practice, connections with students, and where they work, which in turn shape the contexts of their socialization experiences (Delpit, 1995; Lankford, Loeb, & Wyckoff, 2002; Metz, 1990). We consider the teachers' professional preparation because it can influence their practice and culturally and linguistically responsive teaching, especially in programs with strong visions of teaching and explicit social justice agendas (Darling-Hammond, 2000; Kennedy, 1999; Ladson-Billings, 2001).

Researchers have documented the impact of teacher background on cultural/professional roles for teachers of color. Families, mentors and role models, experiences with social injustice, and socioeconomic/political and ethnic role identities shape the beliefs and commitments of teachers of color (Galindo, 1996; Irvine, 2003; Quiocho & Rios, 2000). However, some teachers of color may devalue their cultural backgrounds because their early schooling or preservice education emphasized assimilation and deculturalization (Delpit, 1995; Foster, 1990; McLaughlin, 1993). Alternatively, there are some examples of promising preparation for teachers of color, where novices of color are supported to develop cultural resources.

Three areas of teacher background are highlighted in the literature as influencing the development of teachers of color in enacting cultural/professional roles: (1) cultural, community, and familial experiences; (2) teachers' own schooling; and (3) pathways and preparation.

Cultural, community, and familial experiences. Studies tend to report how teachers of color, in general, enter the profession with cultural, familial, and community experiences that motivate and shape their commitments to enact cultural/professional roles such as role models, culturally/linguistically responsive teachers, and agents of change for students of color. Researchers identify how community experiences shape humanistic commitments of teachers of color to serve students from non-dominant communities. Su's (1997) case study of 56 teacher education candidates who were Asian American, African American, Hispanic, and White reported significant differences between teachers of color and White teachers, with teachers of color wanting to teach in urban schools and make a difference in the lives of low-income students of color. Teachers of color also differed from White teachers in their understandings of being a "change agent." They focused on reducing social and structural inequalities. Other researchers concurred that preservice teachers of color, compared to White teacher candidates, were more likely to report that their primary motivation for joining the profession was their desire to improve the educational opportunities and lives of students of color (Belcher, 2001; Kauchak & Burback, 2003; Rios & Montecinos, 1999; Villegas & Irvine, 2010).

Other researchers identify a community ethos as part of the humanistic orientation of some teachers of color. Dixson and Dingus's (2008) ethnographic study of five Black female teachers (including a novice) identified teaching as "community work" and giving back to their community, highlighting how the decision to enter teaching allowed them to remain connected to Black communities and students. McCray, Sindelar, Kilgore, and Neal (2002) examined African American women's decisions to become teachers and found that mothers, women in the community, and female teachers were significant influences on participants' decisions to teach. These experiences and interpretations shaped their images of good teaching as shared, culturally responsive mothering in their community. These studies thus suggest that some teachers of color are drawn to the profession in order to act on their community commitments to serve students from non-dominant racial and cultural communities by enhancing their opportunities to achieve academic success. These humanistic commitments may also explain the higher rate of retention for teachers of color in low-income, high-minority schools than for their White counterparts (Achinstein, Ogawa, Sexton, & Freitas, 2010). This issue will be taken up further in Chapter 4.

Many studies highlight "community cultural wealth" (Yosso, 2005), familial values, resources, and role models derived from home communities that were drawn on in cultural/professional practices (Basit & McNamara, 2004; Blasi, 2001; Carter, 2005; Case, 1997; Foster, 1993b, 1994; Galindo, 1996; Galindo, Aragon, & Underhill, 1996; Galindo & Olguin, 1996; Irvine, 1989, 2002; Jacullo-Noto, 1994; Lynn, 2006, McCray et al., 2002; Solomon, 1997; Villegas & Lucas, 2004). Some studies emphasize culturally responsive practices derived from such experiences specific to subgroups (e.g., "othermothering" among African American female educators; "respect for the street" among African American male educators; use of "cariño" and values of "la familia" and "educacion" among Latino educators). Other studies reference a common experience of "bridging" or "cultural navigation" that may be reflected across various groups of teachers of color as they interact with the dominant culture and use their resources to support their students in bridging home and school cultures. Still other researchers highlight how experiences with social injustice shape beliefs, commitments, and cultural/professional practices of teachers of color, particularly fostering commitments to being agents of change (Bascia, 1996; Beauboeuf-Lafontant, 1999; Gordon, 1993; Lynn, Johnson, & Hassan, 1999; Michie, 2005; Murrell, 1991; Nieto, 1999; Quiocho & Rios, 2000; Su, 1997; Toppin & Levine, 1992).

Some researchers report important differences among individuals' and groups' ethnic/cultural and professional identifications and how such identifications influence practice (e.g., a range of within- and across-group cultural orientations); this adds complexity rather than essentializing and homogenizing groups (Jones, Young, & Rodriguez, 1999; Clark & Flores, 2001; Sheets, 2002; Ware, 2006; Weisman, 2001; Zitlow & DeCoker, 1994).

Teachers' own schooling. Some research has highlighted how schooling and personal experiences often challenge the ability of teachers of color to perform cultural/professional roles. This is revealed as they face acculturation pressures in dominant-culture schools and seek support beyond the school. Researchers describe how the schooling experiences of some teachers of color caused them to devalue their cultural backgrounds, languages, and practices in the face of the dominant culture represented in schools (Chavers, 1998; Foster, 1990; Galindo & Olguin, 1996; Gordon, 1992; Guitiérrez, Asato, Santos, & Gotanda, 2002; Lipka,

1991; McLaughlin, 1993; Spring, 2007). These were challenges experienced in the contexts of assimilation and deculturalization, for example, among Native Americans and indigenous peoples removed to boarding schools (Spring, 2007) or among Spanish speakers facing English-only policies (Guitiérrez et al., 2002). Other studies reveal that some teachers of color are particularly likely to view themselves as agents of change if they have experienced injustice in their own schooling (Beauboeuf-Lafontant, 1999; Gordon, 1993; Michie, 2005; Murrell, 1991; Nieto, 1999; Quiocho & Rios, 2000; Toppin & Levine, 1992). Michie (2005) chronicled the culturally relevant teaching of five exemplary early-career teachers of color. Most developed a politicized framework for teaching based on their own early schooling, where many identified experiences of racial discrimination and were motivated to create environments where students "felt culturally (and humanly) validated and cared for in genuine ways" (p. 191). Alternatively, in a more positive experience of early schooling, Foster's (1993b) study highlights how participants' experiences with teachers who acted as surrogate parents fostered their current approaches to teaching, focusing on concern for students' cognitive, affective, social, and emotional growth.

Pathway and preparation. Studies report how pathways and teacher preparation offer both promises and challenges for new teachers of color. The leaky pipeline into the profession underscores challenges for teachers of color entering teaching related to underresourced schools, a poor cultural fit with the school, dropout/pushouts in early schooling, tracking and organizational barriers, underrepresentation and challenges in teacher preparation programs, and teacher testing challenges (Clewell & Villegas, 1998; Epstein, 2005; Villegas & Lucas, 2004). Studies document how alternative pathways are growing as a significant route for entry for teachers of color (Clewell & Villegas, 2001; Shen, 1998; Villegas & Davis, 2008; Villegas & Geist, 2008).

Yet some challenges may arise from these routes (although the kinds and qualities of alternative route programs vary significantly, as do traditional programs). Analysis of recent data from the national Schools and Staffing Survey revealed that in contrast to new White teachers, new teachers of color work in settings that are particularly challenging, more often enter through alternative routes, have less than standard certification, and have differences in preparation, with 30% of new teachers of color receiving no practice teaching at all prior to assuming their teaching responsibilities, compared to 13.7% for new White teachers (Villegas & Geist, 2008). This raises concerns when certain pathways allow teaching prior to undertaking coursework in pedagogy and without student teaching experiences, which may ultimately impact teacher efficacy and retention. Still other alternative routes have explicit short-term retention goals (e.g., 2-year commitment).

However, quality varies among university-based and alternative preparation pro-grams, resulting in different outcomes for graduates (cf. Grossman & McDonald, 2008). The bulk of the literature on the preparation of teachers of color focuses on traditional preparation, where the dominant pattern documents marginalization of the voices and experiences of new teachers of color (Delpit, 1995; Foster, 1993c; Murrell, 1991; Quiocho & Rios 2000). Researchers note an "overwhelming pres-ence of Whiteness" in teacher preparation; the resources of new teachers of color are not tapped or developed in many teacher education programs (Montecinos, 1994, 2004; Sleeter, 2001). Even in some studies of teacher preparation programs with an explicit focus on social justice or multicultural education, researchers re-ported the marginalization of the conceptions and experiences of novices of color in addressing culturally and linguistically relevant teaching content (Knight, 2002; Sheets & Chew, 2002).

Alternatively, some significant studies document promising examples of innovative preparation that seeks to build on the cultural resources of candi-dates of color to enact culturally responsive and socially just practices (Bennett, Cole, & Thompson, 2000; Boyle-Baise, 2005; Cox, 1993; Darling-Hammond, French, & García-Lopez , 2002; Hammerness, 2006; Irizarry, 2007; Ladson-Bill-ings, 2001; Oakes, 1996; Oakes, Franke, Quartz, & Rogers, 2002; Quartz & TEP Research Group, 2003; Sleeter & Thao, 2007; Wong et al., 2007). For example, the work of Oakes (1996) and other research on UCLA's Center X highlight a teacher education program with a clear commitment to social justice for urban educators and strong alumni supports. Oakes (1996) and Oakes and colleagues (2002) capture the elements of quality urban teacher education, highlighting the following: embodying a social justice agenda, treating professional education "cradle-to-grave," collaborating across institutions and communities, focusing on professional education and school reform, reinventing the university's role in K–12 schooling, blending research and practice, bringing together educators' and students' needs on teaching and learning, remaining self-renewing, and gen-erating change agents.

Quartz and TEP Research Group (2003) describe how Center X graduates (of whom 59% are teachers of color) tend to stay in teaching at higher rates than oth-ers and sustain commitments to being change agents. From a 7-year study, the TEP Research Group found that Center X graduates stay in urban teaching at higher rates than the national average. Moreover, the study highlights how graduates have learned to build on the strengths of urban communities, developing nondeficit conceptions about students and communities and identifying as agents of change. Eighty-two percent of respondents said they contribute to the learning and growth of other adults (e.g., by mentoring new teachers, sharing curricular resources, and helping parents "stand up for their rights"), and 86% of respondents felt they'd made their school a more just or caring place (e.g., setting high expectations for all students; teaching history from a non-Eurocentric point of view; opening discussions on race, gender, and so on; and facilitating college access).

In another example, a study by Ladson-Billings (2001) highlighted the Teach for Diversity program at the University of Wisconsin, Madison, which focuses on culturally relevant pedagogy. Ladson-Billings describes how teachers focus on students' academic achievement, develop students' cultural competence, and foster students' sense of sociopolitical consciousness. One expectation of the program is that students will develop further awareness of their own multiple group memberships, understand experiences of groups and how they are represented or not in the curriculum, develop an understanding of teaching to foster "situational diversity," understand the home–school context in their approach to teaching, and prepare educators for diversity.

Where Teachers of Color Work

Research reveals that the personal backgrounds and histories of teachers of color shape, among other things, a "humanistic" commitment to enhancing educational opportunities for students of color. This has the further consequence of influencing where teachers of color decide to work. More than 30 years of research documents that teachers of color tend to work in schools with high proportions of students from low-income and racially and culturally non-dominant communities (Achinstein et al., 2010; Murnane, Singer, Willett, Kemple, & Olsen, 1991; National Collaborative on Diversity in the Teaching Force, 2004; Villegas & Lucas, 2004). Richards (1986) reported the interaction of growing rates of students of color with school segregation patterns was a significant predictor of employment patterns of teachers of color in California public schools. Controlling for teacher sex, experience, and credentials, Richards estimated the likelihood of teachers of color being employed in schools with high concentrations (70% to 100%) of African American or Latina/o students. Newly hired teachers of color were most likely to work in rapidly expanding schools with high minority populations. Latina/o teachers employed between 1979 and 1981 were most likely to work in schools with rapidly growing Latina/o student populations and declining Anglo populations of students and teachers. In an earlier analysis of these data, Richards (1982) explained, "this employment pattern persists because the combination of fiscal, demographic and political pressures which keep schools racially and ethnically segregated are stronger than the existing institutional remedies to overcome segregation" (p. 19).

More recent studies indicate that teachers of color continue to be more likely than White teachers to work in urban districts with high percentages of students from low-income and racially and culturally non-dominant communities. Loeb, Darling-Hammond, and Luczak's (2005) study in California and Murnane and colleagues' (1991) study in North Carolina and Michigan indicated that Black teachers were more likely than White teachers to work in large, urban districts. Zumwalt and Craig's (2005) synthesis of research on teacher demographics concluded that teachers of color were more likely to teach in central cities and in schools serving high proportions of students from low-income and non-dominant racial and cultural backgrounds. While more than two-thirds of African American teachers and 79% of Latinos taught in schools where students of color were the majority, 67% of White teachers taught in schools with less than 30% students of color (American Association of Colleges of Teacher Education [AACTE], 1999; Henke, Choy, Geis, & Broughman, 1997). Henke, Chen, and Geis (2000) analyzed national data from the 1993 and 1997 Baccalaureate and Beyond Longitudinal Study; they reported that teachers of color were more likely than Whites to teach in schools with high proportions of students eligible for free and reduced-price lunches, with 51% Black and 63% Latina/o teachers compared to 21% White teachers. Villegas and Geist's (2008) analysis of the 2003–2004 Schools and Staffing Survey found that 53.6% of new teachers of color (in their first 3 years) were concentrated in urban schools as compared to just 27% of their White peers. Further, Villegas and Geist (2008) profiled schools employing new teachers of color. These schools tended to be larger and have larger percentages of students of color; 80% of new teachers of color and 35% of White novices worked in schools where at least 50% of the students were people of color. In addition, a greater percentage of new teachers of color (44%) than new White teachers (6%) worked in schools with at least 50% teachers of color.

Organizational Context

The interpretive and interactionist traditions of research on teacher socialization also highlight the influence of social context on the development of new teachers. Thus, we also examine the organizational contexts of the schools in which the new teachers are socialized, including forms of capital, power structures and relations, and the broader environment. This is crucial because the urban schools in which many teachers of color work often present challenging conditions, including low levels of capital and control-oriented power relations.

Forms of capital. We highlight three forms of school capital that influence teacher socialization (Achinstein & Ogawa, 2006, 2011; Achinstein, Ogawa, & Speiglman, 2004; Ingersoll, 2003; Marsh, 2002; Spillane & Thompson, 1997): (1) human capital, which includes professional knowledge and skills, commitments, and dispositions to learn about and perform professional roles; (2) social capital, which involves relationships and community, sense of trust and collaboration, and professional ties to networks and community within and beyond the school; and (3) cultural capital or cultural knowledge that confers power and status (Bourdieu, 1977) as embodied in what is considered legitimate school knowledge, curriculum, and teaching practices. We consider cultural capital in relation to both dominant and non-dominant cultures, thus identifying a form of "multicultural capital" or resources to navigate and affirm diverse cultural contexts (Achinstein & Aguirre, 2008; Achinstein & Ogawa, 2011).[3] We challenge deficit assumptions behind some conceptualizations of cultural capital that label non-dominant cultures as lacking in powerful resources (Yosso, 2005).

Moreover, we highlight capital as it is exchanged within organizational contexts, rather than embodied by individuals. Exchanges within school organizations involve relations, social systems, practices, norms, and structures that can foster or inhibit individuals' access to resources. Coleman (1988) articulates how social capital "inheres in the structure of relations between actors and among actors. It is not lodged either in the actors themselves or in the physical implements of production" (p. 98). While we describe discrete forms of capital, in fact there are interactions among forms of capital. For example, social capital in the form of teacher collaboration can be exchanged to gain access to human capital in the form of new instructional skills and knowledge.

The amount and types of capital that schools possess and how schools allocate capital can influence the socialization of new teachers of color in enacting cultural/professional roles. Schools with limited social capital can marginalize teachers of color, particularly when their views about education differ from those of colleagues and administrators who maintain the status quo (Carr & Klassen, 1997a; Feuerverger, 1997; Foster, 1994). In one study on advantages and disadvantages that new teachers of color experienced related to their ethnicity, teachers report facing prejudice and negative attitudes from some colleagues, challenges in relating to White parents, and a sense of professional isolation (Basit & McNamara, 2004). In studies of teachers of color and social capital, many participants identify stronger connections with parent and student communities than with colleagues (Bascia, 1996; Driscoll & Kerchner, 1999; Foster, 1993a; Milner & Hoy, 2003). Some research suggests that social capital among teachers—as reflected in collaboration, professional communities, and mentoring—is instrumental to the formation of human capital for teachers (Spillane & Thompson, 1997). Teachers of color often work in schools with little human capital, where colleagues have limited experience and minimal preparation, reducing opportunities for novices to learn and be mentored (Quiocho & Rios, 2000). A few studies examine teachers of color who receive professional development focused on enacting culturally specific teaching practices within culturally matched communities, identifying areas of success (Irvine, 2002, 2003; Lipka, 1994).

Schools lacking multicultural capital can create barriers to resources for navigating and affirming diverse cultural contexts. Studies indicate that issues of race were not discussed in schools where it was deemed inappropriate for faculty discussion (Foster, 1994), and teachers of Mexican descent were unable to incorporate their cultural knowledge in schools with pre-established curricula (Tellez, 1999). Researchers report that teachers, who are primarily identified with students in low-status/capital categories, tend to receive less administrative support; have less influence in school decisions, curriculum control, and professional development; and are afforded less credibility by colleagues and administrators (Bascia, 1996; Finley, 1984; Oakes, 1989; Talbert & Ennis, 1990). This may have implications for new teachers of color, who may work in settings with non-dominant cultural and linguistic student populations. This was particularly seen in a study where teachers of color were marginalized in formal or informal language and ethnic tracks (Bascia, 1996). Furthermore, studies identifying limited multicultural capital that influenced development of cultural practices highlight the following: (1) Teachers of color find that schools do not recognize their cultural resources and thus experience alienation from their schools' goals, particularly concerning issues of diversity, anti-racism, and social justice (Feuerverger, 1997; Foster, 1994); (2) colleagues have negative expectations, and the teachers of color lack access and shared beliefs (Monsivais, 1990); (3) there is informal resistance to racial equity in the form of undervaluing race experiences of teachers and students, and fellow teachers have lower expectations of students of color (Carr & Klassen 1997b; Monsivais, 1990); (4) and teachers of color lack a sense of safety in sharing political views or visions of education with peers (Arce, 2004).

Power structures and relations. These three forms of capital are situated within power structures and relations that formalize and legitimate what counts as capital. Power structures and relations include norms that define the nature of social relations between organizational roles, including decisionmaking and influencing the behaviors of others. Thus, control over decisions and behaviors is included in the framework, highlighting teacher agency to enact cultural/professional roles.

Research documents the importance of teacher control—the power to make decisions and influence behaviors or other individuals (Bacharach & Conley, 1989; Ingersoll, 2003; McDonald, 1992). Teacher discretion and agency are particularly significant given the need to address diverse learners by flexibly drawing on a repertoire of teaching and principles of practice. New teachers may have little power as they enter a new organization, are vulnerable in their status and job security, and are influenced by more senior colleagues. Further, power relations may be a particular challenge to novices, who are not necessarily aware of how to navigate the micropolitics of their schools (Achinstein, 2006; Kelchtermans & Ballet, 2002).

Structural barriers for teachers of color identified in the literature include discrimination in employment practices, culturally discontinuous school climates, taboos about raising issues of racism, lack of promotion opportunities, inequitable power relations, failure of others to recognize the leadership skills of teachers of color, and the lack of racial minorities in key administrative positions (Bascia, 1996; Carr & Klassen, 1997a, 1997b; Lipka, 1994; Quiocho & Rios, 2000). One of these studies highlights how teachers of color were supportive of antiracist education but did not feel empowered to influence it due to the lack of racial minorities in key decisionmaking positions (Carr & Klassen, 1997a).

Broader environment. Teachers and classrooms function in embedded contexts, which can support or constrain teachers from enacting their professional principles (McLaughlin & Talbert, 2001). The school experiences of new teachers of color are shaped by the broader sociopolitical environment of U.S. schooling, which can be manifest in the policies and histories of communities, the profession, and the state.

The socialization of teachers is impacted by the state, including governmental policies at the federal and local levels. Current accountability policies derived from No Child Left Behind, state accountability mechanisms, and school responses to such measures may particularly impact new teachers of color working in low-income settings, limiting their control over instructional decisionmaking and thus their ability to enact culturally and linguistically responsive teaching. While the intention of such accountability measures is to promote educational equity through disaggregation of data by race/ethnicity and language-proficiency to address the historic achievement gap between students from nondominant cultural and linguistic communities and their White, monolingual peers, new teachers of color may find the unintended consequences of such policies constrain efforts to support educational opportunities for students of color.

Research suggests that accountability policies can produce unintended, negative consequences for the instructional practices of teachers, generally, and new teachers and teachers of color, more specifically. For example, high stakes testing has contributed to educators' narrowing the curriculum, de-emphasizing higher order learning, retaining students in-grade, and excluding types of students (e.g., non-dominant cultural and linguistic communities, students with disabilities) who tend to fare poorly on standardized tests (see Darling-Hammond, 2004; McNeil, 2000). Two-thirds of the teachers responding to the Quality Counts Survey reported that their teaching "had become 'somewhat' or 'far too much' focused on state tests" and that they were "concentrating on tested information to the detriment of other important areas of learning" (Doherty, 2001, p. 20). New teachers may face challenges as their schools negotiate the current policy environment of heightened external controls of accountability and standardized or prescriptive curriculum. Accountability and testing pressures can conflict with new teachers' sense of success in enacting the kind of teaching they want to do (Johnson, Berg, & Donaldson, 2005). In one study, accountability environments differentially influenced new teachers in districts and schools with lower and higher forms of financial and human capital, such that new teachers in low-capital schools and districts experienced less control over instructional decisionmaking and fewer opportunities for learning (Achinstein, Ogawa, & Speiglman, 2004). The study identified distinct tracks of new teachers that parallel inequities found in student tracking. New teacher tracks can be distinguished by distinctions based on social class, race, and ethnicity; levels of inputs of professional development opportunities, instructional control, organizational resources, and curriculum and pedagogy; and outcomes in the form of new teachers' sense of competence and efficacy, and their teaching beliefs and practices. Another study characterizes what happens to new teachers who, in the name of equity and cultural responsiveness to their students, resist prescriptive educational policies adopted in response to accountability pressures (Achinstein & Ogawa, 2006). In this environment they found themselves professionally isolated, and schools experienced teacher attrition. A different study of more than 200 new teachers in New York City found that the prescribed instructional programs and a narrowed curriculum, which were adopted in response to high-stakes testing and accountability, limited teachers' autonomy, thwarted their personal and professional identities, diminished opportunities to connect with students, and exacerbated job dissatisfaction and resistance (Crosco & Costigan, 2007).

Moreover, the current policy context of testing and accountability disproportionately impact schools with high percentages of low-income students and students of color and are deemed "under-performing" (Achinstein et al., 2004), which are the types of schools in which new teachers of color tend to work (Villegas & Geist, 2008). Some studies address the experiences of teachers of color in relation to the accountability environment of their schools. Ingersoll and May's (2010) analysis of the nationally representative 2003–2004 and 2007–2008 Schools and Staffing Survey and 2004–2005 and 2008–2009 Teacher Follow-Up Survey found that teachers' concerns over classroom autonomy and faculty input in decisionmaking were predictors for minority teacher turnover. Ingersoll and May note that a possible consequence of accountability policies might be a decrease in teachers' classroom autonomy and teacher decisionmaking at the schoolwide level, which might produce an unintended consequence of increasing turnover among teachers of color. Another study specifically addressed how the policy environment affected teachers of color, restricting their enactment of cultural practices. Ochoa's (2007) narrative study of 18 Latina/o teachers in Los Angeles County reveals how the emphasis on raising test scores that resulted from No Child Left Behind disregarded how language and socioeconomic class influenced test performance. The emphasis on test preparation led many Latina/o teachers to consider leaving the profession because it conflicted with their commitment to being caring teachers who respond to the needs of Latina/o students. The teachers lamented that high-stakes testing reduced their professional autonomy, limiting opportunities to engage students in multicultural curricula and critical pedagogy. Moreover, the teachers reported how they believed that No Child Left Behind Act was actually leaving many Latina/os behind.

The profession plays another significant role in the socialization of teachers, including policies and messages from professional organizations and associations, teacher education institutions, teacher unions, and networks of educators (McLaughlin & Talbert, 1993). Such contexts help articulate what it means to be a professional, teach one's subject, engage with other professionals, and define practice and values in relation to students. It is within the context of such professional communities that teachers make meaning of their professional lives (McLaughlin & Talbert, 2001).

Teacher socialization is also influenced by the macro sociopolitical environment in which it is embedded. Such macro sociopolitical factors that should be taken into consideration include the relationships between institutional context and debates on multiculturalism and Americanization in U.S. schools, language debates (e.g., bilingual education debates such as those surrounding Proposition 227 in California, which focused on English-only approaches), immigration reform, and understandings of race in America (Garcia, 2004). It is important to situate the experiences of new teachers of color within the literature of teachers of color in general, addressing both historical and contemporary sociopolitical contexts that influence the socialization of teachers of color (e.g., the complexities of policies such as desegregation, which promised greater educational attainment for students of color yet resulted in displacement of teachers of color and loss of human/social capital in communities of color, or recent accountability and No Child Left Behind policies linked to equity goals of closing the achievement gap that put teachers of color in a bind about being caring teachers for students of color, narrowing curriculum and pedagogy, and teaching to a test).

A Foreshadowing of the Book's Central Themes

The conceptual framework that initially guided this study and the research on which it is based foreshadow central themes that integrate the findings of our study. The conceptual framework highlights two sets of factors that influence the socialization and development of new teachers: (1) their personal and professional backgrounds, which include families, cultural communities, and the teaching profession, and (2) the contexts in which they work, which include the schools in which they are employed and the broader policy environment. These prefigure the systemic contradiction, or double bind, that confronted the new teachers of color in our study. On the one hand, their families, their cultural communities, and the teaching profession shaped and reinforced their commitments to improving educational opportunities for students of color by being role models, engaging in culturally and linguistically responsive teaching, and thus serving as agents of change in schools. On the other hand, the culturally subtractive structures of the schools in which they worked and their schools' responses to state and federal accountability policies prevented them from acting on their commitments. Thus, the socialization of the new teachers of color resulted in their being changed by the schools and educational system that they intended and continue to work to change. They thus became "change(d) agents."

OVERVIEW OF THE STUDY THAT INFORMS THIS BOOK

The research that informs this book draws from a 5-year study, funded by the Flora Family Foundation that investigated the socialization of new teachers of color. The study research questions included: (1) What supports or challenges for learning to teach do new teachers of color in urban schools experience? (2) What are the career trajectories of the teachers? (3) How do teachers' sociocultural identifications influence teaching and relationships with students? and (4) What factors shape the teachers' conceptions and practices? The case study approach offered an opportunity to describe teachers' conceptions and the nature of classroom practice over time (Yin, 1989). Case study design is used to obtain an in-depth understanding of processes, contexts, and their meanings for those involved (Merriam, 1988). Although not generalizable, findings provide opportunities to generate hypotheses and build theory about relationships that may otherwise remain hidden (Hartley, 1994; Yin, 1989). [See the Methodological Appendix for further discussion of the study.]

Teacher participants for the study were selected based on the following criteria: (1) initially was a teacher candidate in one of two highly regarded credential- and master's-granting teacher preservice programs that are committed to recruiting teachers of color, placing them in urban diverse settings, and providing them with formal classes on issues of diversity and culturally and linguistically responsive and socially just teaching; (2) identified as a teacher of color with a commitment to working in an urban school with a high populations of students of color; (3) represented a spectrum of subject-matter domains and both genders; and (4) worked in California, where the policy context is relatively supportive of new teachers, with a funded mandate for induction and mentoring throughout the state.

We focus on critical cases of new teachers of color. Critical cases present conditions that are most likely or least likely to produce expected outcomes (Fly-vbjerg, 2001). The cases we examine are critical because they focus on teachers who are deeply committed to teaching students of color in high-needs schools and teaching in culturally responsive ways to improve academic achievement and learning outcomes; they also selected and attended highly regarded and highly selective teacher education credential- and master's-granting programs that focus on preparing teachers to work in urban schools with culturally and linguistically responsive practices to improve student outcomes. The professional preparation of the teachers in this book stand out from the national pattern reported in the Schools and Staffing Survey of 2003–2004 of pathways into teaching by new teachers of color. In this national pattern, only 15% attended a master's-granting teacher education program, 40% attended a bachelor's degree traditional program with a required student teaching experience, 27% entered the profession through an alternative program designed to expedite the transition of nonteachers to a teaching career, 8% entered through individual courses that were not part of a program for a degree, 6% entered through a 5th-year program not leading to a master's degree, and 4% entered through other means (Villegas & Geist, 2008). Thus, the teachers in this book reflect critical cases of deeply committed and extensively prepared teachers of color who might be expected to remain in the profession and sustain culturally and linguistically responsive teaching practices.

The initial 21 teachers in the study included 13 Latino/as (predominantly Mexican American), 3 African Americans, 2 Asian Americans (Chinese, Filipino), and 3 mixed-race students (African American/White; Latino/White; Chinese/Vietnamese). There were 8 males and 13 females (most in their 20s). Twelve participants had parents who were born outside the United States, and 4 participants were themselves born in another country. Most grew up in urban, diverse settings, with about half identifying their families as low income (the rest middle or middle to low income). Their subject areas include: 7, math; 5, history; 4, English; 2, science; 2, elementary education; and 1, Spanish (who later switched to math). We recognize the overrepresentation of Latino/a teachers in this study but also note the overrepresentation of Latino students in California (site of the study). (See Chapter 3 for further details on the participants.)

The data reflect 5 years of the teachers' lives (1 year of preservice and 4 years of teaching) and were collected from the following sources: teacher and administrator/support provider interviews, videotaped classroom observations, classroom and school-level documents, teacher focus groups, and student focus groups. Each year, teachers participated in three extensive, semistructured, tape-recorded interviews, which were conducted in the fall, winter, and spring. Interviews ranged in duration from 45 to 120 minutes. In the initial interviews, among other questions, we asked teachers about why they wanted to become a teacher, why they chose to teach in their school, and how they envisioned their role in the school. In follow-up interviews, we asked how, if at all, aspects of the teachers' cultural backgrounds informed their role as a teacher. Without prompting, participants began identifying commitments to being cultural "role models," "culturally and linguistically responsive teachers," and "change agents." In subsequent interviews, we explicitly followed up on emergent themes about these different roles, which were also highlighted in previous research. We rely heavily on these interview data to understand the insiders' perspective. To capture teachers' instruction, researchers videotaped each teacher during 18 lessons (from one to two hours in length each) in the first 3 years of their teaching. At the end of each year, we interviewed an administrator or school support provider. We also interviewed focus groups of students of teachers who participated in the study to describe teacher practice and relationships with students. Member checks were conducted in the form of teacher focus groups, where we brought together participants in the study each summer to reflect on major themes emerging from data, solicited written feedback, and audiotaped the group discussion (Miles & Huberman, 1994). Finally, we sought feedback about the initial findings from new teacher mentors and scholars on teachers of color at professional meetings.

Researchers from diverse cultural and linguistic backgrounds were involved in collecting and analyzing the data. At times, this allowed for a dialogue about the complexities of culture among us and in our understanding of the data. We also understand how cross-cultural research is complicated by perspectives of both researchers and teachers. We sought to address this by also seeking input from other researchers of color, scholars on teachers of color, and most importantly from the participants themselves about the emergent themes.

We analyzed data from the teacher case studies on three levels (Miles & Huberman, 1994). First, we summarized segments of data that referenced (1) teacher background (personal and professional); (2) organizational context factors associated with human, social, and multicultural capital and power structures as well as the broader environment; (3) teacher cultural/professional beliefs and practices in general (then, as participants began to identify specific roles, we categorized data related to being a role model, culturally/linguistically responsive teacher, and agent of change); and (4) teacher retention and career paths. We summarized interview data from teachers, administrators, support providers, and students on the above-mentioned dimensions. We also documented evidence of elements of culturally and linguistically responsive teaching in practice from videotaped classroom practice (e.g., community of learners, cultural responsiveness, and social justice perspective). Here we sought to capture as much evidence as possible of teaching practices aligned with three elements of culturally responsive teaching by using a rubric that captured enactment of the dimensions and by writing vignettes of observed lessons and supplementing these with information from interviews with the teachers.

Second, we generated teacher case vignettes and pattern codes, using the constant comparative method (Strauss & Corbin, 1990) in an iterative process to generate, revise, and regenerate categories and codes (Miles & Huberman, 1994). We examined (1) the commitment to as well as nature and level of role performance of each of the three cultural/professional roles and identified representative examples; (2) kinds of supports for and challenges to engaging in the cultural/professional roles; (3) teacher background and school-level influences on enactment of the roles; and (4) impact on retention decisions. We summarized interview data and documented evidence from videotaped classroom practice based on cultural activities (e.g., community of learners, cultural responsiveness, and social justice perspective).

Third, we conducted a cross-case analysis. We developed matrices and other displays to further condense data and draw comparisons (Miles & Huberman, 1994). We compared teacher background, teacher preparation, teacher beliefs and practice, and school context factors to understand the differences in enactment of the roles and retention. Finally, we incorporated feedback from a member check from participants, mentors, scholars of color, and researchers on teachers of color.

Limitations of this study include the size of the sample and heavy reliance on teachers' self-reports and observations of teaching. While we collected some evidence from other school stakeholders (students, principals, mentors), findings rely heavily on data that reflect teachers' views and experiences from interviews and observations. Alternatively, in-depth case studies and teachers' perspectives are vital for building theory about teacher socialization and cultural/professional roles. Because we sought to understand the ways teachers were making sense of and negotiating these roles, their insider perspectives are vital.

Given a framework for investigating the socialization of new teachers of color, we turn next to meeting the teachers in this study. In Chapter 3 we explore the teachers' personal and professional backgrounds that inform their commitments to teaching and cultural/professional roles.

CHAPTER 3

Meet the Teachers
Their Backgrounds and Commitments

It's really important to me to do something for the community. . . . It's the only thing that I want to do with my life, I want to contribute and alleviate some of the suffering of my fellow people, my community.

By my community I mean people of color. . . . We are all here because we want to help out; we want to be part of the solution, and we have a commitment to these students. We can't abandon them because *they are us*.

—Jose

I value my culture and talk a lot about my culture and I hope that when I'm in a classroom with our students . . . to be able to share my culture with other students and allow the students the opportunity to share with me and with the rest of the class about their culture.

—Inez

I wanted to become a teacher because of the degree of dysfunction that I witnessed while I was in public school. I wanted to somehow mitigate that. I think teaching is a political act and I see my role as being a social agent. I wanted to make some changes somehow and the best way to do that I felt was to directly interact and get involved with students. That's why I wanted to become a teacher.

—Linh

In this chapter we meet the new teachers from the study and examine factors that shaped their initial commitments to teaching in culturally and linguistically non-dominant communities and to enacting cultural/professional roles. In particular, we explore their personal and professional histories, including family backgrounds, schooling experiences, and teacher preparation, in order to understand how the teachers' experiences influenced commitments. As Jose, Inez, and Linh reveal, the teachers held firm beliefs about contributing to communities of color and to culturally responsive and socially just teaching. While individual differences exist in how teachers conceptualize those beliefs, they generally share strong commitments to communities of color and to cultural/professional practices that derive from their personal and professional backgrounds. This echoes previous research about the humanistic commitments of teachers of color and how a community ethos draws them into the profession to work with students of color (Achinstein et al., 2010; Su, 1997; Villegas & Irvine, 2010). The chapter concludes by raising the question: Given the messages that the new teachers of color received and adopted related to their responsibilities to the community and to enacting cultural/professional roles, how will they sustain and develop these commitments in the school contexts they are about to enter?

TEACHER DEMOGRAPHICS

As Table 3.1 reveals, of the 21 teachers in our study, 13 identified as Latina/o (11, Mexican; 1, El Salvadoran; and 1, Guatemalan); 3 as African American (1, Caribbean descent); 2, as Asian American (1 Filipina American, 1 Chinese American); and 3 of mixed cultures (1, African American/White, 1, Mexican American/White, 1, Chinese/Vietnamese American). The overrepresentation of Latina/o teachers in the group reflects the demographic trends in California and its schools. Latinos made up 37% of Californians in the 2008 census (Pew Hispanic Center, 2010). Latino students comprise 50% of California's school population (California Department of Education [CDE], 2010a).

In terms of socioeconomic status, 11 teachers identified as growing up in low-income communities, 4 in low/middle-income communities, and 6 in middle-income communities. Language variation included 12 with Spanish as their first language, 6 with English, 1 with Black English, 1 with Cantonese, and 1 with Mandarin. In terms of immigration status, 13 participants had parent(s) born in another country (10 in Mexico, 1 in the Philippines, 1 in Taiwan, 1 in El Salvador), 2 participants were born outside the United States (1 in Guatemala, 1 in Hong Kong), 1 identified as second-generation U.S.-born (grandparent born in the Caribbean), and 2 identified as third- or fourth-generation U.S.-born (Mexican heritage). Eight of the participants were male and 13 were female. All were relatively young, in their 20s or early 30s. When the participants entered teaching, their initial content subjects included: 7, math; 6, social studies; 3, English; 2, Science; 1, Spanish, and 2, multiple subject. Three of them also taught English as a second language (ESL).

COMPLICATING IDENTIFICATIONS

While the above numbers seem to clearly demarcate demographic groupings, the teachers identify themselves in much more complicated ways, revealing the intersectionality of their identifications (e.g., race/ethnicity, class, language, immigration generation, immigration status, gender, family experiences, religion, and political commitments). For example, Carmen and Manuel are both Latina/o teachers of Mexican descent. However, they differ in how they self-identify. Carmen explains her cultural identification as Chicana, articulating a fusion of U.S. and Mexican culture. She further expresses the political nature of her affiliation as well as her generation, class, and language identifications. She situates these identifications within a complex sociopolitical context in which education may mean greater access but current immigration debates reveal continued challenges:

> I consider myself Chicana. . . . I'm very oriented to my culture and pride in that culture. I have shirts that always say "Brown is beautiful." . . . As a Chicana, I know that my culture within the United States is a mixture of both; it's a fusion. It has influences of both American and Mexican. . . . I'm very proud of my Mexican culture. To me it means recognizing that there are these injustices around us and if you're Chicano you need to be united and fight the systems that are around us. . . . With an education we have our powers, but then on issues of immigration we have our problems. As a people we need to think of how to help our people and do something for our community.

Manuel identifies as a Mexican American, Latino, and Spanish speaker. He was born in the United States but was raised in Mexico by his grandparents and uncle while his parents worked: "I had a pretty good connection overall with my roots and my home culture." He discusses how his family has kept up their traditions in the United States: "Spanish is just such a very strong part of the culture, so it's something that my family doesn't want to lose. They struggle not to lose that but also to learn the new language, which is English." He recalled how his grandparents said, "Always remember to speak Spanish to your family members, and don't forget to speak Spanish to your kids when you have kids. If you're going to have a wedding, make sure [that though] you could be married by the courts, make sure you also have a religious ceremony." He is "proud to be bilingual." Manuel is the first in his family to go to college. He also explains, "I had a pretty good understanding of social injustices just from my family, from their own experiences . . . of certain aspects of our society, here or in Mexico."

TABLE 3.1: Teacher Demographics

Teacher Pseudonym	Ethnicity/Race & Generation	First Language	Income	Subject	Preservice Program
Agustin	El Salvadoran Parents born in El Salvador	Spanish	Low	Math	A
Alejandra	Mexican American Parents born in Mexico	Spanish	Low	Humanities	B
Alicia	Mexican American Parents born in Mexico	Spanish	Low	Spanish (later Math)	B
Angela	Mexican American Parents born in Mexico	Spanish	Low	Social studies	B
Carmen	Mexican American Parents born in Mexico	Spanish	Low/ middle	Social studies, ELL	A
Gabriel	Mexican American 3rd generation	English	Middle	Math	A
Inez	Mexican American Parents born in Mexico	Spanish	Low	Multiple subjects, ESL	A
John	African American & European American	English	Middle	Math	A
Jose	Mexican American 4th generation	English	Middle	Science	B
Linh	Chinese & Vietnamese American Born in Hong Kong	Cantonese	Low	English	B

Teacher Pseudonym	Ethnicity/Race & Generation	First Language	Income	Subject	Preservice Program
Liz	Filipina American Parents born in Philippines	English	Middle	English	B
Liza	Mexican American Parents born in Mexico	Spanish	Low	Math/Economics	B
Lucia	Guatemalan American Born in Guatemala	Spanish	Low	Multiple subjects	A
Manuel	Mexican American Parents born in Mexico	Spanish	Low	Social studies	A
Monica	African American	English	Low	English	A
Mike	Chinese American Parents born in Taiwan	Mandarin	Middle	Science	B
Peter	African American	English	Middle	Math	B
Ricardo	Mexican American Parents born in Mexico	Spanish	Low/middle	Math	A
Sonya	Mexican American & White Mother born in Mexico	Spanish	Low/middle	Social studies	B
Tanya	African American, Caribbean descent	Black-English	Low/middle	Social studies	A
Theresa	Mexican American Parents born in Mexico	Spanish	Low	Math	B

Linh and Liz are both of Asian descent yet describe complex and different affiliations. Linh was born in Hong Kong and identifies as a Chinese, Vietnamese American. At the age of 1, she migrated with her family to the United States, where she grew up in a working-class family and spoke Cantonese as her primary language. As she prepared to become a teacher, Linh explained how coming from a poor family would allow her to connect with students, even though she is Asian American and her students may be from different non-dominant ethnic/racial communities:

> I think that fact that I grew up in [an urban community] and come from a working-class family will contribute to me as a teacher. . . . We definitely need teachers who understand the population that we serve and can build strong relationships with them. I've seen that happen with teachers of color and I've also seen some teachers of color who don't do a good job of it. To tell you the truth, I think the socioeconomic background of the teacher counts more than the race. . . . I think that makes a big difference in how students interact with their teacher. I would say class trumps race.

Linh also described the complexities of her multiple cultural affiliations:

> Chinese people and Vietnamese people in America and coming from different socioeconomic backgrounds and different experiences and some are refugees, some are immigrants—I feel like there's such a wide span of identity of being Chinese American or being Vietnamese American. . . . I just feel like as I grow older I see and recognize the complexities in different cultures and that there's no simple answer. . . . My evolution with my culture and my cultural identity has been shaped by learning about the history and oppression of Chinese and Vietnamese people—maybe more Vietnamese than Chinese. . . . I think growing up it was always really hard being Chinese and Vietnamese because I think my features are more Vietnamese than Chinese, but I speak Chinese. I think being mixed even if it's just culturally, because of that I've had a hard time identifying with just one group. Then as I get older I realize there's no need to identify with strictly one group and with the complexities of everything it's OK that I don't.

While Liz describes herself "ethnically as a Filipina American," she reports that "the Philippines are pretty foreign to me even though I look like I belong there":

> I can't physically deny the fact that I am Asian, nor do I want to, but that's only one way of identifying a person. . . . I feel like my parents made a very

conscious decision to raise us as American because they were first generation and so when I think about my culture, it's American. I know a few words here and there in Tagalog and that's about it. I look Filipino but it's very surface.

She described her childhood growing up in an all-White, middle-class environment, attending a private school, and not being conscious of her culture until college: "All my friends are White and it was never a question to me and I was never concerned about it. I didn't wonder why there weren't other Asian, other Filipino kids running around. . . . There was some weird name-calling . . . but I was unfazed." Liz did describe the significance of her gender identity, explaining that she "feels American, particularly in my way of being an independent female." She identified her level of independence as a female as distinct from gender roles in Filipino culture.

CULTURAL/PROFESSIONAL COMMITMENTS

Overall, the teachers in our study entered the profession with strong commitments to working with students from non-dominant communities and to enacting cultural/professional roles of role model, culturally/linguistically responsive teacher, and change agent. There was also some variation and a range of conceptualizations of these commitments, particularly along a spectrum of more or less transformative visions of the role of education in changing society.

Commitment to Community

The predominant theme throughout our earliest conversations with the teachers about their hopes for becoming teachers and the kinds of schools they planned to teach in was a commitment to teaching in schools serving non-dominant cultural and linguistic communities. The sense of "giving back to community" and "social responsibility" in supporting underserved communities of color resonated throughout our conversations. Further, there was a calling to address inequities found within the communities, particularly in the schools. Moreover, as Jose described it in the epigraph of this chapter, there was a strong sense of moral obligation to youth of color: "We can't abandon them because they are us." Throughout the interviews we heard this sense of calling to community. In many cases, teachers specified wanting to work with students from their specific racial/ethnic background and in a few cases even return to the school they had attended.

Linh explained that she wanted to become a teacher because she had an obligation to give back to her community and reform the failed system:

> I feel like I have a law of obligation and social responsibility to return to my community and somehow give back and contribute. The best way I know how is as a teacher. . . . I've also witnessed how horrible [schools are], how [schools are] terribly run, how underprivileged a lot of the students in [this community] are, with resources and how the curriculum is and how problematic being a student in [this community] is. I really feel like I need to return to that community and somehow fix the situation. So that's a big motivation for me—that I definitely want to reform the system that I came from.

Peter reported his commitment to teaching students of color as a role model:

> I intend to teach at a school that has a large population of African American, Latino, and other minority students. . . . Being an African American, I believe it's very important that the minority children have a role model that can demonstrate that they, too, can learn mathematics and be sharp at those skills of mathematics and science. I believe I have the ability to effectively communicate that message to them. . . . It's clear to me that my role is not just as a teacher; there is a lot of responsibility placed on my shoulders where I am a role model. I become a variety of family figures for the children who lack family in these environments. . . . I've also become aware that I'm also a counselor and a leader.

Others identified the need for teachers of color to serve in communities of color to provide role models and in that way to give back. Ricardo explained:

> I just want to go back and teach [in the high school I attended] and just give back to my community, because there are a lot of Latinos out there. When I was in high school, there weren't too many Latino high school teachers. . . . Kids couldn't really look up to some of the teachers, because they weren't Latino, and to the Latino teachers that were there, I noticed that there was a lot of—the students looked up to them. I see that there's a lack of Latino teachers out there. That's the main reason why I want to go out there.

A number of the teachers returned to teach in the communities where they grew up; some, including Ricardo, ended up teaching in the high schools they had attended as students.

Commitment to Cultural/Professional Roles

The new teachers of color, to a person, expressed a commitment to performing the cultural/professional roles of role model, culturally and linguistically responsive teacher, and agent of change. For example, Jose, a science teacher explained how he hoped serving as a role model would promote going to college among students of color:

> I'm a role model just by my mere existence . . . a Mexican American dressed in a lab coat is a thing that my students don't really see that often, and I think by being there I represent another option to my students. . . . A lot of my students are probably intimidated, thinking that college is a very White place and it's not for them. I went [to college] . . . just being there and showing them, it changes the power dynamic if all the teachers are White and you're a student of color. It implies that higher education is for White people . . . I'm showing them that, "Hey, it's possible."

He also revealed a strong commitment to culturally responsive teaching: "Cultural relevance justifies the reason for studying science, too, to the student and the student being a whole person, which is their culture. They are their culture. I think their culture is their community, the geography, their racial identity, everything, their identity with their friends." He explained that science teaching is culturally problematic for English learners and youth from low-income and culturally non-dominant communities, making the teaching of science an equity issue as students understand the impact of science on their community. Jose explained how he hopes to include community issues in his science teaching to make it culturally responsive and socially just. He wants students "to know more about inequities and science's role in that and how to fight it." Moreover, he is committed to notions of social justice:

> Getting them ready to be able to succeed in real life, in college and beyond and this society. I want everyone to participate in society. I really like Deborah Meier's focus of getting students ready to participate in democracy, and I really take that to heart. I really believe that, too, because I don't really care about high school as much as I do about their participation as adults in this world, and their voice needs to be heard. They need to be in academia, saying what they [believe], giving alternative opinions. They need to be out there and they need to be people creating policy, not just receiving it. They really have to be in there. . . . Our society's going to be unequal as it is and as it's continuing to be, as I'm watching it. I want everyone in there [making a difference].

Carmen chose to become a teacher because of her commitment to students of color and social justice. "There's such a need for Chicana educators and there's not many of us . . . it's just rare, we're very limited out there . . . so it's having more and more of our issues being addressed." Carmen held strong commitments to teaching for social justice prior to entering teaching:

> I really want to become a teacher . . . to promote that philosophy of social justice and having students become more aware of their surroundings, and find something within education that clicks so that they can prepare for their future. . . . I'm hoping that I'll be able to incorporate social justice and not just go by the framework or by what's already said, but actually doing some social change and just promoting critical thinking.

When asked how her identities might inform her teaching, Carmen explained her commitment to shaping her curriculum to address the cultural lives of her students and tap her own "Chicano-ness":

> [My students will] see an educated woman who is Chicana, too. I feel like they relate with me. . . . So East LA is predominantly Mexican, well Latino, so I'm going to try to shape my curriculum to cover the aspects of our Chicano history. That's how I see that they will identify or recognize my Chicano-ness, 'cause I'm going to put it out there. I know they can relate 'cause it's a similar cultural upbringing.

She also explained how she hoped to connect subject content to students' cultures: "If they could see history through the perspective of vital multicultural history, then they might have more interest in history itself." Carmen noted how her cultural identities and commitment would impact what she would do in her role beyond the classroom, in creating after-school programs "to promote cultural pride." She hoped to start up a MEChA chapter, an organization in which she was involved when she was younger, explaining, "I really believe there's never too young an age where you can start being involved in your community."

Before Inez began teaching, she explained that her culture would play a significant role in her teaching, both as a Latina role model and as someone who would share her own and her students' cultural backgrounds in the classroom. She hoped to promote access to higher education for her students:

> There's not very many Latina female teachers. . . . How that's going to play a role in my teaching is becoming a motivator for other Latina students who may still have parents who have these beliefs that women don't go to college,

can't go to college, shouldn't go to college. So I hope to be a motivation to some of these parents and families. I hope to be able to communicate this and allow these Latina female students to make their own educated choices and select whether they want to go to school or not and hope that they do want to go to school and be an inspiration in that sense.

As Inez's quote in the epigraph expressed, she hoped her own and her students' cultures would play a central role in her future teaching.

Angela entered teaching because "I want to be a role model to all my students . . . to show them how important history is, and hopefully they develop . . . the passion I have for it . . . to look at different perspectives." She particularly wanted students to learn about the history of people of color. Angela also expressed her passion for teaching in culturally responsive and socially just ways: "That means teaching about the struggles of different people based on who they are: gender, sexual orientation, socioeconomic status, ethnic minorities, or having some sort of disability." She wants students to know about diversity, social justice, race, oppression, and the experiences of minorities and women. She identified the importance of talking about struggles in order to effect change: "It's important to talk about those struggles, how they were in the past, especially in my subject, and how they continue, and how we could try to change it. By just talking about it, that's one step in the change."

Variation in Conceptions

Teachers varied in how they viewed their cultural/professional commitments, with some pursuing "access to equal opportunities" for students of color and others identifying a more "transformative" vision of social change. Describing a commitment to equal access, Ricardo explained his vision of what equity and social justice teaching meant: "Just being fair with the students, giving every single student the same opportunity to learn, which is very difficult at times. But just being equal to all." Alicia explained that her sense of social justice in teaching made it her calling: "I think once I connected how powerful education is with social mobility and society and opportunity, once I learned more about that, I really felt that that was something I was called to do. . . . I think one of my goals and one of the reasons I went into teaching was to level the playing field and make students aware of what's out there." John explained that he did not feel he approached teaching "from a cultural perspective," but he expressed the importance of providing "equity and access to the material for all students." Moreover, John described his belief in the importance of learning about dominant power structures and providing keys for access:

I don't think the way to go about it is to say, "We as people of color or low SES individuals are battling the man or the system." I think it's more of just an acculturation process of [explaining], the world is the way it is and you know there's a certain dominant power structure right now and this is the way for an individual to get successful or to get ahead or accomplish what they want in the structure and it's not good or bad, or right or wrong. It is what it is and here are the keys and the tricks and everything.

In contrast, other teachers had a more critical or transformative conceptualization of teaching and education. For example, Alejandra explained: "Teaching for social justice . . . means empowering the kids, and I think that means giving them a good idea about the system they live in and how to function within that system, and how to work within that system to change the system." Linh described that "part of the reason why I am a teacher is because I want to mold kids to be social agents of change." She said, "I think teaching is a political act and I see my role as being a social agent." Angela explained wanting to support Latino youth to effect change:

Why I wanted to teach where there's a lot of Latino students (because I felt close to them, obviously I'm Latina)—I felt like one of the things I never received when I was in high school was knowledge about the history, about what's going on, what kind of change has happened, what change is still happening and what can be done. So I felt as a teacher, especially by teaching history, which involves a lot of culture, I felt that I'd have the opportunity to inform students and help them think about the issues, think about their place, their position in society, how they wanted to effect change, if they wanted to effect change.

TEACHER BACKGROUND INFLUENCES ON CULTURAL/PROFESSIONAL COMMITMENTS

Where did these teachers' commitments arise? We turn next to how the teachers' backgrounds—including their families, schooling, and teacher education—shaped their cultural/professional commitments. Both positive and negative experiences informed the teachers' beliefs.

Family Influences on Commitments

Many of the teachers reported how their families influenced their decisions to become teachers and their commitments to pursuing social justice and serving non-dominant cultural and linguistic communities. For some teachers whose families were recent immigrants, education was deemed critical for success; thus, families instilled the importance of a good education, even if the parents themselves did not have high educational attainment. For example, Liza explained that her parents were born in Mexico and immigrated to the United States for economic reasons when they were fairly young. They met at adult school but were never able to stay in school because they had to work. Her father went up to 6th grade; her mother went up to 3rd grade. Liza explained that at home "we pretty much only spoke Spanish . . . my grandmother lived with us, too, . . . it was disrespectful to speak in English." She identified the significance of education: "To my parents education is very important . . . not just the academic part about it but also the religious, like knowledge that we needed to learn to become better [people] . . . " Liza's parents always pushed her and her brother to go to college. Although Liza's parents were not able to help with homework, she described ways they provided support:

> They've always really tried to accommodate us. . . . For example, moving 4 hours away from Los Angeles to a small town was really a big challenge for them, but they did it because they wanted the best education for us. Even though they didn't quite understand what that was. . . . [My father] actually met with my counselor and let him know that he didn't know what I needed to do to go to college, because he never had that opportunity.

Alejandra's parents are immigrants from Mexico. Her dad (1 of 14 children) had a 3rd-grade education in Mexico and her mom (1 of 13 children) was expected to quit school and take care of family after middle school, but she struck a deal to continue her education and then trained as a secretary at the university. But when they came to the United States in their mid-20s, her mother's degree "meant nothing here," so now she cleans apartments for a living; her father is a construction worker. Alejandra's parents are strong advocates of education. She recalled her father saying: "I don't want you working like donkeys, jackasses doing hard labor." So they decided that education was the most important thing. Her parents started letting the children get out of chores if they were doing homework, "which is amazing for my parents, considering all day long my mom cleans and dad is in construction." All four of Alejandra's siblings attended 4-year colleges.

Other teachers had parents who were teachers or involved in education and inspired them to become teachers. Some identified how their parents' understanding of institutional racism in the United States fueled their commitment to becoming a social justice educator. Jose said:

> I must credit my parents; they're both teachers and they both care and are passionate about education. My father really cares a lot about it especially because he had a lot of negative experiences in a racist education system, and

I know that that's something that really speaks true to him. I learned a lot of that from him. I really got that passion from him, and I really agree with his commentary on the state of education, especially for students of color and the racism that can exist. My mom's also a teacher, and she's always dedicated to students, and that's really inspired me and also [gave me] the sense of my community, that when you do something, you do it to serve your community.

Agustin's parents grew up in El Salvador and migrated to the United States in 1980. Agustin was born in 1981 and grew up in southern California with two older brothers. His father told him he used to teach when he was younger; consequently, he encouraged Agustin to become a teacher. His family is very supportive of his pursuit of a teaching credential and master's degree: "They're very excited for me. I would be the first person getting my master's from my family."

In contrast, 6 of the 21 new teachers reported that initially their families did not support their decisions to become teachers because teachers are not paid well or because they wanted their children to pursue higher-status professions. Four of these six teachers indicated that their families grew more supportive over time. Alejandra's family, for example, at first considered it a waste of Alejandra's education if she went into teaching. It simply did not fit their American dream, which was to use education to get a high-paying job. She reported that they said attending an elite college only to go into teaching was like "going to Harvard to become a janitor." Monica was raised by a single mother in a low-income community in South Central Los Angeles. Monica's mother initially wanted her to become a doctor or lawyer because she knew how little teachers were valued in society. Ultimately, Monica's mother did support her passion.

Schooling Experiences

Most of the teachers described negative schooling experiences that inspired them to become teachers and change agents in an educational system that did not serve them well. Others described individual teachers or role models in their own schooling who shaped their later commitments. For some, becoming a teacher/activist was an act of resistance. Lucia faced challenging odds transitioning from a small school in Guatemala to a large urban high school in California, to which she commuted 2 hours a day because it was located in a wealthier community where her grandmother and aunt worked as housekeepers: "I felt really lost . . . I just wanted to go with the people who spoke Spanish." Lucia further explained, "An African American student and I would be together because the others wouldn't really talk to us." She faced challenging teachers, explaining how one even said:

"You're gonna go back to your house and you're gonna tell your mom that you wanna go back to your country because you don't understand anything."

Many teachers described how the schools they attended were characterized by student alienation, high dropout rates, lowered expectations, and failure to prepare students for college. Thus, they wanted to be the kinds of teachers that changed the conditions of schools for students of color. Alejandra incisively captured this motive in noting how observing injustices in her own schooling experiences led her to become a teacher:

> I wanted to become a teacher because of my experiences in high school and seeing my peers, who I believed to be just as smart as I was but they weren't succeeding. Seeing the ridiculous, obscene, dropout rate and seeing the ridiculously low college acceptance rate and college attendance rate, and then the dropouts that happened once in college with the small numbers that even got there. It was really depressing. I wanted to go into teaching to help change that situation and empower kids like me and kids like the ones I grew up with to really take advantage of their education and use it to succeed, and use it to help them become more socially responsible.

Other teachers identified feelings of injustice due to race or language. Agustin felt he was "always dealing with racial issues" in his elementary school, which tried to place him in bilingual classes even though he was an English speaker:

> I knew English, but the school kept on insisting on placing me in bilingual classrooms. My parents fought through that, fought against the school for them to place me in an all-English class. I took an exam, I did well on the exam . . . yet the school would not want to place me in an all-English classroom.

Mike described being teased about the food he brought to school and how other students would make noises like "ching chong." In high school he was a part of the Asian American Christian club, and he learned to have a leadership role. He began to feel proud of being Chinese. He talked about wearing the Asian pride shirts and feeling confused when he and other students got in trouble with the school administration. He remembers questioning, "We're not supposed to be proud of being Asian?" Peter explained that he felt that, because of his race, he wasn't given the attention that other kids received in 2nd grade. When he raised his hand, he wasn't called on. He would say to the teacher, "You're not calling on me because I'm Black." He would get in trouble because of this. Other teachers described the conflict between their home language of Spanish and having to speak English in their schools, creating tensions for them.

Many teachers also described inspiring early schooling experiences, particularly when they had teachers who demonstrated caring attitudes and high expectations (even in schools where other teachers were problematic). Agustin remarked, "Luckily, I've had a lot of positive teachers along my educational path and I think that's what's inspired me to become a teacher, but at the same time I've had those negative teachers that push me and inspire me to become a teacher." Though Lucia had a teacher who questioned her capacity and right to be at the school, she also described the teacher who believed in her regardless of her access to English language. "One of the teachers . . . she really believed in me and she said, 'You know what, I know you don't understand English, but I'm going to have you be in a class where I know you're going to learn.'" She also had a tutor in high school whom she continued to tap even in college. Jose described an honors physics class teacher who "cultivated this sense of wonder that I always had about science." Linh was inspired by her teachers:

> When I was in high school my senior year, I had two really [amazing teachers]. . . . They really ignited a fire within me to go out there and make a difference and do something. . . . I remember thinking to myself, wow, this is awesome, we're in English class and we're learning about issues of race and equity and that's really cool. We're reading cool books like *Othello*. I remember reading this Toni Morrison book and I just remember feeling very empowered by that class and thinking, yeah, that's what I want to do as a teacher, replicate that and create that in my classroom.

Still other teachers recognized how their college experiences raised their cultural and political consciousness and would later inform the kind of teacher they wanted to become. Carmen explained how a growing awareness of her Chicana identity in college, her major in ethnic studies, and her involvement in Chicano organizations resulted in a "whole name transformation: At first I'm Latino, then I become Chicano, and it's just a whole experience of cultural awareness." Manuel described becoming more politicized in college: "You start thinking differently about the society we live in, things that are good about it, bad about it. So definitely the whole college experience politicized me a lot more, made me more aware of the injustices happening here in this country as well as happening around the world." Angela explained how taking an education class in college and finding out that Latinos had the highest dropout rate inspired her to want to become a teacher:

One of the biggest influences, I think it was my second year of college, I was in an education class and I read Latinos had the highest dropout rate and it just blew me away. I remember reading and crying, "That's so sad! Maybe if I'm a teacher I could help some kids not think that 'oh, I'll just drop out.'" So that's what got me into it.

Others faced cultural challenges in college as they realized their minority status. Alicia explained:

Because I grew up in a Latino community, Latino's were all around me. . . . I went to school [college] where I was definitely part of the minority. Race became a larger issue. Things like my accent, which I never even realized I had one up until I went to university and people pointed it out. . . . I was more conscience about not letting an accent come out. . . . [Then] my family and friends . . . every time I came home for vacation, they said, "Oh yeah, you know, you're speaking differently. You're acting differently."

Alejandra also described becoming aware of her accent and how that made her feel different from college peers—and her subsequent attempt to change the way she spoke. Jose was a minority as a Latino in the sciences in college, which informed his desire to become a role model in teaching science to other minorities and in incorporating a social justice agenda:

In college, especially in science, I was a definite minority, and it was difficult. I want my students to succeed. I want them to thrive in that environment, not just get in there. I am not just interested in them just getting in there, so I think that is what fuels my emphasis on [wanting students to understand] when hitting obstacles to keep going, [building] self-sufficiency, working with each other, using this science to fight injustice if it's possible.

Professional Preparation

It is perhaps not surprising that the teachers in this study were committed to a relatively common set of cultural/professional practices because they chose to attend preservice programs that are devoted to teaching about social justice and culturally and linguistically responsive teaching in service of non-dominant communities in urban schools. Thus, teachers shared similar definitions of such teaching. All of the teachers attended one of two well-regarded credential- and master's-granting preservice programs that sought to recruit a diverse group of prospective teachers to become agents of change and educational leaders. The programs involved coursework explicitly focused on meeting the needs of cultur-ally/linguistically diverse youth and provided extended student teaching practice.

One program describes its mission as radically improving urban schooling for California's racially, culturally, and linguistically diverse students. Its key prin-ciples are to foster social justice; create small, long-term-learning communities; promote social inquiry in communities of practice; reflect diverse and socially re-sponsible learning communities; and be attentive to the moral, cultural, and po-litical dimensions of teaching. It seeks to prepare teachers to be agents of change in urban classrooms, schools, and communities. Its courses address issues of cultur-ally and linguistically responsive teaching; teaching in urban schools; social foun-dations and cultural diversity in education, language, and culture; and teachers' roles as change agents.

The other program's key principles include commitment to social justice, un-derstanding the strengths and needs of diverse students, and dedication to excellence for all students. The program and courses emphasize teaching and learning that is culturally and linguistically responsive to diverse learners; sensitive to the family, community, and political contexts of education; explicit about educating for equity and democracy as well as addressing cross-cultural concerns; focused on needs and development of learners; and grounded in subject matter that enables inquiry, criti-cal thinking, and problem solving. It seeks to prepare and support teacher leaders working with diverse learners to achieve high intellectual, academic, and social stan-dards by creating equitable and successful schools and classrooms.

It is notable that this cohort of teachers is unique among new teachers of color nationally, in that these novices entered teaching through a pathway that involved an extensive preparation program resulting in a credential and master's degree, required extended student teaching practice, and promoted culturally/linguisti-cally responsive and socially just teaching. National trends show that only 15% of new teachers of color attended a master's-granting teacher education program and almost 30% entered through alternative routes. Furthermore, many programs do not actively promote a social justice agenda or one that addresses the needs of diverse student.

The teachers in our study reported how their preservice programs focused and developed their commitments to teaching in non-dominant communities and to culturally responsive and socially just teaching practices. Liz described the impact of her preparation program:

> I would definitely say being in [this teacher education program] was
> important because it was about "teaching to change the world, teaching
> for social justice" and I think those things are important. I think if you're a

teacher and you don't think you're changing the world, even if it's a small corner of it, then you either need to go back and reflect or find a different profession.

Jose explained how the program fostered his commitment to social justice:

> [It] helped me claim my social justice dedication. I know leaders like Paulo Freire really affected me. . . . [as well as] Vygotsky, Lisa Delpit, bell hooks. I feel like I've met my intellectual elders or the people I look up to. Then to see teachers, professors that really believe in that as well, like my mentor from [teacher education program], really was helping me just push my expectations and really try to scaffold well. . . . It pushed my activism.

John explained that the teacher education program does not want to just turn out teachers, but "social justice educators." Liza described the program as having a focus on educational equity and student learning, raising questions such as: "How to create equity in your classroom? How to engage and motivate students? What are the best strategies, methods behind learning and understanding and what does that mean? What does it mean in relation to your subject matter, for example, math, and what does it mean to understand math?"

Alternatively, some teachers described limitations of their preparation programs. Linh explained that while the program prepared her to teach in urban schools and the professors were socially conscious, not all of the teacher candidates were committed to working in urban schools. Peter and Tanya identified how their programs could have better addressed the needs of prospective teachers of color, "catering to our concerns," rather than focusing primarily on White teachers as they confronted challenges in urban contexts. Another teacher, Theresa, wished for greater practical guidance in teaching for social justice, particularly in her domain of mathematics:

> How do you teach for social justice, and what teachers are really doing that? Our professor brought in some examples of some readings from a teacher in [an urban setting] that was doing that, where they were actually using math to study how frequently certain groups get denied a loan for housing and things like that. So that was [helpful], but we only spent one class talking about it, and everybody left thinking, "Well, I still don't know how to really do this." I remember feeling like I don't know how to handle a discussion like that, that may become very personal, to come up with discussions about race and injustices. I don't feel qualified to do that yet.

Thus, while committed and inspired to incorporate cultural/linguistic responsiveness and social justice in her teaching, and having been introduced to some concepts in her preparation, Theresa still sought continued support in how to enact such practices more fully.

GABRIEL'S AND TANYA'S
COMMITMENTS AND BACKGROUND INFLUENCES

Each teacher's unique background experiences informed his or her conceptions and commitments to the cultural/professional roles. To understand their individual experiences and influences more deeply, we present two vignettes that reflect the general patterns described across the new teachers of color in this study.

Gabriel's Commitments and Conceptions of Cultural/Professional Roles

Gabriel describes himself as a Chicano, which for him meant someone of "Latin" descent born in the United States and someone who "gives back to the community." Being Chicano, he explained, is about "supporting our culture, especially through education . . . and [someone who] goes back to their community." He describes his commitments: "I wanted to give back to the community. Why that area? Because that community is highly Latino and that's who I am. . . . I'm just bothered and upset by the fact that Latinos, especially those of Mexican descent, have the highest dropout rates and I don't want to see people who look like me uneducated." Ultimately, Gabriel explained his cultural/professional commitments to being a role model as well as a culturally responsive and socially just teacher in terms of providing greater educational opportunity and access for students of color. He identified education as key to such access: "I know that education is key, and I really wanted to give back and try to get more Latinos in college or to get them motivated in education, get an involvement with their community and try to do something productive in their lives other than going the gang route."

As far as being a role model, Gabriel explained how he wants to work with youth from non-dominant cultural communities because he wants them to see someone who "resembles them . . . [showing] that we can succeed as a culture, as a particular ethnic group." In his view of being a culturally responsive teacher, Gabriel explained his high expectations and caring stance: "I want to be the teacher that is their first math teacher that actually cares about [students of color] or pushes them to do well." He recognized the importance of making the math relevant to students, and, by giving them a familiar context, he hoped to get them to pay attention to the math concepts. Gabriel described his concern about the high dropout rates of students of color, particularly Mexican students. He wanted students to have more "choices" like higher education and wants students to have a "better life" with education. Gabriel explained his social justice perspective: "Social justice is very important, especially for students of color that are living in really tough areas. Social justice is being sensitive and trying to engage all students and make sure everyone is given equal opportunities." Gabriel particularly wanted to become a middle school math teacher to effect change early in students' careers so that they will graduate high school, and he viewed math as a significant barrier to getting into a good college for many students of color. Thus, "access" was at the center of Gabriel's commitments to educational change for youth of color. Gabriel described the kind of school he hopes to teach in as a school with a large Latino population, with urban and low-income youth, because he wants to provide them with choices and opportunities in a system that historically has not served them well:

> A lot of these kids are dropping out and there is a reason why . . . pretty much these kids have been let down—students of color—in education for quite some time now and I know that within the students of color, specifically the Mexicans, have the highest dropout rate. With the kids that are dropping out of school, then they won't have their formal education. . . . I want them to be able to have choices, that they could pursue a higher education—just to have a better life within education and realize that there are opportunities out there to go on.

Background Influences on Gabriel's Commitments

Gabriel's commitment to community and his conceptualization of his cultural/professional roles were informed by his family background, schooling, and teacher education experiences. His background experiences reflect the conflicting pressures of immigrant families negotiating bicultural identifications, yet with the twist of being third generation and middle class. His family experiences also highlight both the promises of and the questions about U.S. schooling for the Chicano community. Gabriel identifies as a third-generation Chicano and Mexican American who grew up in a middle-income community that was predominantly of Mexican descent. Gabriel explained the influence that his father had on his own identity, rooted in his father's involvement in the early Chicano movement in Los Angeles. He explained how his father taught him the importance of "protecting your own" and "help[ing] each other out." Gabriel also described conflicts in the larger family, in which Gabriel's paternal grandmother and paternal uncle refer to themselves as "American Mexican," wanting to identify as American first, Mexican second. Gabriel's parents did not teach him or his brothers Spanish because "they did not want to confuse us," wanting them to learn English (he indicated that they later regretted their decision because they saw the importance of being bilingual).

While neither of Gabriel's parents completed college, they engaged in occupations situated in schools and encouraged their children's education. His father was a maintenance worker for a school district, and his mother works as a high school administrative assistant to a vice principal. Initially, Gabriel's mother was not supportive of his becoming a teacher because teachers are not paid well and are not treated well by students, noting many disciplinary problems with students at the high school where she worked. His mother changed her mind once she saw the "teacher in me" and is now excited that Gabriel is interested in teaching. The rest of his family has been very supportive. His younger brother is now attending college. Gabriel identified his older brother as a role model and mentor in education, as the first in the family to attend and complete a 4-year college and now pursuing his doctorate in education administration and policy. His conversations with his brother about educational injustices in the Latino community inspired Gabriel to become a teacher.

Gabriel's own negative schooling experiences (with the exception of a math teacher who was a caring role model) inspired him to become a teacher who provides educational access and role models for students of color. His early schooling experiences opened his eyes to inequities in the educational system in an urban high school with a majority of Mexican American students and some African American, White, and Asian students. He identified how the structural tracking made him want to redress inequities in schooling. He wanted to "give back what I didn't get." While he took a few classes in the honors International Baccalaureate program, he took other classes in what was described as the "college prep" program. He found differences in these two tracks in regard to course content, teacher quality, and teacher attitudes; he did not feel that the college prep program prepared students for college or provided quality teaching. He further wondered about those students in the "regular" track (neither honors nor college prep). The tracking he experienced in high school made him wonder about how students were being prepared for their future as citizens. He wanted to teach regular-track students in an urban school because of their lack of access to school resources. He wanted to let students know he cares about their futures. "I want to be a good teacher for them because I didn't really have any good teachers when I was in the [high school program I was in]. I just want to make sure that they have a chance and that they receive a really good education with a teacher who cares about their future." Gabriel did identify one high school math teacher who inspired him because "he treated us with respect and he really cared about us, as far as succeeding in his class." Thus, care, respect, and high expectations mattered in his vision of becoming a good teacher for students of color.

In college, Gabriel experienced a "huge culture shock" when he left California and attended a state school in Oklahoma, where he was now a minority with few students or faculty of color and no role models in his major. This lack of role models inspired him to want to become a teacher for students of color:

> I was the minority and that was hard. There really weren't any support groups at the university level. . . . I noticed that in my classes, I was pretty much the only student of color and it was very awkward. I didn't feel like I fit in with the group. Even [with] the professors and the department . . . I didn't feel like I can connect with anyone culturally and that's very important to me. The lack of that really [mattered]. . . . I realized education is important. I didn't have any role models in the college setting and it's obvious that a lot of kids also have this. They don't have any role models that resemble them. So I decided, teaching and education would be a good way to prevent kids that look like myself, or other students of color, from lacking a role model that looks like them.

Gabriel was attracted to the social justice perspective of the teacher education program he eventually attended. His preparation program provided a positive experience, inspiring his commitment to teaching youth from non-dominant communities in urban schools, to teaching for social justice, and to understanding more about cultural complexities as a teacher of color. When he explained what he hoped to gain from the program, he said, "I just want to learn more about urban schools and what we can do as social justice educators, what we can do for these kids to prevent them from failing, continuing to fail in this society." He described the program's philosophy:

> To make sure that we teach in a very social justice manner, because that's what this whole [teacher education] program is all about. Just making sure that everyone has a chance to succeed even though the schools may lack the resources, the teachers must bend over backwards and try to help these kids as much as possible with different teaching strategies so these kids don't fall behind as they have in the past and can go forward and go to college.

Finally, Gabriel reported that taking a class on identity issues was a critical experience in his preservice education. He explained that "[it] helped me figure out who I am. . . . They wanted us to figure out who we are as individuals before we teach." It helped him to realize that he is "bicultural." Gabriel explained:

I do have a lot of the Mexican values and traditions, but then also because I'm third generation, I share a lot of American mainstream qualities, too. I realized how important it is, and it was also a very painful experience, too, in not being able to speak Spanish, which was a big issue and I brought it up in class.

However, he realized the importance of learning Spanish to communicate better with parents of the children he wants to teach. Ultimately, his teacher education program helped heighten his own understanding of cultural identifications and strengthened his commitment to teaching for social justice in urban communities of color. In his view, this would provide students of color a "chance to succeed" and access "to go forward."

Tanya's Commitments and Conceptions of Cultural/Professional Roles

Tanya described herself as African American of Caribbean descent with a deep connection to her home community. She identified her commitments to giving back to her own community: "I feel that's my responsibility to my community; that's how it motivates me [to want to teach there]. I think about all of the things that it has given me that helped me get where I wanted to be, and I owe it to my community to do the same thing." She affirmed her sense of commitment to returning to her home community: "I feel as a leader of my community, it is my responsibility. If I am going to be a teacher, I should be a teacher in the community where I received so many of my talents and guides." She plans to teach in a low-income, inner-city school and maintains a mission to support youth whom the system has underserved:

I want to work with the students who the school says can't succeed. . . . I really want to teach and target those students, because I don't believe that students can't make it. I'm clear that it is the system that makes them believe that they can't make it, and so they just got turned from education. . . . I want to teach in a school that's going to be challenging but at the same time allows me to get to the people that need me the most.

While Tanya's commitment to community is similar to Gabriel's, how she conceptualizes her role is different. She wants to be a transformative agent of change in her school and society, someone who reverses injustices in the educational system and the larger society. Tanya cites Paulo Freire in describing her own "liberatory approach of exposing the kids to the reality of their situation or as he phrases it, the reality of their oppression." She envisioned her role as a community advocate and activist:

I believe my role at any school is not only as a teacher. I believe that the teacher has a responsibility to be an advocate in that community and live in that community and be a participant in that community. As a teacher I feel it's not only my role to teach and educate the students, to build friendships with my student and to make the school a better place, so I'm not only a teacher, but I'm an activist. I'm an advocate. I'm a community advocate and community participant.

Tanya envisioned becoming a teacher as becoming a role model in her community:

It is my responsibility to be a role model to my students because they may not see any other positive person in their life or in their community, especially when they go outside or when they turn on the television. They are not portrayed or seen in a positive fashion. They don't see that many positive role models, so I think that is my ultimate responsibility.

Tanya reported that her status as a person of color will inform her role as a teacher, making her more sensitive to the experiences and culture of African American and Latino students. She also identified how being a woman helped her empathize with others in "subordinate" positions. Finally, she identified her commitment to being a socially just and culturally responsive teacher in teaching history to underserved communities:

My beliefs are . . . to make the curriculum as socially and culturally responsive as possible. Students tend to tune out if you present the same type of boring and bland type of history, and they don't see themselves reflected in the history. There is a lot of critical pedagogy written about students from underserved communities . . . how they view the curriculum, how they tune out from education in general just because it is not culturally responsive, and they don't see themselves in the curriculum, and it doesn't relate to them in any way, shape, or form, so they don't see the purpose of learning it.

Background Influences on Tanya's Commitments

Tanya's commitment to community and her transformative conceptualization of her cultural/professional roles were informed by her family background, schooling, and teacher education experiences. Tanya explained that her commitment to being an agent of change derived from her earliest experiences and were reinforced by messages throughout her formative years: "You can't one night wake up and be a change agent. It's something planted in you from the beginning . . . in every single aspect of the realms of my life I heard that message [about being a change agent]."

Tanya's grandmother was from the Caribbean, and Tanya grew up in New Jersey, in what she characterized as a working-class/middle-class African American community. She was an only child and lived with her mother, who had some college education, and a stepdad, who was an engineer. Her father lived nearby. Tanya grew up in Black Islamic activist family. She was always told that "oppression was out there and racism was out there, that there is a racist institution in America." She also recounted how her family celebrated African American traditions and culture so that she knew of contributions of Africans and African Americans: "They just practiced things that would always tell us about our history and our culture, and where we were from." For example, Tanya describes her family celebrating Kwanzaa:

> My family celebrates Kwanzaa. A lot of the principles and things that you learn in Kwanzaa have to do with African American history and African traditions. So you learn a lot about the history of African Americans, the history of Africa; you learn about African languages and traditions. Like I was given books on African American adventure, and I was given books on famous African Americans for Kwanzaa, and I would read those books and my parents would read them to me.

Tanya explained that her "mom is a role model just for the simple fact that she was very strong and very persistent, and she didn't let obstacles stop her from achieving her goals and meeting her aspirations. She always had high expectations for me." Tanya's mother was an advocate for Tanya's early education and moved her from school to school looking for a good education. Her father was an advocate for her as well. Yet her mother was not initially supportive of her becoming a teacher, wanting her instead to go into business or law. Consequently, her mother stopped paying for the private university when Tanya changed direction from her international business major to turn to history and teaching:

> My mom didn't want me to teach; she actually wanted me to go into corporate America. . . . I never really wanted to do [international marketing major] . . . and she said, "I am not paying all of this money for you to go to school . . . " and I at that time was going to a private institution, "for you to go and become a teacher."

Tanya's boyfriend (and later husband) encouraged her to follow her commitment even if her mother wouldn't pay her tuition. When her mother stopped paying tuition, she began to work part time and her husband stopped school for a while to work full time to support her education. Eventually, Tanya finished her undergraduate career at a public university. She was more committed than ever to becoming a teacher in order to give something back to her community rather than make money.

Tanya explained that she was sustained by a broader community of support, including her neighborhood, her extended cultural community, and her racial/ethnic community.

> There were a lot of people in my community that, when I was coming up, helped me in various ways and were teachers to me even if they didn't have college degrees. . . . They always made sure I was getting good grades, checked on me, took me with them to college to see what it was like.

Tanya described both negative and positive early schooling experiences, which informed her political consciousness and inspired her commitment to becoming a teacher in order to redress inequities of schooling in her own community. She highlighted how her racial background was addressed by educators:

> The more sensitive teachers were the African American teachers, and I don't know if it's because they are African Americans, so they are slightly more sensitive to the culture or what exactly it was, but they tended to be more sensitive to my home culture and less critical of some of the cultural things that I brought into the classroom. Whereas my Caucasian teachers, because they didn't understand or they may not have been familiar with the culture I was coming from, would make comments, statements that I felt weren't appropriate.

She described the divide between her home and earliest schooling experiences as "the biggest dichotomy between what I was learning in school and my home experiences, it's just that it was totally irrelevant to what was going on in my house, what was going on in my community." Tanya explained:

> The things that we learned, the way that they went about approaching the curriculum and teaching the curriculum, they never made it relevant to my life experiences and my home experiences. Especially when it came to language acquisition, there was no recognition at all of the dialect of English that we spoke. My family's from the Caribbean, so they speak with an accent. . . . I spoke English but I just spoke a certain dialect of English and there was no sensitivity toward that.

Tanya described a negative experience when she was 7 with a teacher who challenged her Caribbean dialect. She explained that the teacher "made a big scene" about the way Tanya pronounced words in ways that her family communicated, resulting in student teasing and Tanya thinking:

> Well maybe my family members aren't smart or something. I was wondering, "Well, why is it that they pronounce certain words differently than everybody else?" I knew that they were from somewhere else. At that time I didn't know how to make that connection between them pronouncing certain words [and being from somewhere else]. I just assumed that maybe I was stupid or they were stupid.

Tanya attended a magnet program in a public elementary school, but when her mother observed some poor teaching, she moved Tanya to a Catholic junior high school and then later to a public magnet high school where the teachers were not "great," but the principal cared and helped her. Tanya noted that the history curriculum did not address African Americans or their contributions to history, describing it as "racist." She later had an African American teacher who finally included African American and Native American perspectives.

In striking contrast, Tanya felt that her high school principal, a White woman, was a strong advocate for her. Tanya reported that she was a bright student yet was outspoken and "challenging to my teachers." Tanya's principal both supported and encouraged her to not "care about what these people say about you, you need to get your education and keep on going." According to Tanya, the principal cared deeply about students, particularly those who were struggling. Tanya was such a student, and she explained that a lot of her teachers questioned whether "maybe she should leave and we should kick her out." Tanya reported, "The principal really stood by me." Tanya had long conversations with her principal and even visited her principal's home. She remembered, "I ended up graduating with a 3.7 and I was class president. I probably wouldn't have done it if it wasn't for her encouraging me to keep on going and helping me along the way."

Tanya explained how attending a historically Black college (HBC) extended earlier family messages about Black consciousness, becoming a change agent, and contributing to her community:

> It was always instilled in us that we were change agents and that we were supposed to be leaders of our community. W.E.B. DuBois calls it "the talented tenth" and how the responsibility of the talented tenth is to help the other 90% in the community, and that was really driven into us at [my historically Black college] as our role and responsibility. That has always

stuck with me. . . . Then I look back and I looked at all of the people in my community who helped me . . . including my principal. . . . It made me say, I have a responsibility to do the same. If people did it for me, then I should do it for others in my community.

Tanya faced a critical juncture during her junior year at the HBC when she changed her professional goal from business to teaching and realized that helping the community must be her "life commitment." According to Tanya, "That's your job [helping the community]. You are in this position because that is your role, that's why you're at this school."

Tanya chose a teacher education program committed to social justice and urban education. She explained: "It is one of the few programs in the country that teaches you about inner-city students, the dynamics of inner-city communities, social justice, and social injustices. . . . A major advantage of the program is that it prepares you to go into those communities and teach and to persevere in those communities." Tanya explained how the program also focused on issues of culture; always talked about race and culture; and included classes on race, identity and culture as the focus of the curriculum. Tanya identified a limitation of the program: In giving students the drive to teach in urban settings, the program tended to focus on the cultural identity development of White teachers but not African Americans and other people of color. Tanya joined a curriculum committee to address this shortcoming.

Tanya highlighted the significance of a class she took on culturally relevant curriculum. The African American course instructor invited students to come to his house to plan lessons. Through this experience, Tanya developed a network of like-minded practitioners. She explained: "Whenever I was stumped on a lesson and I didn't know how do I tie this into what the kids are doing today, I can e-mail or call someone in that cohort that we developed on our own and they would give me some ideas that they did and what they did to make it relevant." She felt her cohort was made up of "like-minded educators and professionals." She would call on them to sustain her vision in practice.

THE CULTURAL/PROFESSIONAL COMMITMENTS OF TEACHERS OF COLOR: THE POTENTIAL BURDEN OF VIRTUE

Whether it originated in messages they received from their own families, communities, and teachers, from teacher education program, or from the profession, the teachers in this study adopted a strong commitment to giving back to their communities, to teaching to transform the lives of students of color, to culturally and linguistically responsive practices, and to teaching for social change. Their expressions of professional identity were deeply linked to cultural identities and to commitments to teaching students of color. These commitments drew them into the profession, to teacher education programs that reinforced such beliefs, and to work in schools with students from non-dominant cultural and linguistic communities. Such commitments may drive them to want to remain in such teaching environments.

While they each had unique experiences and may have varied in their nuanced conceptions of social change, ranging from access to more transformative stances, it is striking that all of the teachers report similar commitments to teaching to support communities of color and cultural/professional roles. These heightened expectations about their future roles may be a tall order for new teachers, particularly those who have had to struggle within the very systems they hope to change. It is noteworthy that the teachers in this study had the same message reinforced over and over from their earliest experiences and later in their professional preparation. It makes one wonder about whether this may be an extra burden for such novices of color, and one that may prove particularly challenging.

Enacting their commitments will require that they possess and be able to employ pedagogical skills to provide opportunities to learn for students of color, including the skills of culturally and linguistically responsive teaching. The teachers who participated in this study reported that their teacher preparation programs emphasized just such instructional approaches. However, the increasing number of teachers of color who enter the profession through short-term, alternative pathways often receive only limited preparation in general instructional methods, let alone pedagogical approaches for working with students of color (Villegas & Geist, 2008). Additionally, research reveals that new teachers must be supported by their schools in further developing their pedagogical knowledge and skills, which may be particularly important for teachers of color, who work in the challenging environments of urban schools that serve students from low-income and culturally non-dominant communities.

Thus, while the teachers in our study experienced heightened expectations for their cultural/professional roles, the questions remain: Where did the teachers go? What schooling contexts would they enter? And to what degree would such conditions support or undermine their commitments to and retention in schools that serve youth from non-dominant cultural and linguistic communities? These questions are particularly pertinent because, as Peter reminds us, there may need to be a supportive schooling environment to sustain new teachers of color with such commitments:

It's been my experience that not all environments are receptive to African American male teachers, African American teachers and other minority teachers. It appears that that will be a constant challenge throughout my career. . . . Whatever school I'm placed at, I believe they will have to be supportive of having minority teachers . . . that they believe that's important and integral to society and having those types of teachers in the community and supporting them in everyway.

Thus we take up these questions of where the teachers go and the nature of schooling contexts in the next chapters.

CHAPTER 4

Where Do the Teachers Go and Why?

This chapter explores the types of schools to which the new teachers of color were attracted, the retention and turnover rates among the teachers, and the factors that influenced these patterns. We found that the teachers were drawn to work in schools with high proportions of students from low-income communities of color. Overall, the teachers tended to stay in these schools over time at higher rates than national trends in the general new teacher workforce. The teachers reported being motivated by their deep sense of commitment to youth of color, which was fueled by the teachers' personal experiences and professional preparation. Those teachers who moved to other schools attributed this to the lack of support in their initial schools; they moved to other schools that serve low-income students and communities of color, which again runs counter to a trend in the general teacher workforce. Thus, the new teachers of color did not move because they wanted to teach a different student population; rather, they found the conditions at the initial schools untenable. Those few who left teaching described a deep struggle with leaving behind students of color. The results of our study are consistent with findings from previous research on retention patterns among teachers of color nationally that reveal their humanistic commitment to working and remaining in high-minority, "hard-to-staff" schools and document that teachers move to escape unsupportive conditions in schools. The chapter closes by questioning the social justice of promoting policies aimed at attracting and retaining teachers of color in urban, "hard-to-staff" schools but failing to enact policies to alleviate the lack of resources and other poor working conditions that often characterize these schools.

THE SCHOOLS WHERE TEACHERS TAUGHT

Immediately after the first year of preservice education, 18 of the 21 teachers took teaching positions in urban schools serving culturally and linguistically diverse students. One teacher took a leave to take a position to make money for his family but hoped to return to teaching, another had a baby before returning, and two had not completed their credential work (one of whom was teaching full time while seeking to complete her credential). In their first year of teaching, 14 teachers worked in high schools, 7 of which were charter schools, and 4 worked in middle schools. Nine of the schools were located in southern California and 9 in northern California. Some of the schools were charter/magnet schools with philosophies similar to those of the teachers' preservice programs. In other cases, teachers were placed in schools where other new teachers from their teacher education program were working as a cohort to provide support. The schools' enrollments ranged from 297 to 2,903 students. The schools were all "majority minority," ranging from 61% to 100% students of color, with an average of 89%. While all schools included some mix of student cultural backgrounds, in all but 3 schools Latino students made up the majority of the students of color. African Americans made up the largest group of students of color in the other 3 schools. Asian, Filipino, Native American, Pacific Islander, and mixed-race student populations were also reflected in the schools. On average, 61% of the students in these schools qualified for free or reduced-price lunches, and 31% were English language learners. The faculties of the schools ranged from 17% to 76% teachers of color, with an average of 43%. Table 4.1 provides a detailed breakdown of school demographics.

TURNOVER AND RETENTION PATTERNS AND INFLUENCES

Overall, the turnover rate for the new teachers of color in this study was lower than national figures on the general new teacher workforce. The retention of these teachers was positively affected by their commitment to working with students from non-dominant cultural communities. The organizational contexts of schools—namely, the availability of human, social, and multicultural capital and supportive power relations—influenced the teachers' decisions to move from or stay at their initial school placements. All movers went to other schools serving non-dominant communities.

Incomplete Entry

Three of the 21 new teachers of color did not complete the preliminary credentialing process. Agustin left his preservice program for financial reasons, family issues, and challenges with passing the preliminary credentialing test. He went into real estate to support Latinos in becoming homeowners:

Financial issues actually made me think twice about getting into education. Another obstacle that I have had this year has been passing the CSET [California Subject Examinations for Teachers]. . . . I have had to repeat it . . . just going to the schools and seeing children out there and the needs in education motivate me and help me get back up on my feet and want to study for this exam.

Two other prospective teachers began teaching but did not complete initial credentialing requirements and dropped out of the study.

Leavers and Shifters

Of the 18 teachers who completed the credential process and earned master's degrees, 2 left teaching, and 1 shifted to a nonteaching position but remained in education. While each teacher is unique, these teachers explained that low levels of social, multicultural, and human capital, along with top-down power relations in their schools, influenced their decisions.

Theresa moved from her initial school before she left teaching at the end of her 2nd year because of a lack of social capital in her initial placement. She reported a lack of connection and cultural match with her teacher colleagues as well as a need for more support from administrators generally and support in developing as a math teacher specifically:

I haven't made too many friendships with my co-workers. That's one thing that [a colleague] suggested that I need to reach out to more people on the staff, because that's how they survive here. . . . I really don't feel that I have much in common with the people that I work with. . . . I am a Latina female, I speak Spanish. I didn't come from the background that . . . most of my colleagues came from. My parents didn't go to high school or college or anything like that. . . . I never felt like I fit in.

Theresa also identified a lack of human capital in her school and a need for greater support in teaching mathematics: "I want to improve my teaching and I know that I'm going to improve just based on experience, but I would like somebody coming in constantly and observing me. Our principal and our vice principal come in once a month, but they don't have math backgrounds." She also found that two of the four members of her math team were planning on leaving at the end of the year. She struggled with the decision to leave because of her deep commitment to students: "I love the kids, and I don't want to leave them . . . and I know that they have teachers coming in and out of their lives all

Table 4.1. School Demographics

Key: L = Latino; AA = African American; A = Asian; F = Filipino;
N = Native American; P = Pacific Islander; W = White; M = Multiracial

Teacher	School					
Pseudonym	*Student % by Ethnicity/ Race*	*ELL%*	*Free/ Reduced-Price Lunch %*	*School Level*	*# Students*	*Teacher Demographics ToC = % Teachers of Color Breakdown by Race/Ethnicity*
Alejandra	L = 54, AA = 29, P = 5, F = 5, W = 4, M = 3	34	66	High	296	50 ToC W = 50, L = 32, M = 6, A = 6, AA = 6
Alicia	L = 84, W = 13, AA = 2, A = 1, N = 1	13	48	High	2337	39 ToC W = 62, L = 31, A = 5, AA = 2
Angela	W = 39, L = 33, P = 9, A = 8, F = 6, AA = 4, M = 1, N = 1	15	15	High	1137	19 ToC W = 81, L = 13, M = 3, A = 3
Carmen	L = 95, AA = 5	54	88	Middle	2562	61 ToC W = 39, L = 29, AA = 21, F = 6, A = 5
Gabriel	L = 98, AA = 1	54	96	Middle	2798	76 ToC L = 53, M = 24, W = 24, AA = 11, F = 8, A = 4
Inez	AA = 56, L = 44	22	57	Middle	1948	64 ToC AA = 48, W = 36, L = 10, A = 3, N = 2, F = 1
John	L = 59, AA = 27, W = 6, A = 3, F = 3, P = 1, M = 1	14	56	High	1375	50 ToC W = 50, L = 26, A = 10, AA = 9, F = 5
Jose	L = 54, AA = 29, P = 5, F = 5, W = 4, M = 3	34	66	High	296	50 ToC W = 50, L = 32, AA = 6, A = 6, M = 6
Linh	L = 53, AA = 37, W = 5, M = 2, F = 1, A = 1	41	65	High	237	56 ToC W = 44, L = 19, AA = 25, A = 13

Teacher	School					
Pseudonym	Student % by Ethnicity/ Race	ELL%	Free/ Reduced- Price Lunch %	School Level	# Students	Teacher Demographics ToC = % Teachers of Color Breakdown by Race/Ethnicity
Liz	L = 90, W = 3, AA = 3, A = 1, N = 1, F = 1, M = 1	38	75	High	297	50 ToC W = 50, L = 36, M = 14
Lucia	L = 62, AA = 21, W = 11, M = 4, F = 2, A = 1	25	78	Elementary	1050	25 ToC W = 75, AA = 14, L = 9, A = 2
Manuel	L = 81, A = 16, AA = 1, W = 1	44	87	Middle	2018	56 ToC W – 44, L – 31, A – 17, AA = 6, F = 1
Mike	W = 35, L = 32, A = 11, F = 9, AA = 7, M = 4, P = 1, N = 1	19	46	Middle	1090	17 ToC W = 83, M = 8, A = 4, F = 2, L = 2, AA = 1
Monica	AA = 72, L = 28	11	67	High	2890	Incomplete data
Ricardo	L = 75, AA = 15, W = 5, P = 2, A = 2, F = 1	34	64	High	2903	47 ToC W = 53, L = 22, A = 14, AA = 7, M = 2, F = 2
Sonya	L = 61, W = 26, AA = 3, A = 3, P = 3, M = 2, F = 2, N = 1	33	33	High	1687	25 ToC W = 75, L – 13, AA = 5, A = 5, F = 2, N = 1
Tanya	AA = 39, L = 34, W = 24, A = 3	0	63	High	623	20 ToC W = 80, AA = 12, A – 4, N = 3, L = 1
Theresa	L = 35, W = 28, A = 16, F = 14, AA = 5, P = 1, N = 1	23	24	High	1833	32 ToC W = 68, A = 16, L = 10, F = 4, AA = 3

Note: School data reflective of teachers' 2nd year of teaching. Student and teacher demographics are from state database website (http://api.cde.ca.gov/reports/page2.asp?subject=API&level=School&submit1=submit) and sites on districts and schools (http://www.ed-data.k12.ca.us/ and http://education.state.nj.us/). Numbers are rounded to the nearest whole number.

the time, sometimes many a year. . . . I want to add some stability . . . [but] it is really, really hard."

In her 2nd year of teaching, Theresa moved to a different high school that also served students from non-dominant cultural communities, where she thought she would receive more support from colleagues. She grew dissatisfied with the level of social capital and collegial support at the second school, identifying disagreements with math colleagues on how to approach teaching and expectations of students. Furthermore, she described a general lack of social capital due to the size of the school, reporting that a large school created a sense of alienation for both teachers and students. She also identified a lack of multicultural capital when describing her disconnect with some members of the math team, with many of them focused solely on standards and some expressing low expectations for the students: "There were clearly divisions between where people stood on how to teach and what was appropriate for our kids and even what they believed our kids could do." She further noted problematic power relations, reflected in the school's top-down decisionmaking approach.

Though Theresa left her second school, she continued to tutor and coach students at the school and reported that she would like to return to education, indicating that she would like to start her own school. She held high expectations for her teaching, identifying ways in which she did not want to fail in meeting the needs of her students. She felt she was not "doing justice" to her students in her teaching, given the image of good teaching she had developed in her preservice program:

> I also feel like [my preservice program] really showed us and kind of drilled it in our heads what a good teacher looks like and a math classroom that is really working and people are learning, what that looks like. I just feel like I'm nowhere close to that and that's been very hard. That's been tough, too, when I feel like I've been trained to be the best, when I can't do that, or when I feel like I'm not being the best, how do I deal with that?

A second new teacher, Angela, returned to teach in the school she had attended as a student. She took a leave in the middle of her 3rd year of teaching, citing "burnout, physical and emotional exhaustion," and then left teaching at the end of the schoolyear. She said her reasons for leaving did not have to do with students, who continued to motivate and inspire her, or her colleagues and site administrator, whom she found supportive. Rather, her decision involved "personal reasons" of feeling burned out and a sense of being overwhelmed. She also reported challenges that reflected shortages of resources and authoritarian power relations, including budget cuts, benefit cuts, and extensive layoffs in the beginning of the schoolyear, despite the district knowing that there were prior budget concerns, union disagreements, and a possible strike. She reported the guilt she felt in leaving her Latino community:

> I felt a lot of guilt because I thought I'd be a teacher forever. I wanted to especially help my community and do all that good stuff. . . . My goal was to come back and help my community, and especially I felt guilt for leaving my Latino community because I was La Raza club adviser and the liaison to the Latino Parent Club. I wanted to be a teacher so students of color, especially Latinos could be like: "She did this, she did that, she went to college, so can I." That's the part that really hurts.

Angela has not ruled out a return to teaching but is currently working in the computer industry.

The third teacher, Alicia, shifted roles at the end of her 3rd year of teaching, entering a PhD program in educational administration and planning to remain in education. She described issues related to power relations in explaining her desire to take on more of a leadership role and have a voice in educational reform, which she didn't feel was supported in her classroom and school context. She hoped to be an administrator in an alternative school, where she felt she could better connect with students than in a traditional comprehensive school. She continued teaching on Saturdays with Upward Bound while completing her degree. She planned to return to the classroom part time the following year and continue her PhD program: "My long-term goal was always to go into administration or go into more of a leadership capacity." When asked what factors contributed to her shifting roles, she explained: "I really felt like I had much more to contribute than what I was doing in the classroom to education, to reform." She explained what would have sustained her in her school "would have been having more opportunities to be involved in leadership and to take on greater leadership roles. I felt like I wanted to do more and it was just kind of confined to my classroom space in that context."

Alicia also identified a lack of access to multicultural capital in explaining what kinds of support she would have liked as a teacher of color:

> Specifically as a teacher of color, I would have liked to have more administrative support and colleague support for developing new programs to address the needs of students of color. . . . I feel like as a teacher of color . . . I may have a better understanding of what these students are going through and what some of their needs might be. I never really felt supported in the sense of developing my ideas and implementing my ideas.

Of the 18 teachers who completed their credentials, 3 left teaching: 2 as "leavers" and 1 as a "shifter." This meant an attrition rate of 17% after 5 years. Of the 21 individuals who began the study, 3 were leavers or shifters and 3 did not enter the profession, resulting in an overall attrition rate of 29%. By both counts, new teachers of color in this study had lower rates of attrition after 5 years than national projections of attrition rates after 5 years for the overall teacher workforce. Ingersoll and Connor (2009) estimate beginning teacher attrition (those who left teaching) at the following rates based on a national analysis of the 2004–2005 Teacher Follow-Up Study: 11% after 1 year, 20% after 2 years, 27% after 3 years, 36% after 4 years, and 46% after 5 years. The retention of teachers of color in our study is consistent with the findings of previous research that, while teachers of color tend to work in urban schools serving high proportions of students from low income and racially and culturally non-dominant communities, they are more likely to remain there than White teachers (Connor, 2008; Hanushek, Kain, & Rivkin, 2004; Kirby, Berends, & Naftel, 1999; Scafidi, Sjoquist, & Stinebrickner, 2007).

It is notable that the new teachers in our study assumed they would all stay in the profession long term and that on average they intended to remain in classroom teaching for 8 years, with 16 of 21 indicating a minimum of 5 years. Most reported that they planned to move onto an administrative or leadership role in education. Thus, shifters may not represent a net loss to the profession. This pattern held for leavers and the individuals who did not complete their credentials: One who left in her 3rd year of teaching had planned to stay in teaching until retirement, and the other who left at the end of her 2nd year had projected staying for 5 years. The 3 individuals who did not complete their credentials had expected to remain in teaching for 3, 4, and 10 years.

Movers

Six of the teachers moved from their initial schools and, as reported above, one teacher moved after her 1st year and then eventually left teaching. All of the movers went to teach in other urban schools with high proportions of students from low income and non-dominant cultural communities. This pattern contrasts with research on White teachers, who tend to move to schools with lower proportions of students from low income and non-dominant cultural communities.

The predominant reason the new teachers of color gave for leaving schools related to unsupportive organizational contexts, including lack of social capital (weak collegial support), lack of multicultural capital (low expectations for or negative attitudes about students of color and lack of support for culturally responsive or socially just teaching), and challenging power relations (problems with the administration and lack of teacher influence on decisionmaking and instructional autonomy). Some of these elements align with Ingersoll and colleagues' findings from analyses of nationally representative surveys that retention rates of teachers of color are negatively affected by low levels of administrative support, teacher classroom autonomy, and faculty influence in decisionmaking (Ingersoll & Connor, 2009; Ingersoll & May, 2010). In addition, three of the teachers reported moving to reestablish family connections and/or return to their home communities. One moved from a middle school to a high school because he preferred working with older students.

Tanya moved after her 1st year of teaching to return to her home state and the high school she had attended. In explaining why she left her initial school, she gave personal reasons for moving. Early in her career, she had hoped to return to her home community and school and wanted to support her ailing grandmother. In terms of organizational factors influencing her decision to change schools, Tanya specifically identified problematic power relations, a lack of social capital as reflected in low collegial support, and a lack of multicultural capital. She described unsupportive power relations in the school she left: "The administration at our school doesn't support the teachers [or] the decisions the teachers make." She reported that administrators had not supported her when parents complained about her failing students at the end of the 1st term. She felt that "instead of supporting" her and the clear, high expectations she set for her students, the administration "condoned" and "agreed" with the parents.

> I don't think that enough is being done to really prepare the students, so I just can't deal with that anymore. It becomes frustrating to me to deal with and to see it going on, and I just can't deal with that. I'd rather go to a school where . . . it may be in shambles but everybody is working to try to better it for the students, and not go to a school where nobody is really concerned about the students, everybody's concerned about their own individual motives and interests.

Tanya noted a lack of multicultural capital on two levels. First, the school did not support African American males and other students who were not on the path to higher education. Second, she reported that a number of colleagues disagreed with the way she taught, particularly her culturally responsive and socially just focus. She also reported a lack of social capital and support from colleagues. Her department colleagues rarely attended meetings, leaving her with little opportunity for subject-specific development: "I never really get to develop professionally with my department."

Another teacher, Gabriel, moved twice. At the end of his 3rd year of teaching, he moved to a new state and school. He moved again in his 5th year to a different middle school in the same district. He reported leaving his initial school because of a lack of community, family, and administrator support; an over-focus on standardized testing; and the need to support his brother's family, including a new baby and wife, who had moved to a new state. He described problematic power relations with a new principal and lack of organization at the school, including student violence and implementation of new programs that were not yet up and running. "I'm burned out and this year really, really took a toll on me. I definitely need a change, otherwise I'm not going to stay in this profession. It's sad that I've come to that after 3 years. . . . I feel like there's no organization at the school." He also identified a lack of multicultural capital and concern over the administration's focus on testing, which undermined his desire to draw on students' cultural resources and connections:

> They want us to do well and our [state] tests are in 2 weeks. But the school really doesn't focus or when we have people talk to us for professional development, it's never, well this is the type of community your kids are coming from, [here are their] cultural resources, it's just never like that. . . . It's always just changing our instruction so that they can do better on the test. . . . It feels like they ignore what the students are bringing, other than they are below grade level.

Gabriel moved to a new state and took a new position working with a well-regarded math reform project that allowed him to teach innovatively in a middle school with a high proportion of minority students. While he had some positive experiences in the new program and school, by spring he again experienced pressure toward standardized testing that resulted in his wanting to leave the new school. In both his schools, teachers lacked control over instructional issues, which reflected administratively driven power relations, and a lack of access to multicultural capital because the schools focused on teaching to a test. The focus was so strong in his new school that the administrator abandoned involvement in the math reform project and had Gabriel remain in the back of the classroom while another teacher prepared students to take the test beginning 7 weeks before it was administered. Ultimately, Gabriel left this school at the end of the year. He explained:

> All drill and kill and just teaching them the surface, traditional method . . . it was just really sad to see it. If I wanted to step up in this school and really try to do something away from that, then it would go against school culture. . . . I will not, I cannot be part of a school like that. It's sad because the students are the ones that are hurting from this.

He moved in his 5th year to teach in another middle school in the district. Ultimately, he planned to return to teach in his home community in Los Angeles, revealing his sustained commitment to meeting the needs of students of color:

> I [will stay in the profession] for as long as I can. Teachers can still make a difference even though . . . the system is not set up to really help those students who are in the urban settings . . . mainly students of color. I'm gonna stick around in the population and do what I can.

Still another teacher, Jose, moved at the end of his 3rd year. He explained that he moved because of concerns about limited social capital in his department and, more importantly, a lack of multicultural capital as reflected in lowered expectations for students of color:

> I've been frustrated [with the] low standards that are going on for students. . . . I was getting really frustrated 'cause everyone was just talking about how to get people to graduate high school and I think that's not enough. It should be more. It should be college and beyond. . . . I really care about these kids. . . . I hope so much for them and it's deeply saddening when students aren't engaged with education.

He also indicated that he wished his staff could talk about issues of race and expectations of students:

> There's a certain kind of reflective teacher that thinks a lot about racial issues and really digs into it, and I just haven't had that conversation with colleagues. . . . I'm just frustrated with low academics and behavioral expectations and then [educators] kind of saying, "That's the way the kids are."

Jose moved to another urban school with a high percentage of students from nondominant cultural communities, noting how he felt that the staff at the new site held higher expectations for students.

Another mover, Liz, appreciated the multicultural capital in her school, noting its founder's social justice mission of enabling students of color to become first-generation college goers. She decided to move to become a founding teacher in a charter middle school that spun off the high school where she had taught for 4 years. She reported challenging power relations in her initial school, with limitations in the leadership after the founder left and limited social capital due to an estimated 50% turnover of teachers. She explained her reason for leaving her initial site: "This year in terms of wanting to leave, it's a lot about school context and school leadership. I've just been disillusioned by seeing behind the door of administration. . . . I worry that the leadership for whatever reason is not inspiring. . . . [It's a] lack of vision on the leadership's part." Liz plans to take a school leadership position in the future.

Stayers

Two themes are reflected in the reasons that nine teachers gave for remaining in their schools through their 5th year of teaching: (1) a commitment to work in schools with students from non-dominant communities and (2) supportive school contexts.

These teachers reported having a strong commitment to making a difference in the lives of students from culturally non-dominant communities. For example, Inez, a Latina bilingual English as a second language (ESL) teacher, explained a significant reason for staying at her school, though the administration was not supportive of her continued efforts to engage the ESL parent community:

> The reason is because my students, our population, the ESL group needs me and I feel that I'm a resource to them. They make me feel this, and I think I've also grown to see that there is a need for lots of things in this school, and it's not going to happen if I get up and go to a different school where they might already have this or that.

Another teacher, Ricardo, explained that he remained at his school because of his long-term commitment to following his AVID students (Advancement Via Individual Determination project, made up of first-generation college goers, 90% of whom are Latinos) from freshman year to senior year and getting them into college. He explained that if he did decide to change schools, it would only be to return to his home community and teach in the high school from which he had graduated: "The whole idea is about giving back to the community, just helping others that are coming from the same background and situation that I was in when I was in high school."

Linh, who had considered leaving her school due to administrative turnover and lack of support, explained that she remained into her 5th year because she was committed to teaching and to her students from low-income and non-dominant backgrounds:

> Teaching for me is a calling. . . . I feel like I'm not really getting paid that much and so I'd do it for free regardless. . . . I love the connection that I have

with my students, I love the fact that I'm giving them this opportunity to learn and to grow as human beings. I think it's very important and I'm just very committed to this population that I'm serving.

Teachers also identified factors in their school contexts that affected their decisions to stay: supportive colleagues and administrators (a form of social capital) and opportunities for their voices to be heard (a reflection of positive power relations). Sonya explained that she had leadership opportunities and avenues for learning: "I still feel like there are opportunities to grow, and I definitely feel like I'm a voice that's heard. And that is really redeeming. . . . I feel like I have a place here." She also identified a supportive working environment, including colleagues with whom she collaborated and developed curriculum: "I think knowing that in school we can teach with our doors open so that if I had a question I could ask [colleagues] and if I wanted to explore something new they would give me the support to do so." Linh echoed the importance of her school context: "I guess my reason for wanting to continue in this profession and teaching specifically at my school is directly connected to how competent my administrators are and how I feel like I'm being respected and my ideas are heard by the staff." Carmen noted that after many years of lacking school support, in her 4th year of teaching she finally had a stable team of teachers at her grade level who came from the community and were Latino. She also mentioned that money was a motivating force for remaining in her school; she received a CAL grant for teaching for 5 years in a high-needs school. Ultimately, she reported, it was her commitment to her students that kept her at the school.

IMPLICATIONS OF NATIONAL PATTERNS
OF RETENTION AND TURNOVER OF TEACHERS OF COLOR

Our findings are consistent with national trends of retention and turnover among teachers of color, particularly in two domains: (1) Humanistic commitments draw teachers of color to work in and possibly remain in high-minority, "hard-to-staff" schools, and (2) school movers are impacted by schooling conditions that are policy amenable.

Several studies indicates that higher proportions of teachers of color work and remain in high-minority, "hard-to-staff" schools compared to White colleagues, suggesting that the stability and quality of the teacher workforce in urban schools might be enhanced by increasing retention rates among teachers of color (Adams & Dial, 1993; Darling-Hammond, Dilworth, & Bullmaster, 1996; Hanushek, Kain, & Rivkin, 2004; Harris & Associates, 1998; King, 1993; Kirby et al.,

1999). Studies report that in the general teacher workforce higher rates of teacher turnover are associated with higher proportions of students from low-income and non-dominant racial and cultural backgrounds (Borman & Dowling, 2008). However, several studies reveal that teachers of color are less likely than White colleagues to leave these schools (e.g., Connor, 2008; Dworkin, 1980; Hanushek et al., 2004; Horng, 2005; Kirby et al., 1999; Scafidi et al., 2007; Texas Education Agency, 1995). In a slight variation, Ingersoll & May (2010) reported that while increases in the percent of low-income students, minority students and minority teachers in schools were each related to higher White teacher turnover, there was no relationship between the likelihood of minority teachers departing and any of these demographic characteristics of their schools. Thus, the retention of teachers of color may be a strategy for addressing the problem of "hard-to-staff" schools. Alternatively, it also raises an equity challenge when teachers of color tend to work and remain in schools that may have unsupportive working conditions. This could reproduce the historic pattern of unequal access to resources experienced by people of color in U.S. schools.

Research suggests that a factor not emphasized by studies of the general teacher workforce might impact the retention of teachers of color: the humanistic commitments of teachers of color. For example, Lewis (2006) surveyed 147 new male, African American teachers in three urban districts in Louisiana about their views of factors that affected recruitment and retention. While the teachers rated "job security" as the most important retention factor, this was followed closely by "contributions to humanity." Kottkamp, Cohn, McCloskey, and Provenzo (1987) surveyed 2,718 teachers in Dade County, Florida, and similarly found that, while intrinsic rewards related to "reaching" students were primary for all teachers, African American teachers perceived its importance at higher rates than Whites.

A primary reason that teachers in our study gave for remaining in their schools through the 5th year of teaching was a commitment to working in schools with students from low-income and non-dominant cultural and linguistic communities. These teachers saw themselves as cultural and linguistic resources to youth and their families and wanted to give back to their communities by making a difference in the lives of students of color.

An emerging body of research suggests that school context can affect the retention of teachers of color. Ingersoll and colleagues' work on three recent cycles of the nationally representative Schools and Staffing Survey (1999–2000; 2003–2004; 2007–2008) and Teacher Follow-Up Survey (2000–2001; 2004–2005; 2008–2009) revealed that dissatisfaction with school conditions was the major factor in explaining turnover for minority teachers (Ingersoll & Connor, 2009; Ingersoll & May, 2010). In a recent review of research on retention of teachers of color, the few studies that directly examined factors contributing to turnover among teachers of color identified the following characteristics of schools: financial capital in the form of teacher salaries and other resources, including instructional materials and facilities; social capital in the form of professional development opportunities, mentoring, and participation of new teachers in induction programs; and power relations in the form of administrative support and teachers' classroom autonomy and influence in schoolwide decisionmaking (see Achinstein, Ogawa, Sexton, & Freitas, 2010, for a full review of research). All of these conditions can be changed by policymakers or local administrators and thus potentially provide mechanisms for increasing the retention of teachers of color (Borman & Dowling, 2008).

Findings from our study point to another organizational quality that may impact career decisions of new teachers of color: schools' cultural capital. The most common reason teachers in this study gave for moving from their schools was that their schools were characterized by low expectations or negative attitudes about students of color, lack of support for culturally responsive or socially just teaching, and limited dialogue about race and equity. That is, they left schools that lacked multicultural capital. It is telling that all of the movers transferred to other schools that served non-dominant racial and cultural communities. This suggests that the retention of teachers of color may be affected by the interaction of the humanistic orientation of some teachers of color and the presence of multicultural capital in the schools where they work.

Moreover, a mismatch between the humanistic commitments of teachers of color and schools' capacity to affirm non-dominant and dominant cultures may result in deep conflicts for teachers of color. Bascia's (1996) study identifies a professional conflict for teachers of color who were drawn to support students of color but faced challenges of status and organizational access. The empathy of teachers of color for students of color, which was reported to be rooted in a common experience, resulted in teachers feeling isolated, having few colleagues with whom they shared the same orientation toward students, and being excluded from certain professional and social encounters that could foster a sense of belonging, help their teaching, and impact organizational decisionmaking. Foster (1994) described how African American teachers committed to being agents of change can be undermined by those in power. Teachers of color may find that schools do not recognize their cultural resources and thus experience alienation from their schools' goals, particularly concerning issues of diversity, antiracism, and social justice (Feuerverger, 1997; Foster, 1994). Thus, it is critical to understand the interaction between a commitment to serve students of color (a teacher background factor) and the presence of multicultural capital, along with other forms of organizational capital (a school condition) and its impact on the retention of teachers of color in "hard-to-staff" schools with high proportions of students of color.

Research on retaining teachers of color in urban "hard-to-staff" schools raises a social justice dilemma for practice and policy, pointing to the possible unintended consequence of racially segregated and educationally unequal schools that were deemed unconstitutional by *Brown v. Board of Education* more than half a century ago. Is it problematic to promote retention policies that persuade teachers of color to continue to work and remain in such schools when these are the very schools that are often characterized as underresourced with poor working conditions? How can policies support the retention of teachers of color, particularly in high-needs schools, without reproducing patterns that can be associated with unequal access to learning opportunities for both students and teachers of color? How can educational leaders and policymakers build on the humanistic commitments of teachers of color while simultaneously supporting improved schooling conditions that allow teachers of color to develop and support youth of color?

Beyond retention, we are also concerned with understanding the conditions that support new teachers of color in enacting their cultural/professional commitments. While addressing the *demographic* imperative by retaining new teachers of color, it is only through supporting them in tapping their and their students' cultural resources that the *democratic* imperative can be addressed in order to support learning opportunities for students of color. In the next chapter we examine the conditions in schools that served to either support or challenge the teachers' commitments to enacting cultural/professional roles that drew them into the profession.

CHAPTER 5

Subtractive or Additive Schooling of New Teachers of Color

The Impact of Organizational Contexts on Cultural/Professional Roles

We introduced two imperatives at the beginning of the book: a demographic imperative to close the numerical gap between teachers and students of color and a democratic imperative to close the achievement gap between low-income students of color and more affluent White students. The focus on teacher retention and the demographic imperative, highlighted in the previous chapter, overlooks an important point that is emphasized by proponents of the democratic imperative: Teachers of color may promote educational opportunities and positive outcomes for students of color by accessing cultural and linguistic resources in themselves and their students. This begs the question: Is it enough to simply increase the number of teachers of color who work with students of color?

The National Collaborative on Diversity in the Teaching Force concludes, "Although teacher quality has been accepted and internalized as a mantra for school reform, the imperative for diversity is often marginalized rather than accepted as central to the quality equation in teaching" (NCDTF, 2004, p. 3). A mounting body of research documents the "power of the presence" of teachers of color (Quiocho & Rios, 2000). A recent review of research on retention among teachers of color notes that many teachers of color are motivated by a "humanistic orientation," which reflects the belief that they can improve educational outcomes for students of color (Achinstein, Ogawa, Sexton, & Freitas, 2010). Indeed, an emerging body of research suggests that teachers of color can produce more favorable academic results on standardized test scores, attendance, retention, advanced-level course enrollment, and college-going rates for students of color than can White colleagues (Clewell, Puma, & McKay, 2005; Dee, 2004; Hanushek, Kain, O'Brien, & Rivkin, 2005; Klopfenstein, 2005; Villegas & Irvine, 2010). Studies also report that teachers of color may be able to improve educational opportunities for students of color by serving as role models, culturally and linguistically responsive teachers, and agents of change in the educational system because teachers of color understand the cultural and linguistic experiences of students of color and thus can build cultural bridges between school and students' homes and communities (Gándara & Maxwell-Jolley, 2000; Quiocho & Rios, 2000; Valencia, 2002; Villegas & Irvine, 2010; Villegas & Lucas, 2004).

However, research indicates that new teachers of color may not cultivate the cultural resources needed to perform cultural/professional roles (Villegas & Lucas, 2004). They must be supported in determining ways to develop and employ their own and their students' cultural/linguistic resources (Quiocho & Rios, 2000). Thus, teachers must be supported by communities, schools, and educational policies that encourage their development as teachers who "'stay the course' of work for social justice across multiple roles and responsibilities" (Cochran-Smith, 2004b, p. 391). Yet little research has examined conditions that support or challenge the efforts of new teachers of color to perform cultural/professional roles for students of color.

INFLUENCES ON CULTURAL/PROFESSIONAL ROLES

In this chapter we seek to answer the following questions: How and to what extent are the personal and professional backgrounds of new teachers of color associated with their performance as role models, culturally/linguistically responsive teachers, and agents of change? How and to what extent are conditions in schools associated with the performance of new teachers of color as role models, culturally/linguistically responsive teachers, and agents of change?

A pattern emerged from the cohort of teachers in our study. All of the teachers expressed a commitment to performing cultural/professional roles—such as culturally and linguistically responsive teacher, role model, and change agent—and felt prepared through preservice programs to engage in culturally responsive teaching. However, they varied in the extent to which they were able to engage in these roles. They identified pivotal forces in their school contexts that constrained or supported their roles. Among the 17 teachers active in the study in their 2nd year of teaching, 13 described challenges in enacting culturally and linguistically responsive teaching. Only 1 teacher reported receiving professional support focused on the needs of students of color. Nine reported little to no professional supports for connecting their teaching of content to students' cultures, and no teachers reported support focused on meeting the needs of new teachers of color.

By their 3rd year of teaching, only 4 teachers reported that they engage in high levels of culturally/linguistically responsive teaching. Teachers who reported lower-end enactment of this approach to teaching tended to describe their school contexts as constrained by curriculum, standards, and pacing plans; lacking professional development and learning opportunities generally and regarding issues of culturally/linguistically responsive teaching specifically; lacking administrative and/or collegial support to talk about issues of culture and equity; and, in some cases, exhibiting instances of institutional inequities such as tracking and lowered expectations for students of color. The challenges they reported were linked to their lack of agency, constraints on instructional decisionmaking, limited opportunities to learn, and a school climate unsupportive of addressing issues of culture and equity. Alternatively, some teachers described conditions in their schools that enabled them to access their cultural resources and supported their commitments. They characterized their schools as organizations that made available all forms of capital and that reflected power relations that supported the teachers' cultural and professional commitments to serve the needs of students of color.

To conduct a deeper examination of the enactment of culturally/linguistically responsive teaching, we analyzed videotaped classroom instructional interactions of the 11 Latina/o teachers in the study. While no teacher consistently demonstrated higher enactment in all domains of culturally/linguistically responsive teaching, we noted a general trend: Teachers with lower levels of enactment were in schools that generally exhibited fewer organizational forms of capital and power structures that supported the teachers' commitments to serve students of color. A smaller group of teachers with moderate enactment of culturally/linguistically responsive teaching worked in schools that tended to have more supportive forms of capital and greater teacher control in support of their commitments. Thus, the teachers' experiences in their schools led us to formulate a spectrum of schools, ranging from lower to higher organizational support for enacting cultural/professional roles.

There were a few instances of schools that were less supportive of teachers' cultural/professional roles but where new teachers received some support from outside agencies or individual sponsors or advocates. Sponsors sustain teachers by providing access to human, social, and/or multicultural capital that may not be abundant or even available in teachers' schools, enabling teachers to perform cultural/professional roles. Advocates actively advance a new teacher's efforts in enacting cultural/professional roles to which they are committed by removing barriers, buffering the teacher from sources of resistance, or placing the teacher in a position in which the teacher could work to change his or her school. Gabriel moved to a new school in his 3rd year of teaching and was excited to be working with a national reform effort that he identified as equity-focused in supporting students of color to access and succeed in mathematics courses that often stood as barriers to college. He worked alongside project leaders developing new curriculum and piloting new ideas. Ricardo felt supported by the nationally sponsored AVID (Advancement Via Individual Determination) project, which allowed him to play a critical role in getting his predominantly Latino students into college by working with them from their freshman year through their senior year. Inez felt excited about participating in a new district professional development initiative focused on meeting the needs of culturally and linguistically diverse students with a focus on academic language and culturally responsive literature. Carmen participated in a group of Latino teachers from her preservice program who were committed to raising funds so other Latina/os could go to college to become teachers.

Tanya received support from educators who functioned as sponsors and advocates for her efforts to change the education system to engage the cultural resources of students of color. Tanya returned to teach in the high school she attended in her hometown, which brought her into contact with an extended professional community of veteran teachers who had been her teachers and an administrator who had been her strong supporter (both as a student and now as a teacher). Tanya described how the principal buffered her as a new teacher when a group of teachers wanted her to be "reprimanded" for advocating "too much" for the students and when colleagues challenged her approaches to teaching. In other instances, the principal acted as a power broker by supporting changes that Tanya sought to make in the school or district. Some of Tanya's former teachers still worked for the district in leadership positions and sponsored her: "They take me under their wing . . . pushing me . . . to take on more leadership roles." District administrators were interested in Tanya's teaching and observed her classroom to get new ideas about how to infuse African American and multicultural perspectives into history classes. Tanya was appointed to serve on a district team to rewrite the history curriculum and also became involved with curriculum reform at the state level, creating more of an African American curriculum. Tanya explained: "I'm not only trying to effect change in my school and make my culture more represented in my school, but I'm also trying to effect change on a wider view and a broader view and across the state and if possible maybe even the country." The sponsorship and advocacy of key individuals in leadership roles was a critical element of support for Tanya in her successful attempts to enact culturally responsive and socially just teaching.

In some ways these instances of sponsorship reveal exceptions that prove the rule of the more dominant pattern, where the ability of teachers to act on their commitments to being culturally responsive teachers is blocked by conditions in their schools. While a few teachers received support from sources outside their schools, these supports were often precarious. In the cases of Gabriel and Inez, their outside sources of support were overshadowed by challenges in their schools that undermined their ability to perform their cultural/professional roles. Carmen, who also found herself overwhelmed by the challenges in her school, discontinued participation in the outside school network. Tanya, who received support from district and state sources, was often unable to change her school because of the resistance she met from colleagues. Thus, despite the support these teachers received from external sources, they continued to face school conditions that undermined their ability to act on their cultural/professional commitments.

To examine this organizational phenomenon more deeply, we analyze two cases of Latina teachers who worked in schools that provided lower and higher levels of organizational support for the cultural/professional roles to which the teachers were committed. We selected these two teachers because their cases differed along the spectrum of enactment and organizational support, thus offering the basis for theory building about new teachers of color and contexts that support or inhibit the performance of cultural/professional roles. (For further discussion of the spectrum and these cases, see Achinstein & Ogawa, 2011).

THE CASES OF INEZ AND ALEJANDRA

We examine the cases of Inez and Alejandra, new teachers of Mexican descent who are deeply committed to performing cultural/professional roles. First, we describe how these teachers drew from their personal backgrounds and teacher preparation to fuel their commitments to performing as role models, culturally/linguistically responsive teachers, and agents of change. Second, we describe how the teachers enacted the three roles, disclosing differences in their approaches to changing the education system. Finally, we reveal the complexity of performing these cultural/professional roles and identify dimensions of school contexts, including multiple forms of organizational capital and power relations that challenged or supported these teachers' attempts to perform these roles. By identifying school conditions that affected the ability of these teachers to perform their cultural/professional roles, this study reveals that many of the same conditions that characterize "subtractive schooling," which divests students of color of their cultural resources (Valenzuela, 1999), also affected the capacity of teachers of color to engage the cultural and linguistic resources in which their performances as role models, culturally/linguistically responsive teachers, and agents of change are rooted.

Personal and Professional Backgrounds and Commitments

Inez and Alejandra shared similar ethnic, linguistic, socioeconomic, and schooling backgrounds that shaped their cultural/professional roles in urban schools with high concentrations of students from non-dominant cultural and linguistic communities. Inez was the first of nine siblings born in the United States.

Her parents migrated from Mexico and left school by the 3rd grade to support their families. Her father came to the United States as an undocumented worker and later brought his family. Inez grew up in a low-income, Latina/o neighborhood in California and stayed in that community throughout her schooling, including college and graduate school. Alejandra identified as a first-generation, bilingual Mexican American. Her parents were born in Mexico and came to the United States in their early 20s. Her father was a recently unemployed construction worker; her mother cleaned houses. Alejandra's family, including four siblings, lived in a low-income, Latina/o community in Texas.

Both Inez and Alejandra were influenced by early experiences in school to become teachers and improve opportunities for Latina/o youth. Inez was motivated by her negative experiences as a student who encountered low expectations and limited opportunities. In high school, Inez had her earliest exposure to teaching at her church and through tutoring youth in a housing project in south Los Angeles, where she found students had lost their motivation to learn because "teachers just didn't care." She became committed to being a teacher who cared and held high expectations for urban youth, providing them with a role model and opportunities to succeed. Inez was particularly committed to youth who, like her, were English learners.

Similarly, Alejandra's recognition of the shortcomings of her schooling and sense of injustice inspired her to teach: "I didn't understand why it was that I was the one succeeding while all my friends were getting pregnant, dropping out, and getting into drugs. It wasn't until college that I realized it's because we work within a system that makes it so that most people from my background fail." This realization was catalyzed by her experience at a math camp, where she, as one of the few Latinas, felt woefully unprepared.

Both Inez and Alejandra were inspired by teachers, most of whom were Latina role models, to become educators. Inez explained:

> I was fortunate to have two professors who touched my life, set high expectations for me, and allowed me to get to where I am with resources they provided. How will I motivate other students? . . . I hope students will realize that everyone who puts their mind and heart to it can go to college.

Alejandra's role models were a Latina math teacher and a White history teacher: "With the Latina, I was able to see myself in her and figured, if she could do it, I could do it, too."

Inez and Alejandra attended university-based teacher education credential- and master's-granting programs whose missions were consistent with their commitments to work with students from non-dominant cultural and linguistic sharing language and culture enabled her to support a struggling Latina student: "The fact that I am Latina, speak Spanish, and came from her background gave me a very strong in to talk to her. . . . The turning point in the conversation was when I was able to speak to some of my experiences and how they were similar to hers."

Inez and Alejandra described how they knew they had become role models for their Latina/o students. Inez's students copied her behavior: "I even see students mimicking things I say . . . one of the students said, 'Well, remember we have to be responsible students, and we have to be responsible for our education.' I think I had said that." Alejandra recalled a particular incident at student poetry night for the community: "At the end of it one of my students came up to me and she hugged me and she told me, 'When I grow up, I wanna be just like you.'"

Inez and Alejandra believed they provided examples of Latinas who had been successful in college. Inez said, "I see myself as a role model for these students because . . . I talk to them about going to college and what I experienced entering college, challenges, barriers, and how one is able to overcome these." Alejandra described herself as a counterexample:

I am this Latina who graduated from [a university] and is the daughter of immigrants. That in itself is a role model . . . because they can see themselves in me. They can conclude that, "if she did it so can I." . . . When they think of somebody who went to college, graduate school, who works in an office and drives a nice car, they usually think of White people. . . . I want them to know that isn't the standard. . . . They know I'm proud I went to college and graduate school . . . but they also know I'm very proud of my background.

Alejandra also acted as a role model as a senior adviser and talked with students about tensions in negotiating the college-going experience:

In the community where I teach, people don't go to college. It's a big deal if people go to college. [For] many people who are first timers . . . there's a tension like you're breaking away from what the rest of the family is doing and . . . [college] is not exactly jam-packed with people who look like you and come from your background. . . . My choosing to be a senior adviser is a huge way to advocate for them because one of the biggest roles you play is helping kids choose colleges and the [negotiate the] application process.

Beyond being an individual who acted as role model, Alejandra described how her colleagues had been models for a newcomer freshman from Mexico who was contemplating dropping out of school. Alejandra explained:

communities. Inez's preservice program, located in a prestigious public university, describes its mission as providing high-quality education and improving urban schooling for California's racially, culturally, and linguistically diverse students. Its courses address issues of culturally and linguistically responsive teaching and teachers' roles as change agents. Inez's student teaching experience deepened her commitment to working with students who, like herself, were second-language learners. Inez was prohibited from speaking Spanish to students who were native Spanish speakers because her school enforced an English-only policy.

Alejandra entered the teacher education program at the prestigious private university where she had earned her undergraduate degree. That program suited Alejandra's interests by preparing her to teach with cultural relevance, to be sensitive to the community and political contexts of education, to focus on the needs and development of learners, and to ground instruction in subject matter that encourages inquiry. She also had a student teaching experience that inspired her to work with English learners, where she felt a connection with the students.

Inez and Alejandra were drawn to working in schools with high proportions of students from low-income and culturally and linguistically non-dominant communities. Inez accepted a teaching position in a school because "It's within the community that I live, which is very important to me because I feel that I need to be able to relate to my kids and know their surroundings." She taught English as a second language (ESL) to 6th, 7th, and 8th graders as well as math, social studies, and science to 6th-grade English learner students. Seventy-five percent of her students were from Mexico; 25% were from Central America. City Middle School is a large district-run public school located in an urban community, where most of the residents are African American or Latina/o. All of the school's 1,948 students are members of non-dominant racial and cultural communities—56% African American and 44% Latina/o—and 22% of the students are English language learners (ELLs). At this Title 1 school, 57% of students receive free or reduced-price lunches.

Alejandra, too, was attracted to work in a school with a large proportion of students from non-dominant racial and cultural communities. She student-taught and took a teaching position in a small, public charter high school that had opened 2 years earlier and was sponsored by the university where she had been an undergraduate and graduate student. Southside High School is racially diverse, with a student body of 296 that is 54% Latina/o, 29% African American, 5% Filipino, 5% Pacific Islander, 4% White, and 3% multiracial. Sixty-six percent of the students receive free or reduced-price lunches, and 34% are ELLs. The staff is also diverse, with 50% White, 32% Latina/o, 6% African American, 6% Asian, and 6% multiracial. Alejandra taught 9th- and 10th-grade humanities (mostly classes for the general population and one sheltered ELL class in humanities). Unlike Inez, Alejandra did not teach in the community in which she was raised.

Inez and Alejandra confronted different personal challenges to performing cultural/professional roles. Because Inez lived in the community where her school was located, she found it difficult to separate her personal life from her roles as teacher and role model: "Because I am . . . a public figure in the eyes of my kids and their parents . . . I feel that it's a little hard for students to see me outside of the class, to see me as a normal human . . . so the role model figure that is presented in the classroom . . . can change."

For Alejandra, the challenges began with resistance she encountered in her family toward her choice of profession. Her family had considered it a waste of Alejandra's education to go into teaching. It "did not fit their American dream," which was to use education to get a high-paying job. Her own high school teachers were concerned that she wanted to return to her high school to teach; they feared that she would suffer burnout from working in such a dysfunctional place and that the school culture would conflict with the "liberal mentality that [the preservice program] would give her."

Alejandra's challenges also stemmed from her multifaceted and shifting identities as she negotiated her schooling experiences, which complicated the cultural match between herself and her Latina/o students. While Alejandra relied on her cultural knowledge to connect with Latina/o students, she acknowledged that going to college and becoming a teacher shifted her social and economic status, distancing her from her cultural and community roots: "I have a feeling of disconnect sometimes because the last time I really lived in the barrio, in the kind of place where [my students] live, I was 18 years old." Alejandra characterized the contrast between her life before college and her life as a middle-class professional as a "contradiction" that made her feel "disjointed" from her community and "culturally suspect" in the eyes of some Latina/o students. Some Latina/o students challenged her for "talking White" and using "Americanized Spanish." Alejandra described the tension she faced as a role model:

> Be prepared to have your race be called into question. . . . You will be criticized for that background as well as admired for that background. Be prepared to be criticized for your education and admired for it. Everything you have, your identity, [students] will see it as a positive and a negative.

Another manifestation of the challenge presented by Alejandra's shifting identities is reflected in a dilemma she confronted in attempting to change the educational system while working within it. She had moved from an "angry stage" where she recognized injustice as a high school student to deciding in college to "work within the system to change it." She explained, "One of my first transformations into being a person who's very passionate about social justice was going

through the angry stage. I was very angry at White people, very angry at the system. . . . Slowly I started to realize that to change the system, you have to work within the system." To gain social acceptance, she altered the way she spoke and gestured: "I didn't want people to judge me by my accent. I made a conscious effort to change the way I spoke, and I learned to have mannerisms of the people who were surrounding me, most of whom were White."

Performing Cultural/Professional Roles

Both Inez and Alejandra sought to perform the cultural/professional roles of role model, culturally and linguistically responsive teacher, and agent of change. However, they performed these roles to different degrees and with different approaches to change.

Role Model

Inez and Alejandra served as role models, with Alejandra having more opportunities to perform this role. Both teachers connected with Latina/o students through shared cultural experiences and language. Inez identified dimensions on which she related to the experiences of her students: "I see myself as a role model because I connect with the experiences and backgrounds . . . of my students and their parents. I grew up in a surrounding neighborhood." Alejandra recalled how she connected to the experiences of her Latina/o students: "Because I look like the students, [they] know immediately that in many ways I am one of them. . . . [I connect to their] socioeconomic status simply because I know what they are going through." She was also afforded opportunities to perform as a role model by parts of the curriculum. For example, Alejandra's grade-level team developed an assignment for all 9th-grade students to write autobiographies about turning points in their lives. In introducing this activity, she recounted her own life story: "It's my way of letting them know that I share some of the stuff they've gone through." She hoped to use her own experience of understanding violence in the community to help students "become more critical about the experiences in their lives . . . so [the violence] is not seen as normal. Giving them tools to understand that . . . to make it better."

Inez and Alejandra emphasized that sharing Spanish as their first language provided a special connection with their Spanish-speaking students. Inez recounted, "I've noticed that a lot of the Latino kids . . . feel that connection because they're able to speak Spanish to someone in the school." Alejandra similarly recalled, "When I'm talking to them one-on-one, I speak in Spanglish or all Spanish and I'll use more slang. I think that that shows them that they don't have to give up their identity to become a successful academic person." Alejandra also explained how

We had a conversation with him . . . [about] what we needed to do as a school and what I needed to do specifically as a teacher to ensure that he could get into community college and succeed. I think that really impacted me just because only 5 months ago he was thinking of stopping school altogether. Now he's thinking of how to further his education. I attribute that to the school and to the environment that it's created in which there's a lot of adult support and adult models. It feels like that's the reason he succeeded.

Culturally and Linguistically Responsive Teacher

Inez and Alejandra were committed to, and to different degrees enacted, the three elements of culturally/linguistically responsive teaching: establish a community of learners, draw on students' cultural/linguistic experiences in teaching, and promote a social justice perspective.

Community of learners. Inez described how she worked at "building that community of learners within the classroom . . . where the students are the experts and they're providing information and we are learning together." When Inez did find time to engage in collaborative activities, she arranged desks for group work, supported student-to-student exchanges in both Spanish and English, and had students report what they learned as group members. Inez also established a cultural center where students brought books, pictures, and other items to share.

Alejandra's classroom had high levels of student engagement, with group work being the norm for her and her colleagues at the school. She worked closely with her grade-level and subject-area teams to construct activities and structures that involved collaborative learning, group problem solving, and reciprocal teaching. She had students jointly develop a newscast on the Great Depression, develop collaborative lesson plans to teach the rest of the class about slavery and women's rights, and work together on writing an essay on a novel. In one lesson Alejandra supported learning about different forms of democracy by employing a simulation about negotiations between "yellow" and "green" people (workers and owners), who were represented by two groups. When students presented the results of their group work, an animated debate ensued. Alejandra described her use of *cariño* (caring similar to the environment created in a Latino family) to create community: "I call students *mijo* and *mija* . . . this mostly happens with advisees. It shows a lot of love and care. It literally means my son and my daughter."

Students' cultural and linguistic experiences. In teaching, both Inez and Alejandra incorporated their cultural and linguistic experiences and those of their students. While Inez used a required textbook and "a set curriculum," pacing plan, and "mandated components" from her district and school, she made connections to her students' cultures and language. For example, Inez taught a unit on family tales: "From talking about my home experiences and connections to this lesson on 'tales across time,' some of the kids went home and talked to their families about different tales. It's Luis Moll who talks about 'funds of knowledge.'" In another class, students brought family guests to the class to discuss agricultural practices in their home cultures. Inez explained: "That lesson relates to my beliefs that it's important to connect knowledge and skills that students already have from their home to new learning." In one lesson, Inez linked a story about an Indian immigrant to her students' immigrant experiences, noting how they, like the book character, were socially and culturally isolated. Inez also employed linguistic code-switching between English and Spanish to connect with students.

Alejandra connected her teaching to students' cultures and languages. She worked closely with her humanities team to incorporate texts that tapped her students' cultural experiences:

> The texts we choose to teach are culturally relevant. *Parrot in the Oven* is about this coming-of-age story of a 14-year-old boy. He's a Latino boy and the kind of experiences he has within his family mirror a lot of the experiences that the students have. We're going to end the year with a unit on Latin America and we're going to read *In the Time of the Butterflies,* which has some Spanglish in it, apart from being a book focused on Latin America. There's also culturally relevant things going on within the story.

Alejandra had her students write and discuss the biggest challenges they experienced in learning English. Alejandra often code-switched during teaching, helping students make connections through home language. They read texts that included Spanish-language referents and discussed the common roots of words.

While Alejandra's teaching embraced her students' cultures, she was also committed to providing students access to the dominant culture:

> Most of my kids are Latino . . . so [our humanities team] debated . . . whether we should teach Shakespeare. It seems very inaccessible sometimes. . . . But there are a couple of reasons we decided to teach them. The biggest one, I think, was the "culture of power." We wanted students to know that we

value their culture, but we also know that there is a certain culture that they need to be able to work with to experience success.

Alejandra explained, "We talk about this dual identity that kids are supposed to have. We don't want them to erase the identity that they have now, but we also need them . . . [to have access to] this idea of the culture of power." She was concerned with teaching her students how to present themselves in an academic setting without losing their identity. They discussed the importance of using "academic language" while maintaining their own voice and being able to code-switch in different settings. The school had a final exhibition in which students presented their work to community members, staff, partner university faculty, and parents. Alejandra recounted:

> In preparing for the exhibition, I was really proud of them because they're able to use all this academic language and present themselves very professionally, but they're able to keep their identity. A lot of minorities, myself included, when we're put in the situation where we have to present something to a group of people, we turn on a different attitude. It's just like turning on your "White voice." The kids didn't do that for the most part. They were able to be professional, but they never let go of their identity of who they are.

Social justice perspective. In pursuing social justice through her teaching, Inez worked to gain access to educational opportunities for her ESL students. For example, she was concerned that students were being placed at the wrong level of ESL class and thus not learning. Inez also worked to inform parents of her ESL students about how they could help their children gain greater access to educational opportunities in school. As we discuss in the section on school contexts later in this chapter, Inez's efforts were stifled by the school's administration.

Alejandra imbued her teaching with social justice by discussing controversial subjects. For example, along with her department team, she had students read a book about a heroine from the Dominican Republic and tied it to Latin American history, human rights, and social justice. The class discussed what it meant to improve people's lives by fighting for equality and freedom. In another lesson, students reflected on their field trip to a migrant worker camp, where they interviewed Latina/o agricultural workers about conditions related to those in their class reading. The class compared the conditions that they witnessed while picking strawberries with migrant workers to those they read about in their book on migrant laborers in an earlier era, discussing how Cesar Chavez, who had organized in these very fields, changed the lives of today's workers.

Agents of Change

Both Inez and Alejandra saw themselves as agents of change but pursued different strategies. Inez took an adaptive stance, emphasizing "access" to schooling. Alejandra took a more transformative stance, explaining her goal as "empowering students to . . . work within the system to change the system." In addition, Alejandra enjoyed more opportunities to perform the role of change agent. Inez's approach was to work with Latina/o students and their parents to increase their access to schooling. She informed her ESL students and their parents about how the school limited their access to educational opportunities and spurred them to take action:

> I believe that making a change in society begins in your house with dialogue, talking about what you can do to improve things in society and school. Working [at this school] is my house. . . . I have lots of children here, and a lot of these children and families are in need of information and direction. Once you give them that, they can do a lot more.

Inez advocated for the parents of her ESL students, working to eliminate the language barrier that stood between the school and Spanish-speaking parents. She organized workshops in the evenings, when parents could attend, to inform them about the school's ESL program and address their concerns. She also served as a translator for Spanish-speaking parents and tutored parents and students of Mexican descent before and after school. While not intent on "organizing my kids to go and rebel," Inez helped her students recognize that they could take action when the school did not serve them. For example, Inez recounted a conversation with students about what they could do if the school did not appropriately transition them out of the ESL class:

> If somebody tells you, "Sorry, it's not going to happen this year [even though you tested out of ESL]," you're going to sit for the rest of 9 weeks knowing that you could have been in regular English classes? What are you going to do? So we had a conversation . . . to motivate and organize my kids or have them organize themselves to do something.

Alejandra's more transformative strategy centered on her students in two ways. First, she exposed students to the culture of power so that they could participate in and thus change social institutions, including schools: "There are certain things that society as a whole value[s] and [my students] need to be able to function within that society. If they can function, they're more likely to change it in some positive way." Second, Alejandra drew on her experiences to teach students to recognize injustice in the educational system. She shared how tracking affected her schooling, discussing inequalities that resulted from placing Latina/o new immigrants in low tracks:

> I talked to them about how tracking plays out at big, comprehensive high schools, how it played out in my high school, which was 97% Latino. There was still tracking even though everybody looked the same. There was tracking by generation, so first-generation kids would be in the lower track and kids here the longest were in the upper track.

In one class, Alejandra engaged her students in a discussion about the Civil War and abolitionism. Alejandra encouraged students to participate in the school-sponsored activity Sojourn to the Past, where students visited historic sites and learned about activism associated with the civil rights movement. The conversation evolved to discuss hate groups and racism in current times, including racial conflicts between local minority groups. On another occasion, Alejandra confronted students about the use of derogatory racial slurs with one another, making it part of classroom discussion when lighter-skinned Latino students were called names by darker-skinned Latino students. She also discussed institutional racism and local instances of oppression. In one discussion, students challenged Alejandra's distinction between individual and institutional racism, arguing that "White people run the system." Alejandra's response reflected her purpose in raising the issue: to engage students in changing society. She explained, "The system has a lot of problems, but you can't just write it off, because then you're never going to change it." She described how she felt enabled at her school to address social justice: "We don't shy away from controversial issues that are not necessarily presented at other schools." Alejandra was careful not to be seen as an "angry Chicana" but as a person "who worked to change the system from within." Her view of how teaching contributes to change mirrors this:

> Society isn't perfect. There's still a lot of racist beliefs and structures in place and a lot of socioeconomic discrimination. . . . I know my students are very angry at who they think gets privilege and who gets all the resources. . . . I need to be able to give them the tools so . . . they can build the path so there can be more people like them [who] can succeed.

In the spring of 2006, the United States was engaged in a debate over legislation that, in the minds of some, posed a threat to undocumented immigrants and Latina/o immigrants in particular. Inez's and Alejandra's schools served communities that were heavily populated by Latina/os and, thus, deeply affected by the debate. In this cultural and political crucible, differences in Inez's and Alejandra's approaches to being agents of change were heightened.

The community surrounding Inez's school reacted strongly to the immigration debates by staging marches and demonstrations. Three hundred students from Inez's school walked out to join the protests. Students jumped over fences; others opened gates although the school was in lockdown. Inez acted on her obligation to ensure her students' safety by enforcing school rules. She described a challenging moment when she tried to keep students from jumping over the school gate: "I just see a huge crowd of kids with signs. I was in their way. . . . I tried to hold them back. I stood by the gate. . . . I can't make choices for the kids. I was there to protect them." At one point during this exchange, Inez exhorted students to get off the fence and remain in school. A student responded by yelling, "You're a traitor. You're also Latina, also Mexican, and why aren't you allowing us to do this?" Inez explained that she "didn't take it personal" but admitted, "I felt bad about what they screamed at me, but I wanted them to know that it's not right to leave the campus. . . . I felt bad and I couldn't do anything to talk to them."

Alejandra's response to the immigration debates reflected her approach to pursuing change within the system. Many students initially wanted to walk out and join protests in the community. Alejandra sought to provide her students with an alternative that would enable them to learn about the immigration issues as well as give them voice. On the day when many students planned to walk out in solidarity with an economic protest, Alejandra debated whether she should join them. She decided that she was needed at school to teach students who chose to attend. Alejandra planned to discuss the immigration issues in her advisory. She discovered that students were "passionate" about the issue and willing to take action: "I had to do something 'cause . . . I had to practice what I preached in class. I couldn't just say you gotta get involved, get your voices heard, and then have this opportunity come up and just sit in the background." Thus, Alejandra and her students formulated a strategy to educate other students about the immigration debate by developing a flyer and having pairs of students visit other advisories in a "teach in."

After Alejandra's students completed their presentations, they told her that they now wanted to march. She took this to the school's administrators, who were apprehensive because the school was located in an affluent neighborhood outside of the low-income community where the students lived. Alejandra informed her students of the concern. A student who had participated in Sojourn to the Past suggested they model their march after the civil rights march from Selma to Montgomery. When another student asked how they could control the marchers, the student suggested that everyone sign a contract, which yet another student insisted include the six principles of nonviolence. On a Friday afternoon, about 100 students, or one-third of the student body, and a number of teachers assembled to march. Alejandra led the marchers, who silently walked in pairs down the main street and passed out flyers. The students marched peacefully, even when some local bystanders made harassing gestures. Alejandra reflected on her role: "I always say you need to care, you need to be passionate. . . . [My role is] to allow the students to get their voices heard and to make them feel like they can mobilize."

School Contexts: The Influence of Capital and Power Relations

Inez and Alejandra taught in very different schools. Inez worked in a large, district-run public school; Alejandra worked in a small public charter school affiliated with a university that had greater local autonomy than traditional schools. More importantly, the two schools differed in the availability of organizational capital and in the nature of power relations. Inez's school provided little social, human, or multicultural capital and was characterized by power relations that emphasized little teacher control. These conditions presented major challenges to Inez in performing the three cultural/professional roles. Alejandra worked in a school whose mission focused on advancing the academic interests of students from non-dominant cultural and linguistic communities. Alejandra's school tended to invest in social, human, and multicultural capital and engage in power relations that supported her performing the three cultural/professional roles. Yet even in Alejandra's school there were conditions that produced some challenges.

School Capital

The lack of social, human, and multicultural capital at Inez's school hindered her ability to perform as a role model and culturally/linguistically responsive teacher. A relative absence of social capital challenged Inez's efforts to be a role model for Latina/o students. She found it difficult to develop social links in school because she had little time to engage students outside of class: "Building relationships you need time, and unfortunately I have so many things going on that sometimes I can't spend . . . after-school time or before-school or lunch time." A shortage of human capital exacerbated Inez's situation. Because few staff members possessed the human and multicultural capital of fluency in Spanish, Inez was called on daily to serve as translator between school officials and Spanish-speaking parents, reducing her time to spend with students. When her ESL coordinator left in the middle of Inez's 2nd year, she was made ESL co-coordinator but given no release-time because high faculty turnover left Inez as the most senior teacher in the department, further reducing her time to meet with students.

The shortage of social capital also hindered Inez's efforts to engage in culturally and linguistically responsive teaching by not providing avenues through which she could tap the knowledge of senior colleagues. This was reflected in the isolation and marginalization of the ESL Department. Initially, Inez felt supported by the ESL coordinator and ESL Department colleagues, with whom she met every 2 weeks and shared teaching strategies. The coordinator left midyear and was not replaced. Inez attributed his departure to "a hostile environment where anything he fought for in our ESL Department was shut down [by administration]." She added, "I do feel a sense of isolation because I belong to the ESL Department, which is the minority at this school. We don't have a coordinator and he was our support . . . now things are not getting done . . . we don't meet actually as a department anymore." The absence of social capital was also evident in the school's approach to professional development. Teachers had requested time to share knowledge about instructional strategies (a form of human capital) during professional development. However, Inez observed that administrator-driven sessions did not provide time for teachers to interact and share ideas.

Another manifestation of the lack of social capital was the absence of support for new teachers. Inez did not begin teaching until the middle of the year and was not assigned a mentor, which is mandated by the state. Nor did Inez have a mentor in subsequent years because, as an administrator reported, support for new teachers had been eliminated due to funding constraints. In the absence of a formal mentor, the ESL coordinator supported Inez during the first part of her 2nd year, observing her practice and providing some materials. However, he left midyear. Inez hoped that professional communities would develop when, in her 3rd year, the school adopted a small communities model. However, Inez was moved to a different area in the school, distancing her from ESL colleagues. She also explained that because her colleagues had different lunch periods, "We can't get together and talk about our work and help each other out." Moreover, the large size of her school made connecting with students and colleagues a challenge.

It appeared that Inez would receive support in the form of social and human capital from the Academic English Mastery Program (AEMP), which was adopted by her district and school. The school's website indicates that AEMP focuses on "acquisition of school language, literacy and learning in students for whom Standard English is not native." In her 3rd year of teaching, Inez attended AEMP seminars, which provided social capital through contact with colleagues and trainers and human capital in the form of reading materials and teaching strategies. She also had access to social capital in her school by meeting with a colleague in her ESL Department to discuss AEMP strategies and materials that related to the students' cultures. However, Inez reported that the program had "not been as successful in implementation," estimating that only about 6 of the approximately 100 teachers at her school participated in any of the AEMP workshops.

Furthermore, the school's lack of multicultural capital was evident in limitations to curricular and pedagogical approaches that met the needs of non-dominant cultural/linguistic students; a hostile environment toward ESL that, according to Inez, was the reason that her chair left; and resistance to connecting with parents and their cultural resources. Inez grew up and lived in the community where her school was located. Thus, she worked to build bridges to her students' families. She engaged in activities that tapped parents' knowledge, asking students to bring their families' perspectives into the classroom. She sought support from her students' parents: "So parents are now my source of communication, who I can talk to, and they talk to me, and we can try to brainstorm ideas on improving [the school]." Because Inez's school did not value multicultural capital, she met with resistance from the administration for trying to engage ESL parents (discussed below). Inez began to wonder if she should remain at the school, given the administration's resistance to her work with parents. In the end, she remained committed to her ESL students and the community: "Doors are being shut and there's all these different barriers [between parents and the school]. . . . I've decided to stay and to work around these issues because my parents and my kids do need me. I need them also, so I have motivation and support." Despite or perhaps because of Inez's strained relations with her school's administration, she was pursuing an administrative credential: "A lot of what I'm studying . . . as an [administrative] student . . . I come here and I see it. Then I want to do something about it."

In contrast to Inez's experiences, Alejandra's school provided social capital that enabled teachers to build close relations with students and receive support from colleagues. The school was a product of the small schools movement and was designed to take advantage of opportunities provided by its small enrollment and small staff to develop interpersonal relations. A daily advisory program enabled teachers to remain connected with a cohort of students and families for 4 years. "The advisory system makes sure that every teacher has some strong connection with a group of students. That's where my background comes in helping me build those connections with the . . . ELL kids. . . . You become much more family-like in advisory since you know the kids for so long." In whole-staff and grade-level meetings, the faculty discussed what it meant to establish relationships with their students. In these meetings, Alejandra used the school's social capital to access colleagues' knowledge, or human capital, about building relations with students.

Alejandra was supported by her school's commitment to culturally and linguistically responsive teaching, which is reflected in its mission, its emphasis on multicultural capital, and its considerable investment of social capital and power relations to support such approaches to teaching. The school's mission is to prepare students from non-dominant cultures for the world beyond high school, including college and work. Alejandra noted, "This is a focus of the school. They try to make things culturally relevant to . . . the kids that we serve . . . the school connects its curriculum to the cultural backgrounds of its students." This was reflected in a norm that encouraged the staff to discuss issues of race. Alejandra observed, "A culture of talking about race/ethnicity in staff meetings . . . even one-on-one informally people [are] talking about this." She added, "Cultural relevance and social justice are embedded in everything we do, in the way we run the school, and the way we talk about students."

The school's mission was evident in the investment of multicultural capital in the school's curriculum. For example, seniors were engaged in a voter-registration project to educate community members about ballot issues and candidates and to register people in the community to vote. The school was also involved in Sojourn to the Past, a program that took students to Birmingham, Alabama, to visit historic sites and activists associated with the civil rights movement. Alejandra noted, "[Students] don't have to abandon their culture to get an education. They are not entering a White people's world. It can be their world, too, and they can maneuver within it and still be Black or still be Mexican."

Teachers in Alejandra's school had access to considerable social capital that supported culturally/linguistically responsive teaching by providing access to knowledge and skills (a form of human capital), through teacher collaboration and formal efforts to support new teachers. Teachers exerted significant influence in making decisions about curriculum and instruction. Alejandra drew strength from her 9th- and 10th-grade humanities team, which met frequently to discuss issues and share human capital related to culture and teaching. She explained: "Every time we choose a book, we think very deeply about why [are we] going [to] choose it. Would students be able to tap into it? What are we going to teach them and what are we going to prioritize?" As the founding principal explained, the school was committed to building a professional culture that supported culturally and linguistically responsive teaching: "The interest in building a professional culture at our school is pretty central to our mission." She continued, "I have no problem going up to [teachers] or talking about English language development or talking about specific students or talking about curriculum."

Alejandra's school provided strong support for novice teachers. In addition to being supported by a grade-level team, Alejandra received support from two sources beyond her school: mentors provided by a new teacher project and faculty in her teacher education program. She met weekly with her mentor, who, in the mentor's words, "[put] into place whatever is needed for [Alejandra] to be successful in the classroom." She also remained linked to university faculty, who "assist us in delivering appropriate curriculum to these kids."

Alejandra faced some school challenges to teaching in culturally/linguistically responsive ways. A minor deficit in social capital arose when her humanities team had difficulty scheduling a meeting with a music teacher to develop a multidisciplinary, multicultural unit. A drawback for teachers who had the freedom to develop a culturally/linguistically responsive curriculum was the lack of textbooks. Alejandra explained that the teachers had to collect materials because multicultural texts were not available. A more serious challenge for Alejandra was balancing two components of the school's multicultural capital: her students' cultures and the culture of power. She observed, "It is hard to strike a balance between having [students] be proud of who they are in their culture, but at the same time having them accept the mainstream culture and how to work within the mainstream culture." She recognized that students could not identify with the culture of power and that it threatened their identity: "It's not their culture. It's not what they know, so why should they be expected to take it up . . . if they don't see a connection . . . they feel like . . . we're trying to give them a different identity, forget where they come from."

This tension was reflected in two school conditions that challenged Alejandra as a culturally/linguistically responsive teacher. First, the school culture reflected both the students' home cultures and the culture of power. The school supported the inclusion of students' cultures in the curriculum. However, the school and its sponsoring university emphasized the traditional goal of having its students attend college, which was symbolized by the placement of the logos of elite colleges and universities on classroom doors. Included was the crest of the elite university that Alejandra attended (the school's sponsoring university), which, as she explained, distanced her from her Latina/o students. Thus, the school embodied the tension that Alejandra experienced: being a change agent in the education system, while being changed by the system in which she worked. Second, in the final year of this study, Alejandra's school was placed in "Program Improvement" status by the state's accountability system because it failed to meet its target test score in Language Arts. She explained: "To keep the charter we need to have a certain "Annual Yearly Progress," so there is definitely a big push. . . . We have staff meetings devoted to analyzing scores, what can we do, what specific strategies can we use schoolwide . . . to help increase scores." She found that the focus on raising test scores had reduced cultural responsiveness in the curriculum: "We have a whole unit developed, this huge unit devoted to the civil rights movement and this huge unit devoted to South Africa because it's very much culturally relevant . . . those units have to get pushed to later because they're not on the test." Reflecting on the accountability pressure, Alejandra revisited the delicate balance that she maintained between cultural responsiveness and the culture of power: "I feel that we found a way to work with it. . . . I think this is a reality that the kids are gonna have to face. . . . Standardized testing is just a part of educational life." She acknowledged that the longer she taught, the less angry she got about the tests because she realized that "it's not productive" and found herself accommodating. Again, Alejandra had been changed by the school and the education system in which she worked.

Alejandra explained that her school supported teachers who were agents of change, "Because our whole school is built around the premise of social justice, you just do things that are social justice-y." The overall culture of social justice and change was reflected in the multicultural capital with which the school infused many activities. For example, Alejandra cited several projects through which the school pursued change in the racially and culturally non-dominant communities from which it drew most of its students: registering voters, tutoring elementary-aged children, and providing civil rights activities and education.

Alejandra's school presented two challenges to performing as a change agent. First, the small school's faculty was burdened by its many responsibilities, thus taxing its human capital:

> [This school] thrusts anybody . . . into leadership roles very quickly. It's just the nature of teaching at a small school that's underfunded and doesn't have all the adults it needs to run it. There is a tension . . . you have these young energetic people who want to do great things but don't realize the effect it's having, and before you know it you're burnt out.

This contributed to high teacher turnover, further taxing its human capital with so many novices.

Second, the school had a tenuous relationship with the community from which it drew students, thus limiting social capital: "It's been a huge challenge for us to get parents involved. We have done parent meetings and we don't have very good turnout and we're trying to get parents to take on leadership roles in the parent meetings, but it's really difficult." She explained that the school was not located in the community where students lived but in a neighboring, more affluent community, and how one administrator "did a lot of talking in the community, so he would go to the churches and community centers. . . . He received really good feedback about that, 'cause we're not in [the community] . . . and for the most part we expect parents to come to us." She noted how this geographic anomaly created a challenge: "We're not in the community, so it's harder to see us as the community school." This literal distance revealed a figurative distance that Alejandra at times experienced between herself and the community as reflected in her sense of no longer being of the community since having attended college and become a teacher.

Power Structures and Relations

Because of Inez's school's large size and racial tensions, power relations there emphasized controlling students, which restricted the relationships Inez could have with them. She noted, "We at times treat . . . our students in a very boot camp–like way." Inez and her colleagues exerted little influence in making decisions about curriculum and instruction in their school, elements commonly found in large, district-run urban schools. This undermined her efforts to engage in culturally and linguistically responsive teaching. While a site council ostensibly governed the school, for the most part the administration adopted and enforced policies and programs with which teachers were expected to comply. Inez explained, "Most of curriculum comes from up in the top and trickles down. We are told we have to teach this and that." Inez and her colleagues largely attributed these power relations to the school's "Program Improvement" status as a low-performing school. In attempting to raise test scores, the district and school required teachers to use what the ESL coordinator characterized as a "set curriculum," which included a pacing guide. Inez explained that the district "mandated" specific outcomes, including portfolios with certain components that students had to master linked to a pacing plan. She noted that this pacing plan posed difficulties because she found it necessary to slow down and review material with her ESL students. All materials were in English, forcing Inez to translate and create Spanish forms. Inez said the school's emphasis on test scores compromised cultural relevance:

> Our kids have these funds of knowledge. When you bring that to class
> . . . a lot of kids can relate. Once you take them out of that context, give
> them testing, and read something not that relevant, then they are at a
> disadvantage. . . . When it comes to testing, I have no control . . . I have to set
> aside anything I believe is more important or . . . culturally relevant.

Power relations also confronted Inez with two challenges to acting as an agent of change. First, Inez believed the small number of Latina/o teachers in her school prevented them from having much impact, leading her to emphasize the need for involving Latina/o parents: "We are a small population of Latino teachers at this school, so it's really hard to get anything done for our kids unless we get parent involvement." Second, Inez faced a control-oriented administration that challenged her efforts to develop social capital with parents and the community:

> There's a little tension between [the] administration and myself . . . because
> I'm providing parents with information in reference to what they can do to
> help their kids or how they can become more involved in the school. I'm not

sure . . . that I'm getting support for holding these parent meetings. On the contrary . . . I'm being looked at [as] you're not supposed to be doing this or why are you getting parents too informed.

Indeed, an assistant principal explained that Inez had difficulty "understanding policy and procedure." When Inez wanted to take families to a local restaurant to hold a meeting, this administrator emphasized that Inez needed to "make sure you're not liable if something happens." Inez noted that during her 2nd year no administrator had observed her teaching until the conflict arose regarding her work with parents. Then the assistant principal visited her class four times in one week. The administrator did not explain how Inez was to be evaluated, nor did she receive feedback. By the end of her 3rd year, she lamented the difficulty of sustaining relationships with parents given the school's policy of "closed gates."

The administration's response to the immigration debates and subsequent student activism reflected this same control orientation. The school was placed on lockdown, gates were closed, and students were confined to their classrooms. Inez recalled, "There's helicopters, there's police officers surrounding us, and basically it's impacted our community as a whole." The following day, the principal gave a 25-minute lecture over the intercom about the facts of immigration and the importance of staying on campus, explaining that, if students left campus, the school would have to contact the police because it was responsible for the students' safety.

Power relations were quite different in Alejandra's school. She had direct access to and the support of her school's administrators. This provided Alejandra with social capital through which she gained access to human capital in the form of knowledge that supported her performance as a role model. She explained how the principal, a Latina, and the dean of students discussed role modeling: "In conversations [we discuss] what my role is in setting an example for the students, how responsible should I feel, what's my role." The school's commitment to culturally and linguistically responsive teaching was evident in relatively egalitarian power relations. Alejandra directly benefited from consulting with the school's administrators. She reported receiving support from her principal, a Latina: "[She] is an amazing principal. . . . I really feel like she looks out for our best interest." In Alejandra's monthly meetings with the principal, she discussed challenges confronting her as a teacher. She also met with the dean of students, who had been her cooperating teacher during student teaching, about cultural issues and teaching. The school's approach to hiring teachers reflected its dedication to culturally/ linguistically responsive teaching. Teachers joined administrators on interview teams. Alejandra noted that to be a good fit, one needed to be a culturally/linguistically responsive teacher: "In some of the interview questions we ask, that comes up. We get a feel for the teachers, how they will fit in, how they are going to work with curriculum and expand it to reach the needs of all students." Alejandra may also have been able to pursue social justice approaches with high school students more readily than Inez, who taught in a middle school.

Power relations in Alejandra's small charter school also supported teachers' efforts to act as agents of change. Alejandra reported that the school encouraged teachers to advocate for and empower students: "I think the fact that they give us so much power to empower the students really allows . . . students to then advocate for themselves." This was evident in the administration's response to the march that Alejandra and her advisory students organized. Alejandra felt she needed to go to the administrators, who expressed misgivings about the potential impact on the affluent neighborhood surrounding the school. After Alejandra and her students shared their plans for conducting a silent, nonviolent march and responded to the concerns expressed, the administration gave its support. After the march, the principal recounted, "I was really proud of them, that they did it so smoothly and without any incident and were nonviolent and thoughtful." The school credited the work of students who taught others or organized the march as part of the senior exhibition graduation requirement.

MAKING SENSE OF THE CASES: SUBTRACTIVE AND ADDITIVE SCHOOLING

The cases of Inez and Alejandra highlight two themes. First, these teachers are committed to increasing learning opportunities for Latina/o students by performing as role models, culturally and linguistically responsive teachers, and thus as agents of change in education, finding inspiration in their early schooling experiences and direction from their teacher preparation programs. Second, the teachers' ability to perform these cultural/professional roles is shaped by the schools in which they work, marking the challenges and supports that school capital and power relations can present. These findings reveal parallels between non-dominant youth's experiences of "subtractive schooling," which previous research reported as divesting cultural resources of students from non-dominant communities, and experiences of new teachers of color in their organizational contexts.

Influence of Personal and Professional Backgrounds

Inez and Alejandra were deeply committed to improving educational opportunities for Latina/o students by performing the three cultural/professional roles identified by research as having a positive impact on students from non-dominant cultural and linguistic communities (Gándara & Maxwell-Jolley, 2000; Quiocho & Rios, 2000; Valencia, 2002; Villegas & Lucas, 2002, 2004). Their commitments were fueled by early personal and professional experiences. Inez and Alejandra succeeded academically despite an absence of educational opportunities and the depreciation of the cultural resources of students from non-dominant cultural and linguistic communities. Both were inspired by teachers who served as role models and motivated them to do the same for their students. Moreover, both Inez and Alejandra graduated from teacher education programs with strong social justice orientations and coursework that encouraged and supported culturally/ linguistically responsive teaching.

Acting on their personal and professional commitments, Inez and Alejandra sought to perform the three cultural/professional roles. There were differences in the degree to which and how Inez and Alejandra enacted these roles. While both new teachers drew on cultural and linguistic resources to serve as role models for their Latina/o and Spanish-speaking students and to engage in culturally/linguistically responsive teaching, Inez had fewer opportunities than Alejandra to perform these roles. While both teachers identified as agents of change, they pursued different strategies. Inez sought to gain access for her Latina/o students and their parents to the education system; Alejandra employed a more transformative strategy that exposed students to the culture of power and enabled them to recognize injustice so that they could participate in and thus change social institutions, including schools. Even with such commitments, Alejandra faced internal tensions in terms of being a Latina trying to change the system from within and being changed by that very system.

Subtractive and Additive Schooling for New Teachers of Color

A comparison of Inez's and Alejandra's case studies sheds light on the relationship between organizational conditions and the cultural/professional roles of new teachers of color, revealing a spectrum of more and less supportive contexts (see Table 5.1). Inez faced more daunting challenges, while on the whole Alejandra received substantial support in the form of social, human, and multicultural capital as well as positive power relations.

Subtractive Schooling

Inez's school did not provide her with social, human, or multicultural capital, and its power relations, which concentrated on controlling students and teachers, provided few opportunities to perform the three cultural/professional roles

TABLE 5.1: Spectrum of Organizational Contexts in Relation to Cultural/ Professional Roles of New Teachers of Color

←——————————————————————————————→

	Less Supportive Contexts	More Supportive Contexts
Social capital	Culture of isolation, low collaboration, and little professional support for new teachers; little opportunity to build relationships with students; low levels of connection between school and parent communities; barriers to relationship building with community	Systems, norms, and structures for and enactment of collaborative professional culture and community building; extensive new teacher support; opportunities to build ties with students; school norms, structures, and practices that bridge to parent communities; school accesses community resources/knowledge for student and professional learning
Human capital	Few culturally and linguistically diverse teachers and staff; limited professional development and mentoring opportunities for new teachers of color to access cultural resources; overburdened faculty, resulting in burnout and turnover	Policies for recruitment and hiring of culturally and linguistically diverse faculty committed to cultural/professional roles; access to expertise and professional development through partner institutions, instructional leaders, and mentors
Multicultural capital	School orientation that does not advance culturally/linguistically responsive teaching; limited resources related to cultural practices; school culture and norms that do not address issues of race/culture; school responses to accountability that limit teachers' capacity to meet needs of diverse learners	School orientation, practices, and enactment that affirm culturally/ linguistically responsive teaching; schoolwide engagement with issues of race/culture of teachers and students; equitable climate; professional development related to culture; policies that support teachers of color
Power structures and relations	Top-down control over decision making; low teacher control over curriculum and pedagogy; culture of control and compliance	Systems for and enactment of shared decisionmaking, teacher voice in curriculum and pedagogy

to which she was committed. The challenges that Inez faced as a Latina teacher resembled the conditions that Valenzuela (1999) characterizes as "subtractive schooling," which builds upon theories on the "subtractive cultural assimilation" of immigrant/ethnic minority youth and concepts of "schooling" as socially reproductive (Cummins, 1984; Gibson, 1993; Giroux, 1988; Suárez-Orozco & Suárez-Orozco, 1997).

Valenzuela's 3-year ethnographic study of a Houston public school whose students were predominantly Mexican documents how the school subtracted social and cultural resources from U.S.–Mexican youth, making them vulnerable to academic failure. Valenzuela describes how subtractive schools are organized to perpetuate inequality in three ways. First, school structures, such as academic tracking, deprive students of Mexican descent of equal educational opportunities, and "cultural tracking" separates ESL students from other students of Mexican descent, resulting in status hierarchy, limited mobility, and undermining the accumulation of social capital and ultimately human capital through their exchanges. Second, the curriculum is biased against Mexican culture and the Spanish language, thus divesting Mexican students of their culture and language, which are necessary for learning. The school's "informal curriculum" undermines youth's definition of *educación* as building a sense of moral, personal, and social responsibility among Mexican youth and a culture of authentic caring among students and between students and teachers. Third, weak relations exist between schools and the Latina/o communities they serve. The school is characterized by a lack of communication between school and home, typically including no translations, insufficient numbers of bilingual counselors, and PTA parents reporting that faculty have little interest in their participation. Inez's case reveals that these same three organizational characteristics were present in her school, challenging her ability to perform the cultural/professional roles that inspired her to enter teaching.

Tracking challenges: Social and human capital. Inez's sense of "isolation" in the marginalized ESL program was a structured form of "teacher tracking" that limited her access to social capital (connection to other colleagues and parents), which along with the loss of her ESL coordinator limited access to developing human capital. While Inez was drawn to teach in the ESL program because of her commitment to utilizing her linguistic resources, she encountered resistance from the school in her attempts to support ESL students and their families. Inez explained that the ESL coordinator left the school because of a hostile environment in which advocating for the ESL Department was shut down by the administration. She lost his professional support and mentoring, and she received no other formal mentoring (although such mentoring was mandated by the state). The absence of teacher-centered professional development and new teacher mentoring deprived Inez of access to colleagues who might possess knowledge and skills pertinent to teaching in culturally and linguistically responsive ways. In her 2nd year of teaching, she was the most senior in her department because of high turnover in their program, made co-coordinator, not given release-time, and continued to act as the school's sole translator. She was physically isolated from ESL colleagues and did not share a lunch period with them; thus, they could not coordinate their work. Moreover, Inez described how ESL parents were marginalized by the school and how her attempts to connect with and support them were undermined by administrators.

Curriculum challenges: Multicultural capital and power relations. Inez also experienced the kind of curriculum bias against non-dominant culture and language that Valenzuela described. The absence of multicultural capital and teacher influence in decisionmaking on curriculum and instruction, the school's mandated curriculum and pacing guide, and the focus on testing left little room for content that was culturally and linguistically responsive to her Latina/o Spanish speakers. All instructional materials were in English, forcing Inez to translate and create Spanish materials. Further, she was tied to a set curriculum and pacing guide that did not meet the needs of English learners. Teaching focused on testing did not draw on students' funds of knowledge and forced her to "set aside" teaching in culturally responsive ways. While her school was involved in the AEMP program that provided strategies related to the students' cultures, Inez reported that the program had "not been as successful in implementation," with only six teachers involved.

Even in the informal or "hidden curriculum" (Giroux & Purpel, 1983) in schools that promote norms of behavior and interaction in accord with the dominant culture, Inez faced constraints that undermined her commitment to being a role model and building the authentic caring relations with Latina/o youth that Valenzuela described. Inez's original reason for entering teaching was based on her experience tutoring in a housing project, where she found that students had lost their motivation to learn because "teachers just didn't care." Inez wanted to care for her students, serve as a role model, and connect with and support them. However, she also faced barriers to this due to the way the school was structured, which limited opportunities to connect with students outside of class, and additional responsibilities (translating, serving as co-coordinator of ESL program) that pulled her from her classroom. Inez also identified power relations and a "culture of control" with students because of the school's large size and racial tensions, which restricted the relationships she could have with students. Inez described how teachers at times treated students in a "boot camp–like way." Finally, her experience during the immigration debates, when she stood at the schoolhouse gates and found students questioning her loyalty and connection to their cause as she enforced the school's lockdown policy, revealed the double bind that she faced as her school pitted her against the community.

School–community divisions: Social and multicultural capital. Inez experienced weak relations between school and the Latina/o community it served. Ultimately, this limited access to social capital (and parent allies) and multicultural capital (from the resources the community offered). The administration's efforts to limit Inez's connections to Latina/o and ESL parents and the lack of bilingual staff also undermined accessing cultural resources from the broader community. The school's lockdown response when community members and students organized during the immigration debates echoed the barriers to community access and interests. The small number of teachers and staff members who were Spanish/ English bilingual compromised the school's relations with its students' families and community. Few members of the school's staff could even speak with the majority of the parent community. Inez was questioned about meeting with parents in the community (i.e., meeting with parents at a local restaurant seemed to break the rules), and administrators directly challenged her about her organizing ESL parents to educate and connect them to the school.

The prevalence of these challenges is evident in the findings of other studies about Latina/o teachers specifically and teachers of color generally. New teachers of color may not be supported in ways that acknowledge, value, and develop their cultural practices (Irvine, 2003; Sheets, 2005). Thus, becoming a professional can mean leaving one's cultural assets at the schoolhouse door. People of color may enter teaching with a vision of using their cultural and linguistic resources to contribute to transforming the educational system and may even have experienced a teacher education program that fostered such approaches. However, new teachers of color may find themselves working in schools that do not support cultural/ professional roles.

Additive Schooling

In contrast to Inez's school, Alejandra's school invested capital in all forms and cultivated power relations that tended to support her performing the three cultural/professional roles. This school might be viewed as providing a more "additive" organizational context, which affords opportunities to tap rather than suppress cultural and linguistic resources and commitments of new teachers of color. Alejandra's school emphasized social capital through building community, which linked teachers to students and their families through advisories, and through professional norms, structures of teacher collaboration, and new teacher support.

The school's human capital was exhibited through the hiring of faculty committed to culturally and linguistically responsive teaching, access to the expertise of faculty from its partner university, and provision of mentoring for new teachers to help them develop culturally/linguistically responsive and socially just practices. Alejandra's school's multicultural capital was revealed in its social justice mission, its curricular focus on culturally/linguistically responsive teaching, and its teacher and student activities that fostered activism. Moreover, Alejandra's school supported positive power relations through consensus-based, shared decisionmaking and teacher control over curriculum development, which enabled teachers to engage in culturally and linguistically responsive teaching.

Studies of schools where Latina/o students are successful identify school characteristics that parallel the conditions that supported Alejandra's performance of cultural/professional roles and help to articulate "additive schooling" for teachers. Garcia (2004) notes that schools structured toward more culturally and linguistically responsive approaches: (1) value diversity, thus encouraging teachers to access students' cultural resources; (2) treat teachers as professionals and colleagues in making school decisions, thus fostering relations among professionals that mirror instructional activities that build on prior knowledge and collaboration; (3) eliminate policies that categorize diverse students in ways that render their educational experiences inferior, thus establishing norms that encourage academically challenging work; and (4) connect to parents and community, thus revealing norms that support instruction built on students' cultural resources.

It is important to note that Alejandra's school, with its clear mission of social justice and culturally/linguistically responsive teaching, also presented challenges to drawing on her cultural resources and the cultural and linguistic resources of Latina/o students. Although teachers were supported in developing culturally/ linguistically responsive curriculum, they had difficulty obtaining instructional materials and were limited in their ability to incorporate culturally and linguistically responsive content at times because their school, like Inez's, faced the pressure of having to raise test scores. In addition, Alejandra's school struggled to establish authentic and sustained relations with parents and serve as a source of social capital. The school building was not situated in the community it served (creating both a literal and figurative distance), and parent engagement in school-based activities remained an ongoing challenge. While Alejandra's school supported the inclusion of students' cultures in the curriculum, it also emphasizes the traditional goal of having its students attend college, symbolized by the placement of the logos of elite colleges and universities on classroom doors. One of those logos was that of Alejandra's alma mater, which she viewed as a place that had created a distance between herself and her home culture. Alejandra described the challenge of balancing the inclusion of students' home cultures with the culture of power, explaining that students resisted the culture of power because they could not identify with it and it threatened their identity. Thus, while Alejandra's school empowered teachers to engage in culturally/linguistically responsive teaching, it also expected teachers to adhere to traditional school norms.

CONCLUSIONS

Culturally subtractive conditions are endemic to schools in the United States; they are reinforced by the historic purposes and structures of public education and by contemporary educational policies. The contrasts between culturally subtractive and additive conditions in schools are rooted in the historic tensions between the reproductive and transformational purposes of U.S. schools (Giroux, 1983). Schools tend to emphasize reproduction, reinforcing dominant forms of cultural capital and thus working against the interests of non-dominant cultural and linguistic communities (Apple, 1990; Bourdieu, 1984; McEneaney & Meyer, 2000). Ladson-Billings and Tate (1995) document that institutional and structural racism continue to mark schools, as reflected in the subtractive nature of schools documented by Valenzuela (1999). These conditions impact teachers of color and the students of color that many teachers of color, including Inez and Alejandra, are committed to serving. The experiences of Inez and Alejandra reveal a pattern that is the focus of the next chapter: Subtractive schooling can be reinforced by the broader policy environment. Specifically, while these teachers' schools differed significantly in their capital and power relations, both responded to state and federal accountability policies in ways that challenged the ability of these new teachers of color to teach in culturally responsive ways.

CHAPTER 6

New Teachers of Color and Culturally Responsive Teaching in an Era of Educational Accountability

I value my culture. . . . I hope to be able to share my culture with other students and allow students the opportunity to share with me and the rest of the class about their culture.
—Inez, prior to beginning teaching

Our kids live in communities and they have these funds of knowledge. When you bring that to class . . . a lot of kids can really connect, and they're very, very smart. Once you take them out of that context, give them testing and ask them to read something not that relevant, then they might be at a disadvantage. . . . When it comes to testing I have no control, we can't help students, or translate, then it puts me in a situation I feel it's unfair. . . . I'm in a bind.
—Inez in her 3rd year teaching
English language learners in a "Program Improvement" school

The new teachers of color who participated in this study were attracted to teaching in urban schools with high percentages of students from low-income and non-dominant cultural and linguistic communities. Despite the challenging conditions that most of these teachers confronted, they tended to remain in these schools. Those who did move switched to other schools with similar student demographic profiles. Research has long documented the challenging conditions that these types of schools often present to students and teachers. As we explained in Chapter 5, many of the teachers indeed were employed by schools that lacked much of the social, human, and multicultural capital and collaborative power relations needed to support their performances as role models, culturally responsive teachers, and agents of change. Moreover, and not coincidentally, many of these schools were deemed "underperforming" under state and federal school accountability policies. The commitment of many teachers of color to serve students from non-dominant cultural communities may help to explain why high proportions of teachers of color work and remain in low-performing urban schools with high percentages of students of color (Achinstein, Ogawa, Sexton, & Freitas, 2010). It is well documented that these schools are the focus of accountability policies aimed at improving the academic performance of schools and reducing the achievement gap between students from different racial and cultural backgrounds (Darling-Hammond, 2004; Diamond & Spillane, 2004; Haycock, 2006; Mintrop, 2004).

In this chapter, we reveal how the teachers' schools responded to these accountability policies and how these responses affected the ability of these teachers to perform one, arguably the most important, cultural/professional role: culturally responsive teacher. The purpose of this chapter is to examine how and to what extent the ability of new teachers of color to draw on their own and their students' cultural resources to engage in culturally responsive teaching is affected by their schools' responses to accountability policies. This chapter is not intended to assess the effectiveness of school accountability policies. Rather, it presents the accounts of teachers who attempt to improve educational opportunities by engaging in culturally responsive teaching in the current policy environment. We examine the dilemma described in the epigraph by Inez and confronted by many new teachers of color. On the one hand, they are committed to engaging in culturally responsive teaching to enhance learning opportunities for students from low-income and culturally non-dominant communities. On the other hand, in order to work with such students, many of these teachers work in urban schools that often are deemed "underperforming" according to state and federal accountability policies and consequently adopt programs and practices that restrict the ability of teachers to engage their students' cultural and linguistic backgrounds. Thus, the schools' responses to accountability pressures exacerbated the experience of subtractive schooling described in the previous chapter, presenting even further tensions for the new teachers of color.

RESPONSES TO ACCOUNTABILITY POLICIES: UNINTENDED CONSEQUENCES

Educational reform in the United States has focused increasingly on holding schools and districts accountable in order to create more equitable schooling. The logic of such policies holds that the academic performance of students will improve and disparities in the achievement levels of students from different racial, cultural, and linguistic backgrounds will disappear if the following measures are taken: (1) Uniform curriculum standards are adopted, (2) standardized tests are used to assess whether students attain the standards, and (3) schools and districts are held accountable for student performance on standardized tests (Berger, 2000; Thompson, 2001). Supporters explain that the disaggregation of data by race/ethnicity and language proficiency will motivate educators to address the historic achievement gap between students of color and English language learners on the one hand and their White, English-speaking peers on the other. Thus, federal accountability policies of the No Child Left Behind Act of 2001 (NCLB) require states to set standards and measurable assessments of skills in order to promote high-quality teaching and equitable learning outcomes for all students.

In 1999, California adopted the Public Schools Accountability Act, which established a statewide assessment and accountability system. That system annually ranks schools on the Academic Performance Index (API), which is tied largely to scores on the state-adopted, standardized achievement test, and specifies sanctions for schools that chronically "underperform." The state also enacted the Immediate Intervention/Underperforming Schools Program, which was intended to underwrite underperforming schools' efforts to assess their conditions and develop improvement plans. Beginning in the late 1990s, California adopted educational policies that define content standards, align curricula with standards, and regulate textbook adoption. The impact of these measures differed across districts and schools depending on their student populations. Schools serving higher percentages of students from low-income and culturally non-dominant communities tended to adopt more prescriptive programs that emphasize direct instruction (Achinstein, Ogawa, & Speiglman, 2004).

It is noteworthy that a growing body of research suggests that accountability reforms can produce unintended consequences that maintain, rather than diminish, inequality. Such research highlights negative consequences for the instructional practices of teachers generally and new teachers and teachers of color specifically. For example, high-stakes testing and restrictive accountability measures have contributed to educators' narrowing the curriculum, teaching to the test, de-emphasizing higher-order learning, retaining students in-grade, and excluding types of students who tend to fare poorly on standardized tests (Darling-Hammond, 2004; Doherty, 2001; McNeil, 2000). Test-taking strategies are emphasized at the expense of deeper instruction particularly in low-income, low-performing schools (Diamond & Spillane, 2004).

New teachers may face challenges as their schools negotiate the current policy environment in which accountability measures and standardized (and, at times, prescriptive) curricula increase external control of schools (Achinstein et al., 2004; Achinstein & Ogawa, 2006). Prescribed instructional programs and a narrowed curriculum, which were adopted in response to high-stakes testing and accountability, limited new teachers' autonomy, challenged their personal and professional identities, diminished connections with students, and increased job dissatisfaction and resistance in a study of New York City (Crosco & Costigan, 2007).

The emphasis on testing and accountability disproportionately impacts schools where new teachers of color tend to work—schools with high percentages of low-income students and students of color, which are often deemed "underperforming" (Achinstein et al., 2004; Villegas & Geist, 2008). Research suggests that teachers of color may face particular challenges in the current accountability climate. Ochoa (2007) revealed that Latina/o teachers in Los Angeles County viewed the pressure of high-stakes testing linked to No Child Left Behind as oppositional to being caring teachers and supporting the needs of Latino students, limiting opportunities to engage students in multicultural curricula and critical pedagogy, and as placing unfair burdens on their students. Ingersoll and May (2010) noted that accountability policies might increase turnover among teachers of color because their analysis of data from a national sample indicates that two school factors that might be negatively affected by accountability policies—teacher classroom autonomy and teacher participation in schoolwide decisionmaking—were significant predictors of minority teacher turnover.

NEW TEACHERS OF COLOR: CULTURALLY RESPONSIVE TEACHING IN THE CONTEXT OF ACCOUNTABILITY

In meeting the 17 teachers who remained in teaching and in our study for at least 2 years, we learned that all of them were committed to enhancing learning opportunities for students from non-dominant cultural and linguistic communities by engaging in culturally responsive instructional practices. Strikingly, 16 of the 17 reported that their efforts to teach in culturally responsive ways were, to some degree, constrained by accountability measures. The new teachers taught in schools that were located in districts serving large urban areas. Many of these schools were determined to be underperforming by state and national accountability standards and, thus, were confronted with having to increase test scores (with approximately half the schools in "Program Improvement" status and 11 of 17 teacher participants in districts identified as in need of "Program Improvement") (see Table 6.1). While districts and schools varied in their particular responses to these accountability pressures, many adopted prescriptive curriculum programs and instructional pacing guidelines in order to increase standardized test score performance.

In this chapter, we examine in greater detail how schools' responses to accountability policies support and challenge teachers' efforts to enact culturally

TABLE 6.1: School and District Accountability Status

Teacher	School	District
	Accountability Status	
Pseudonym	P = Program Improvement Status (under high accountability scrutiny)	
Alejandra	P	P
Alicia		
Angela		
Carmen	P	P
Gabriel	P	P
Inez	P	P
John		P
Jose	P	P
Linh		P
Liz		
Lucia	P	P
Manuel	P	P
Mike		
Ricardo	P	P
Sonya		
Tanya		P
Theresa		

responsive teaching. We focus on two issues: The first involves three tensions that the new teachers faced in enacting this cultural/professional role. The second concerns the enforcement mechanisms that affected their instructional practices.

Tensions in Enacting Culturally Responsive Teaching

The new teachers of color in this study characterized the challenges of navigating between their desire to engage in culturally responsive teaching and accountability-based barriers as contradictions and tensions. Many teachers identified three principal tensions, which correspond to the three dimensions of culturally responsive teaching: (1) Whose knowledge counts—cultural and linguistic responsiveness or standardization? (2) What type of classroom climate prevails—community of learners or teacher transmission? (3) What gets left behind—social justice or enhanced test scores?

Whose knowledge counts? Standardization versus cultural and linguis-tic relevance. Many of the new teachers of color experienced a tension between the desire to reflect the cultural backgrounds of their students and themselves in their teaching and their schools' emphasis on a uniform, standards-based curriculum. This raises the question: Whose knowledge counts? It also affects an element of culturally responsive teaching: engaging the cultural knowledge of students. Teachers identified two elements of accountability policies: standardized testing and curriculum standards that limited culturally responsive teaching.

Several teachers believed that the state's use of standardized test scores as the basis for educational accountability worked against including the cultural knowledge of their students from non-dominant cultural communities. Inez, a middle school ESL teacher of Mexican descent, was committed to connecting the curriculum to her students' "funds of knowledge":

> My belief [is] that it's important to connect knowledge and skills that students already have from their homes to new learning. . . . It's what Luis Moll talks about—"funds of knowledge." . . . [My students and I] share similar cultures, similar backgrounds and experiences, so being able to discuss and bring a lot more of our personal backgrounds or families and experiences into the content [means] that students can relate.

However, her students' funds of knowledge were not tapped by the standardized test. She explained that "students are smart and have of lot of funds of knowledge that they can demonstrate in other ways other than filling in bubbles on Scantron sheets. I believe that students can demonstrate knowledge in various ways, including verbally acting out, demonstrating projects." But she found that "once we take them out of that context and once we give them testing and just ask them to read something that might not be relevant, that might not be necessarily connected to their life, and answer that, then they might be at a disadvantage." Inez noted that the failure of the standardized test to adequately assess her students' knowledge was compounded by language differences, creating a situation in which she could not help students or support them through translations.

Gabriel, a new math teacher of Mexican descent, after having taught in California for 2 years, moved to a new state and school and was excited to be involved in a math reform initiative focused on helping students from non-dominant communities to gain access to higher-order thinking and constructivist approaches to math. Yet Gabriel reported how the principal "pulled the plug on us" by replacing him with another teacher prior to the administration of the state standardized test, leaving Gabriel to sit at the back of the classroom:

> We pretty much didn't have control over the class for about 7 weeks. . . . [The other teacher] did a very quick, very traditional, really lousy prep for our students. It was very drill and kill. Everything he did went against what we, as the [math reform] project, feel is appropriate in teaching.

Gabriel felt that this undermined the approaches and philosophy of the math reform: to enable students from non-dominant cultural communities to see math as relevant, construct knowledge, and engage in higher-order thinking. Ultimately, he left this school at the end of the year, attributing his decision to the focus on testing: "It's the policies. It's making it hard to stick around . . . mainly the testing and just the direction of where I think schools are going, and it's just sad."

Jose, a high school teacher of Mexican-descent, was deeply committed to making science relevant and accessible to students of color. He noted that access to scientific knowledge was an equity issue because people of color should be able to understand the impact of science on their communities. Jose explained why cultural responsiveness is crucial to supporting students of color in learning science:

> A lot of students are averse to the dominant culture [and have] experienced a lot of racism and negative schooling. So it's important to respect their intellect and foster it rather than regurgitate into [it], which a lot of science courses do. My approach with experiments and having them draw their own conclusions encourages them to see they have a place in the scientific world, a place they might not [initially] identify as where they belong; this is not just a place for White males.

Jose hoped to include community issues in his science teaching to make it culturally responsive. He taught about how communities of color are unduly impacted by environmental racism, identifying toxic sites located near their neighborhood. Like Inez and Gabriel, Jose saw standardized tests as biased against and thus "a trap" for students of color:

> I like the idea of accountability, but having tests as the measures is problematic. It's normalized to the dominant culture, so the test is biased and very language-based, which excludes a lot of students, students of color. . . . The ways of measuring are inequitable. . . . Accountability measures [are] not culturally relevant to students of color, not normalized to them. . . . It's a trap I think.

Therein lay a tension for Jose, who wanted students to do well on a test in which he did not believe: "Because I don't believe in the test, I don't teach to test, but I teach the subject. I teach beyond the test. It was a tension. I want them to do well on it, but I don't believe in it."

Other new teachers expressed concerns that state curriculum standards limited their ability to engage students' cultural knowledge. Carmen, an English language learner and social studies teacher of Mexican descent, envisioned incorporating her own culture and that of her students into the classroom. She also viewed herself as a role model for students of Mexican descent. Prior to teaching, Carmen explained how she hoped her culture and Chicano history would be reflected in her curriculum. Once she began teaching, Carmen noted that Latinos were underrepresented in the history she had to teach. She reported that Latino students consequently were not interested "'cause they don't see themselves in it" and they asked, "Why are we learning this?" Carmen tried to connect the curriculum to her students' cultural backgrounds. For example, she linked a discussion on colonial America to the issue of immigration. However, she found that the state's curriculum standards for American history excluded Latinos and other non-dominant cultural groups: "The standards . . . are not inclusive of all minority groups or at least Blacks and Latinos, which make up my school. . . . If [students] could see history through the perspective of vital multicultural history, then they might have more interest in history itself." By Carmen's 2nd year of teaching, she admitted: "I kind of focus a lot on the standards, and that sways me away from teaching in culturally relevant ways. But wherever I see it's necessary and also possible to do so, I do throw in a few facts that aren't commonly known." Midway through Carmen's 3rd year of teaching, state standards continued to stifle her attempts to connect the curriculum to her students' cultural backgrounds:

> The curriculum is not culturally relevant. . . . You could see it in a lot of [the students'] eyes, that they want to learn about their history and being Chicano and Latino. There is no time. . . . At our [staff] meetings they always talk about standards, standards. So that's why I kind of shy away from [culturally responsive teaching]. I know [the students] want to learn about other things, but the state of California says what you need to teach.

While a few of the new teachers reported that their schools supported culturally responsive teaching (see contrasting cases below), they, too, felt constrained by state curriculum standards and testing. For example, Sonya, a biracial history teacher, explained her commitment to teaching for social justice: "I think that [it] is easy teaching social studies because all you hear is, 'I teach social justice,' it's talking about different parts of the world and keeping kids aware that throughout the world what the human rights issues there are, what the actual experience of people there are." Yet she described the tension presented by standardized tests that undermined social justice perspectives for interpreting history:

> As we move toward testing, history is more about learning facts, not themes, but facts. This happened and this happened and then this happened. This takes away from individuals and choice. It takes away from the questions: "How do people decide what their future should be? Are certain people in power and others disempowered? In places where they can't make decisions, how do you get to that powerful position?" That approach takes out critical thinking.

Alejandra, a humanities teacher of Mexican descent, wanted to bridge home and school cultures, giving students access to both:

> I personally think that Shakespeare is very important, but he is an old, dead, White man, and I want to make sure they appreciate Shakespeare as much as they appreciate the author of *Parrot in the Oven* [a book about Latino youth]. It is also hard to strike a balance between having them be proud of who they are in their culture, but at the same time having them accept [and] work within the mainstream culture.

In many ways, Alejandra's school supported her commitments and provideed opportunities for her to decide course content and to collaborate with colleagues. Yet even in this supportive setting, Alejandra identified constraints that accountability placed on her teaching. She found that the state's testing program undermined culturally responsive practices. She asked:

> If I think culturally relevant teaching is important and embedded in our curriculum, why can't the state see it and judge us on that? We have . . . this huge unit devoted to the civil rights movements and this huge unit devoted to South Africa because it's very much culturally relevant, it's very easy to make the connections. Those units have to get pushed to later because they're not on the test.

She added, "When you have to teach the kids how to read a [standardized test] question, that's less time we spend on connecting the kids' lives to what you're learning."

This section on knowledge reveals how the new teachers of color faced a tension when confronted with the curriculum of schooling that historically has not included perspectives of non-dominant cultural and linguistic communities. They were bound by the focus on testing and curriculum standards but recognized that both de-legitimated the funds of knowledge of students of color. The novices in our study sought to engage perspectives, pedagogy, and content that reflected their lives and the experiences of their students. Yet, they found that the emphasis on raising standardized test scores and teaching to the state's curriculum standards left little, if any, room to include their own cultural resources or those of their students of color.

What type of classroom climate prevails? Community versus transmission.

A second tension for new teachers of color in the study lies in the conflict between teachers' commitment to creating communities of learners in their classrooms and accountability measures that dictate what individual students must learn at a standardized pace. Teachers wanted to build caring bonds with and among students so that students could collaborate and build knowledge together. However, many were compelled to adhere to district-mandated pacing guidelines in order to cover material on the state-mandated, standardized test. Thus, teachers were pulled between building community to enable students to co-construct knowledge and engaging in teacher-directed instruction according to district timelines in order to cover content, which promoted a transmission mode of teaching and learning.

Sonya, a biracial history teacher, explained her commitment to fostering a community of learners: "I really try to create a community in my classroom and try to create a place where students feel like they can speak up and their opinions won't be bashed down by the teacher." She articulated a commitment to student voice and hearing different perspectives as a way to enhance learning:

> It is really important for me that they know that their opinion matters, so I start my class mixing up who talks because I think it is really important for them to hear each other's voices, and know why it is an important rule that they should be listening while others are talking.

Yet Sonya reported that preparing for standardized tests undermined the learning community in class by focusing on "individual accountability" and teacher-directed knowledge transmission. "Testing is a challenge in building a community of learners in class . . . it results in teaching to the test, where we give them knowledge and do not have them think through it and work through it."

Manuel, a history teacher of Mexican descent, described his commitment to culturally responsive teaching and his dedication to fostering a community of learners in his classroom: "I'm really trying to focus on . . . cooperative learning. I'm really trying to know all the kids' backgrounds . . . and use . . . their prior knowledge . . . to integrate it with cooperative learning to create a community environment in the classroom." He explained why he sought to build a community of learners: "My belief is that kids learn best when they're interacting with one another and the material." He continued, "I'm really big on cooperative groups and having kids count on each other for knowledge." However, the district's pacing guidelines prevented him from building a community of learners:

> The pacing, just the fact that you have to cover so much in the time period, I think that kids missed out so much. You can't really do too much stuff because you have to move so fast and so sometimes you can't have all these [group] conversations. . . . So that does affect your style because you want to create a sense of community . . . but then you're getting deep into a topic, and then you're like, "Well, now you gotta move on."

Two mathematics teachers similarly found that their district's and school's responses to accountability inhibited their ability to engage students in collaborative work. Gabriel, when he first began his teaching in California, expressed a commitment to developing communities of learners in his classes. This stemmed from his constructivist beliefs about learning: "Students need to discover the material instead of me telling them." It was also fostered by his teacher education program: "My [preservice] program. They're always telling me, 'Try group work, and see how that may help.'" Consequently, Gabriel introduced more group work during the second semester of his 1st year of teaching. He hoped that students would learn to work as teams: "I really wanted the kids to grasp the concept and not do the whole drill-and-kill-type procedure."

Despite Gabriel's renewed effort to engage students in collaborative group work, the district's instructional pacing guidelines and the need to cover course content posed difficulties, compelling him to focus on transmitting procedures rather than encouraging critical thinking:

> Because of the pressures from the district, I was kind of forced to have to go that route . . . being told, "Hey, you're running out of time." . . . I'm just gonna teach it the traditional way just so [students] can be exposed to it and see it and know how to do the problem. It's more like a procedural thing, like how do you do this. . . . It wasn't ever like, "Well, why is it that we distribute? What is it that we're actually trying to find?"

John, a biracial African American teacher, also expressed a commitment to engaging students in collaborative group work. He explained how he struggled to engage students in "activities that I've done that involve them getting up and communicating with each other and explaining to each other." John linked one's pedagogical approach and teaching with cultural responsiveness: "I could make every activity culturally relevant . . . from what I've learned of learning theory, they would remember it better if I could find a different way to teach it."

However, John's efforts to build communities of learners in his classes were stymied by having to cover a large number of curriculum standards in a prescribed timeframe:

> The real problem comes from . . . state testing and standards . . . with the amount that we have and the breadth that we have. . . . Let's say in 3 weeks I'm supposed to cover ten standards, I might be able to think of a cool 3-week activity, but if I don't cover . . . all ten of those standards in that 3-week activity, I'm behind because I have to somehow get to those standards because they're going to be tested.

John identified the tension that he confronted:

> Any [culturally responsive] activity that I could find that was of absolute value that would take longer than for me to just give them the steps, so therefore I'm already falling behind on the next standard unless I can include that with that activity. . . . So it's a two-pronged problem where even if I could find a great activity, I'd have to find a great activity that fits in the time that's allotted for me to cover everything.

This section reveals a tension between fostering a community of learners and the more traditional transmission model of instruction. The teachers of color hoped to create caring classrooms that built collaboration, yet faced pressures to emphasize individualism, keeping up with pacing guides, and direct instruction. These two approaches to teaching were at philosophical odds. Furthermore, the notions of building community and caring ties were linked to the teachers' cultural/professional commitments that drew them into the profession and were reinforced in their teacher education programs.

Leaving no children behind? Pursuing social justice versus raising test scores. Educational accountability is touted as a policy measure that will enhance educational equity. This is evident in the use of language, such as "No Child Left Behind," which reflects the intention of providing equal educational opportunities for students from all socioeconomic, racial, cultural, and linguistic backgrounds. The experiences of the new teachers in this study belied this promise of equity. Many found themselves confronted by a third tension: These teachers were committed to enhancing educational opportunities for all students, particularly those from non-dominant cultural and linguistic communities. However, their schools responded to accountability pressures by focusing on improving schoolwide test scores. Thus, teachers often found themselves having to "leave behind" students who were unable to learn the prescribed content within district-mandated time-frames, raising the questions: Which children are being left behind and why?

Alicia, a Spanish and math teacher of Mexican descent, believed in the importance of teaching for social justice:

> Teaching in socially just ways I think definitely incorporates making our students aware of their situations, aware of their conditions, making them conscious of their own opinions and their own choices and what they're doing in their own society, in their own community and teaching them about how furthering their education will help either change or inhibit progress.

However, Alicia noted that her school's response to accountability did not allow for flexibility to adapt to individual student's needs and, thus, left many students behind. Moreover, Alicia reported that the school literally left certain students behind by holding them back in classes they had already passed in order to improve schoolwide performance on the state's standardized test: "What kind of message is it sending to me as a teacher when they're saying, 'Well, it's to help the [standardized test] scores anyways. It doesn't matter that he already passed that class and he should be trying this one.'"

John expressed his belief in "providing everyone with equitable access to education." He explained that his preservice program had emphasized teaching for social justice: "The program does not want to turn out teachers, but 'social justice educators.'" Thus, the program prepared teachers to deliver the curriculum "in a manner that is fair to every student." John focused his efforts on conveying the importance of attending college to his students because, as he explained, "It's a gateway into success later in life." He added, "The college education is their gateway out of poverty or out of a poor neighborhood . . . so it's not just themselves, but for their future generations and for minorities in particular." His approach to conveying his message was direct. For example, in a mathematics course, John showed students a table that revealed differences in the incomes of high school dropouts and graduates and college dropouts and graduates.

To raise test scores, however, John's school adopted practices that presented obstacles to providing students with "equitable access to education." He described how targeting student subpopulations whose test scores could be easily raised meant leaving other students behind:

> We have the same push toward getting more proficiency and . . . they gave us a list of all the students who were real close to moving up from "below

basic" to "basic [proficiency]" and we're supposed to focus on those kids. . . .
Should I not teach the kids who aren't on this list?

Thus, teachers were expected to play a numbers game by focusing on students who
would most impact schoolwide test scores, leaving behind students who might
have been in greatest need.

Gabriel explained that he chose to work with Latino/a youth because he wanted them to see someone who "resembles them . . . that we can succeed as a culture,
as a particular ethnic group." He also wanted to give back to the Latino community. Gabriel wanted students to have more "choices" like "higher education." He
wanted students to have a "better life" through education.

Thus, Gabriel felt that he was doing his students a "disservice" in leaving many
behind by adhering to instructional pacing guidelines in order to prepare students
for the standardized test:

> I felt like I couldn't really . . . slow down, I just felt pressured . . . to move on.
> Oh, sorry, kids, we didn't get this? We gotta move on because the test is in
> 3 weeks. . . . So I felt like I was really doing a disservice to them, because of
> the pressures I had from the tests. . . . I was so stricken by this deadline every
> time that I really couldn't elaborate or try to use additional material because
> I didn't have time for it.

Inez's school mandated teachers to use a scripted program, which included a
pacing guide. Thus, in teaching her English as a second language (ESL) students,
Inez had to use a set curriculum. She explained that the district "mandated" specific outcomes, including portfolios with certain components that students had to
master before moving on. She remarked that this pacing plan posed difficulties for
her students. She found it necessary to slow down and review material with her
ESL students, while being expected to cover a set amount of material in a given
timeframe. But she believed that everyone learns at a different pace and that it's
difficult to allow for that with the pacing restrictions: "I feel that everyone learns
at a different pace. It's really difficult in a classroom of 30 students to say, 'Well, we
didn't finish it but we gotta move on.' It's really difficult, because of the pacing plan
many times we do this."

Contrasting Experiences: Supportive Schooling Contexts

A smaller number of the new teachers of color who participated in this study
were far less affected by accountability pressures and, thus, able to engage in culturally responsive teaching. Some were buffered from the need to improve test scores

for a variety of reasons: Their grade level was not tested, they taught advanced courses, or they taught in high-achieving schools. Others worked in schools, some of which were high-achieving, where teachers exercised a great deal of discretion over the curriculum. These cases are essentially exceptions that prove the rule: Teachers of color who work in schools that are underperforming—and thus facing greater accountability pressures—and that have high proportions of students from non-dominant communities confront tensions between their commitment to culturally responsive teaching and the barriers presented by their schools' responses to accountability pressures.

A few teachers in this study were not affected by accountability measures because they taught advanced courses, which were not the focus of statewide testing. Thus, they did not have to incorporate state-mandated standards, adhere to pacing guidelines, or prepare students to take a standardized test. For example, Ricardo, a math teacher of Mexican descent, felt that he "has to follow the plan in algebra. But anything above geometry, it's a different story" John described having more freedom in teaching courses such as Advanced Placement physics.

Sonya, unlike other teachers in her school, felt buffered from accountability pressures because the subjects and grade levels she taught were not tested. She taught sophomore social studies and senior government; neither subject was tested by the state. Not surprisingly, Sonya was not bound by instructional pacing guides. She explained that she was "lucky in social studies by teaching freshman and seniors. I'm not as tightly held to the California standards that sophomores and junior teachers feel. They don't get tested on standards until 10th grade. They don't take state testing in the years I teach."

A few of the other new teachers in this study also had extensive curricular and instructional freedom and used this to support culturally responsive teaching. Alejandra explained, "We have total freedom . . . we look a lot at culturally relevant teaching and the culture of power." Alejandra taught at a small charter school operated by a nearby university. The school and its leadership maintained a strong commitment to culturally responsive teaching and a professionalized culture where teachers retained control over instructional and curricular decisions, both of which sustained her principles of practice. The school's mission was to leave no students behind, regardless of social class or racial, cultural, or linguistic background. Moreover, the school embraced a broad view of what counts as knowledge. Alejandra explained:

> This is a focus of the school. They try to make things culturally relevant to
> people, to the kids that we serve . . . the school connects its curriculum to
> the cultural backgrounds of its students. We make a strong point of teaching
> cultural relevance, tap students' previous knowledge, and use [it] to develop

lessons, and texts we choose. For social justice, two of [the] habits we focus on are social responsibility. We also want them to have access to [the] culture of power and resources to be successful. . . . It's never questioned, it's expected . . .

Alejandra's orientation was evident in her teaching. For example, in a unit we observed, she had students interview Latino migrant laborers and link that to the text they were reading.

Similarly, Liz, an English teacher of Filipina descent, enjoyed the freedom to make her teaching culturally responsive. She, too, taught in a small charter high school. The school's mission centered on cultural relevance and social justice; its purpose was to get its students, all of whom are members of non-dominant cultural and linguistic communities, to become the first members of their families to attend college. Liz described the curricular autonomy at her school that supported culturally responsive teaching:

> It's a given that you should be considering the standards in your curriculum, it shouldn't be just sort of random, but other than that, as long as you're within those sort of constraints . . . then you and your team of teachers have the right to create curriculum that you think is relevant or that's useful for students, which I think is fantastic.

Teachers in higher-performing schools tended to have greater discretion to incorporate culturally responsive teaching. This stemmed from generally having control of instructional decisionmaking and not confronting the accountability pressures that faced lower-performing schools. Five of the seven teachers who reported having instructional control and support for culturally responsive teaching worked in higher-performing schools (not in "Program Improvement" status). For example, Tanya, a history teacher of African American/Caribbean descent, contrasted her experience with the experiences of teachers in lower-performing schools: "[Accountability] impacted my school very little. We were a high-achieving school, so we didn't have all of those mandates and things that they place on low-performing schools. It didn't impact my school at all." Tanya actively engaged in culturally responsive teaching. In one unit of study, she taught her students to critique the textbook for upholding perspectives from dominant communities. Tanya included an "African American perspective," which was relevant to the lives of her students.

Angela, a history teacher of Mexican descent, returned to teach in a school she had attended, where students performed well academically. The teachers in her grade level organized and pressured the school to change the world history curriculum to be more multicultural in focus:

That's why the freshman course was developed in the district because modern world history in sophomore year just focuses on European history, with some area studies, but teachers spoke up. They're like "that's not enough," considering we have so many minorities in our district, and especially in our community. The purpose of my freshman course is to start with geography, culture and teach kids about Latin America, China, and then the Middle East.

In one lesson we observed, Angela shared her family's immigrant experience, linking it to the curriculum. Moreover, Angela felt free to teach in the way she chose, which was focused on cultural responsiveness. She did not find herself at all affected by the state's accountability program.

Enforcement Mechanisms

The new teachers of color reported two factors that reinforced the influence of accountability on their practices: (1) the fear of monitoring and (2) internalizing the link between test performance and access to educational opportunity. Both contributed to teachers' complying with their schools' responses to accountability pressures.

Fear of monitoring. Several new teachers of color reported that administrators closely monitored them for compliance with district-mandated practices that were adopted in response to accountability pressures. Monitoring often produced a sense of fear and intimidation for the teachers. For example, Carmen, who taught in a "Program Improvement" school, explained:

> I have to state all content standards because I know that our principal and our assistant principals do walk around the classrooms, peek their heads in and check out the standards, ask students what our standard is. . . . That kind of intimidates me not to go outside of it.

Similarly, Inez, who also worked in a "Program Improvement" school, reported that teachers were constantly informed that they would be monitored by administrators through random classroom visits, causing teachers to become "worried about their positions":

> We hear about ["Program Improvement" status] every Tuesday during our staff development meetings or department meetings. Administration reminds us constantly that we're under the big light at the district. We're going to have visitors randomly coming in and observing our classrooms,

monitoring that things are being done according to how they should be getting done. . . . When we hear this constantly like you're under a big light, everybody is looking at you. We want to make sure that this gets done. If not, there's going to be lots of changes, including teachers will be displaced or moved on to other schools [through the mandated reconstitution of the school].

Lucia, a teacher of Guatemalan descent, recounted similar experiences. She explained that because her school was on probation (in "Program Improvement" status), teachers had to follow the prescribed text and pacing plans. She was required to use one of the prescriptive, state-adopted literacy programs, complete with ten teacher guides and scripted lessons. Lucia reported that the vice principal told her that all of her lessons must be "by the book":

I was observed a couple of times and I was talking to the vice principal, who was going to come and observe me. I was going over what I was going to do and her first question was, "Is everything here in the manual?" I said, well, the vocabulary is not. She said, "Well, there must be something in the manual that could go along with the vocabulary because you're supposed to use everything that's in for the Language Arts."

Gabriel, in his first school context in California, described how his district's pacing plan meant that he had to be in sync with his colleagues. Consequently, he feared telling his colleagues that he was not doing the same multiple-choice tests in preparation for the district exams because of his commitment to helping students explain their thinking. Gabriel also reported that his mathematics coach did not observe or coach him, but collected standards assessments and transmitted them to the district office. While Gabriel proceeded with his own approach, he noted the mechanisms of compliance and his fear of going public with his practices:

We're all supposed to be giving the chapter tests. . . . We're all pretty much supposed to be in sync with each other. But . . . I'm not using the chapter tests anymore. I started to . . . but I don't like multiple-choice tests, because the kids can't write down [their thinking]. They bubble any number they want. What I want to see is where are they making the mistakes. Where in the math problem are they having the problem? So all my tests are show all your work and I grade it. . . . I'm sure [my colleagues] won't yell at me that I'm not doing that . . . I don't bring it up. I'm very hesitant. I guess I'm a little scared to.

The monitoring of teachers has heightened the press of accountability policies. Some have likened the intensified scrutiny of teachers to a climate of surveillance (Bushnell, 2003). This form of monitoring may contribute to a sense of de-professionalization, and in the case of these new teachers of color, vulnerable as untenured staff, promote a climate of fear.

Internalizing the promise of access. Some teachers came to accept that accountability, standards, and testing might provide students of color with access to the dominant culture and, thus, educational success. Others reported the pragmatics of having students learn to navigate the accountability system. This was not an uncritical analysis, as many of the teachers realized it was "a game," and others understood the costs of buying into that game. These teachers internalized the discourse of the promise of accountability to provide access and equity as a means of enforcing norms and practices associated with raising the performance of students on standardized tests.

Liz understood the significance of achievement on the state standardized test (STAR) and college access for her students, all of whom were students of color, in a school whose principal mission was to get its students to become the first members of their families to attend college. She described how she had students analyze test scores and rates of graduation and college attendance and compare their school to others with higher percentages of White and Asian students:

> We did this mini research project about STAR scores in the area and what were the demographics of the schools, for their particular scores as well as for what were their graduation rates and then matched up [our school] against those numbers. It was a pre-STAR testing inspiration. . . . The statistics that they had found showed that a lot of the higher-performing schools were dominantly White and Asian. When they showed the graduation rates and the percentage by race at different colleges [they saw] how at highly competitive colleges it was predominantly White and Asian.

Despite Liz's use of standardized test scores to reveal educational inequity, she described her "mixed feelings" about the limitations of testing:

> Testing is really important this year and I have mixed feelings about that all the time. Because I understand the importance of testing in terms of being able to share data and have an even way of comparing students, our cohorts from year to year. I get that. At the same time, I don't personally care terribly much if my kids are basic or proficient or advanced. I think there are other ways for kids to prove their college readiness.

Such "mixed feelings," which reflect the tensions confronting these teachers, were relatively common among the new teachers in this study. These teachers reported a pragmatic accommodation to accountability, knowing that students would have to learn how to do testing. However, they also described their strong beliefs against such measures. Before Linh, an English teacher of Chinese/Vietnamese descent, began to teach, she described her beliefs: "I see teaching as a political act because education has the potential to be empowering and I see myself as an agent for change in this society." When she began to teach, Linh explained the challenge posed by accountability and standardized testing to culturally responsive teaching:

> I find that with my school and No Child Left Behind and the values of the organization where we care about the standards, we want to have benchmark assessments every 13 weeks, we want all these things to happen involving STAR testing ... [such] that the idea of culturally relevant teaching ... it's obsolete within our organization. So I guess that's been a challenge where I feel like these philosophies [of cultural relevance] aren't supported ... [and are] not even discussed.

Linh was outspoken in describing how NCLB and state accountability policies undermined culturally responsive teaching. Yet she also indicated that students needed to be able to take standardized tests in order to graduate and gain admission to college, which she saw as ultimately advancing social justice by improving the students' opportunities in life. To succeed, though, she remarked, "They are going to have to learn to conform." Linh ended by describing her pragmatic approach to test preparation:

> I feel like my students being able to take standardized tests is a part of a larger game that they have to play and participate in as a student in the public school system and as a student that is going to go on to college, and maybe even graduate school. . . . It is a reality that students have and in order for them to succeed in this society, they're going to have to conform to taking these standardized tests. . . . I guess 'keeping it real' with the kids . . . and [telling them] how it's going to indirectly or directly impact them I think is empowering for the kids and culturally relevant in the sense that this will ultimately impact your life.

Alejandra similarly explained how standardized tests undermined some of her ability to teach and assess her students' academic performance in culturally responsive ways. However, she, too, realized that she had to prepare her students for the test. She acknowledged that the longer she taught, the less angry she was about the tests because she realized that "it's not productive" and that standardized testing was just a reality in her students' educational lives. She explained:

> The longer and longer I teach, I get less angry at the tests just because it's not productive. I still think the tests are not exactly the best indicator of student success, but I've now come to the point where I accept the test as a reality.
> . . . I think I'm learning to embed it within the curriculum in such a way that I don't feel like it's totally taking away from what I can do as a teacher. . . . I mean standardized testing is just a part of educational life, so I guess at least in that sense I'm preparing them for that.

Alejandra accommodated this tension by developing a unit test that included questions taken from previous STAR tests while also conducting an innovative performance assessment in which she felt students could better demonstrate their understanding.

Ultimately, internalizing the discourse of equity through accountability may be a source of deep tension for teachers. They find that they are both critical of the dominant discourse on accountability as it impacts students of color, while adopting or accommodating accountability messages and practices in hopes of greater equity.

CONCLUSIONS

Many of the teachers in this study described how school responses to district, state, and federal accountability policies reduced their professional discretion and thus limited their ability to engage in culturally resp-+onsive teaching, highlighting the impact of standards, district-adopted curricula, the pressure of testing, "Program Improvement" status, and accountability policies. An unintended consequence of accountability policies, which were intended to enhance educational equity, was that they constrained teachers from engaging in instructional practices that they believed would provide more equitable educational opportunities for their students of color. Thus, the accountability environment of the schools in which the teachers of color chose to teach in order to serve the needs of underserved students of color exacerbated the effects of subtractive schooling by undermining efforts to teach in culturally responsive and socially just ways.

The teachers identified three tensions between their commitment to engage in culturally responsive teaching and their schools' responses to district policies that standardize curriculum and instruction in order to improve student performance on state-mandated, standardized tests: cultural responsiveness versus curriculum standardization, community of learners versus transmission, and teaching for social justice versus enhanced test scores. They also described two enforcement mechanisms: administrative monitoring and teacher internalization of the accountability logic.

The teachers explained that elements of accountability policies—curriculum standards and standardized testing—challenged their ability to engage in culturally responsive teaching because state standards and standardized tests do not reflect the cultural resources and histories of students from non-dominant cultural communities. In addition, these teachers explained that the standardized instructional programs and instructional pacing guides that were adopted by their districts and schools to improve test scores forced them to engage in transmission-oriented teaching instead of the collaborative and culturally responsive approaches to which they were committed and and in which they were trained.

A smaller group of teachers in this study provide exceptions that prove the rule. Some worked in schools with extensive curricular and instructional freedom and used this to support culturally responsive teaching. Others felt buffered from accountability pressures because they taught grade levels or advanced topics that were not covered by the state's standardized achievement test. Still others were supported by strong professional cultures, often in higher-performing schools that experienced little pressure from the state's accountability system. These are exceptions because they reveal that in the absence of accountability pressures (e.g., working in schools or having instructional situations that exempted or buffered them from accountability pressures) teachers are more able to teach in culturally responsive ways.

Accountability-based enforcement mechanisms created a sense of fear and intimidation for some of the teachers. School administrators monitored teachers for compliance with district- and school-adopted instructional practices and pacing guides aimed at increasing test scores. Teachers were threatened with sanctions for deviating from these programs and policies. This resulted in teachers complying with institutional demands and thus not acting on their commitment to teach in culturally responsive ways and hindered their development as teachers. Fear also undermined teacher control. Many of the new teachers of color explained that strict administrative oversight kept them from engaging in instructional strategies that they otherwise would have employed.

Teachers reported a second mechanism by which accountability measures were enforced. They indicated that they internalized the rationale of district and school accountability measures, especially the focus on preparing students for the state-mandated, standardized test. Teachers noted how tests were important "gate-keepers" to greater access to higher education and how they had a responsibility to support students of color in gaining that access. These teachers reported a pragmatic accommodation to accountability measures, accepting that students would have to learn to play the testing game. The internalization of the accountability rationale by many of the teachers in this study reveals a dimension of enforcement that exacerbated the tensions with which these teachers were confronted. This form of enforcement has been characterized as ideological or normative, where the cultural constructions created in institutions and the social realities that underlie institutions provide justification or legitimation (Berger & Luckmann 1966; Thompson 1980). These normative controls shape the nature of discourse, determining what is "right." Ultimately, messages of accountability become internalized within some of the new teachers of color in ways that may be deeply at odds with their cultural/professional commitments.

CHAPTER 7

Change(d) Agents
New Teachers of Color in a Double Bind

The experiences of the new teachers of color who participated in this study reveal a paradox. As we described in Chapters 3 and 4, their commitments to working as change agents, who transform schools to improve educational opportunities for low-income students of color, were shaped by family, community, and professional influences. Thus, they were attracted to working in schools that served these communities. However, as we documented in Chapters 5 and 6, the teachers were often kept from acting on their commitments by the culturally subtractive conditions of the schools in which they worked and by the schools' responses to state and federal accountability policies. In this chapter, by applying the metaphor of "double bind," we develop two themes that illuminate this paradox: (1) The paradox arises from the systemic, not personal, contradiction in which the teachers are caught, and (2) the teachers become "changed" agents, who internalize the systemic contradiction and thus become compromised by the very schools and educational system they seek to change.

Previous research began to focus on teachers of color for the "power of their presence" (Quiocho & Rios, 2000). That work reveals experiences that were largely missing from research by documenting the cultural assets and commitments to social change that teachers of color bring to classrooms to serve students of color (Beauboeuf-LaFontant, 1999; Foster, 1997; Irvine, 2002; Michie, 2005). Subsequent studies render a deeper understanding of teachers of color as change agents by identifying constraints and complexities (Bascia, 1996; Ochoa, 2007; Quiocho & Rios, 2000; Tellez, 1999). We build on this previous work by expanding the scope to examine the systemic origins of the bind new teachers of color face: They are supported in their efforts to be agents of change by their families, communities, and the teaching profession, on the one hand. On the other hand, they are challenged by the historically reproductive function of schools, which is reflected in the culturally subtractive nature of schools that is reinforced by accountability policies. This chapter also raises concerns about the impact of the systemic tension on the new teachers of color and how they have had to change to negotiate living in this double bind. In the end, the teachers, who intended to be change agents, were altered by the system, thus becoming change(d) agents.

A DOUBLE BIND

Bateson (1972) coined the term *double bind* to characterize dilemmas or untenable positions created by communication patterns within some complex family systems. He described interactions between family members that resulted in contradictory messages whereby a successful response to one message results in a failed response to the other. The person trapped in the bind cannot confront, comment on, opt out of, or resolve the dilemma. Bateson presents an ecological approach, which reveals that the psychological state and thus behavior of individuals do not develop in isolation but develop through interactions and reinforcement within a social system. Bateson describes a systemic condition that can lead to dysfunction for individuals because contradictions in a social system can become internalized by people involved in that system. Thus, the concept of a double bind explains that difficulties experienced by individuals can originate in dysfunctional aspects of their social environments.

While Bateson examined family interactions in order to explain the onset of schizophrenia, we neither seek a psychological explanation for the paradox confronted by teachers in our study nor imply that the paradox resulted in mental illness. Rather, we use "double bind" as a metaphor to more deeply understand the nature of the paradox confronting the new teachers of color in this study. On the one hand, these teachers identified strongly with the low-income, non-dominant cultural and linguistic communities where they taught and were committed to acting as role models, culturally and linguistically responsive teachers, and agents of change to improve educational opportunities for students in these communities. On the other hand, the ability of teachers to act on their commitments was challenged by culturally subtractive conditions in the schools where they worked and by many of their schools' responses to state and federal accountability policies.

The paradox confronting the teachers bears two key features of the double bind described by Bateson (1972). First, the paradox is rooted in the *systemic contradiction* of the transformational versus reproductive functions of schooling in the United States, which are reflected in the educational philosophy expressed by the teachers' families, communities, and profession, on the one hand, and by the educational programs of most of the schools in which the teachers work and policies of state and federal government, on the other. Second, the teachers *internalized* this systemic contradiction, contributing to their becoming "change(d) agents." This was reflected in the teachers' shifting personal and professional identities, issues concerning their cultural match with students, and their involvement in pursuing mainstream goals of the educational system.

Systemic Origins of the Contradiction

The paradox confronting the new teachers of color is embedded in several institutional layers of the U.S. education system. At a foundational level, the paradox is rooted in the historic tension between the transformational and reproductive purposes of U.S. schools (Giroux, 1983). Schools have been and continue to be viewed as vehicles for improving the social, economic, and political status of marginalized groups, including females, immigrants, and non-dominant racial, cultural, and linguistic communities. In this sense, schooling may be said to be transformative of current social relations in promoting equity and challenging society's status quo. However, schools tend to emphasize reproduction, reinforcing dominant forms of cultural capital and thus working against the interests of non-dominant cultural communities (Bourdieu, 1984; McEneaney & Meyer, 2000). Ladson-Billings and Tate (1995) document that institutional and structural racism continue to mark schools, which is evidenced in "subtractive schooling" (Valenzuela, 1999). Thus, schooling reproduces society's current divides and limits access to non-dominant communities.

The two poles of the paradox confronting the new teachers of color in this study reflect this historical and deeply institutionalized tension and are supported by different sets of stakeholders in the education system. The commitment of teachers to improve educational opportunities for students from low-income and culturally/linguistically non-dominant communities reflects the transformational view of schooling and was supported systemically by the teachers' families and cultural communities and by the education profession. The challenges that teachers faced in attempting to act on their commitments reflect the reproductive purpose of schooling as embedded in the "subtractive" structures of schools and reinforced by responses to state and federal accountability policies.

Systemic Supports for Teachers' Commitments

In previous chapters we noted that the new teachers of color were deeply committed to enhancing educational opportunities for students from non-dominant cultural/linguistic communities and that these commitments were largely shaped by the teachers' personal histories. This might lead to the conclusion that this aspect of the paradox confronting these teachers is a matter of individual persuasion: Personal experience led each teacher to develop an abiding commitment to serve students from culturally non-dominant communities. However, the "double bind" metaphor illuminates the multiple and embedded social contexts that contributed to shaping the teachers' experiences and thus their commitments. The early experiences that shaped the teachers' professional commitments were embedded in their families and cultural communities and in schools. Later influential experiences involved various aspects of the teaching profession, including teacher preparation programs, professional sponsors and advocates, extramural educational programs, and educational research. The influences of these embedded social spheres together shaped the teachers' commitments to improving educational opportunities for non-dominant communities and to changing schools and the educational system. As Tanya explained: "You can't one night wake up and be a change agent, it's something planted in you from the beginning . . . in every single aspect of the realms of my life I heard that message [about being a change agent]."

Families. Teachers' families were the first social influence contributing to their commitment to serve students from culturally/linguistically non-dominant communities through education. In a variety of ways, families introduced the new teachers of color to and reinforced the transformational view of schooling. Many teachers explained that their parents deeply valued education, viewing it as the means to upward social mobility and affluence. New teachers of color who participated in this study reported that their families had encouraged them to serve their cultural communities, which historically had encountered injustice and social and economic inequality. This parallels some previous research about how the decisions of teachers of color to teach are influenced by family. For example, McCray, Sindelar, Kilgore, and Neal (2002) describe the impact that mothers have on teachers' decision to teach and their image of good teaching as culturally responsive mothering in the community. However, 6 of the 21 new teachers in our study reported that initially their families were not supportive of their career choices because the parents thought that becoming a teacher was a waste of a college education because it did not afford prestige or a high salary. Four of these six teachers explained that their families did come around to support their career choices.

Communities. The commitments of the teachers of color were also shaped by the cultural communities with which they identified. For many teachers, this meant wanting to work with students who shared their racial or cultural backgrounds and, in a few cases, returning to the schools that they themselves had attended. Like the teachers' families, their communities drew them to the transformational possibilities of education. The teachers often expressed a sense of "social responsibility" and a desire to "give back to community." They sought to serve their communities by addressing injustices and inequities, particularly those found in schools. Throughout the interviews, teachers described a sense of calling to serve their communities. As Jose explained, the call to serve had its roots in identifying strongly with his cultural communities: "We can't abandon them because they are us." This finding echoes previous research about how community experiences shape commitments of teachers of color to serve students from non-dominant communities, identifying teaching as "community work" (Achinstein, Ogawa, Sexton, & Freitas, 2010; Dixson & Dingus, 2008; McCray et al., 2002; Su, 1997).

Early school experiences. Families and communities focused the new teachers of color on the transformational potential of education for students from low-income and culturally/linguistically non-dominant backgrounds. The link to education was made explicit by the teachers' own early experiences in school, influencing their professional commitments in two contrasting ways. First, these early experiences revealed injustices and inequities that compromised education's transformational capacity. Teachers explained that they had been inspired to become teachers because, as members of culturally and linguistically non-dominant communities, they had faced "culturally subtractive" conditions in their schools. Many reported that they had attended schools that alienated students of color, had high dropout rates, and failed to prepare students for college. Several of the teachers cited specific instances of suffering injustices because they were members of racially, culturally, and/or linguistically non-dominant communities. They reported being misplaced in programs for non-English speakers and ridiculed for utilizing non-dominant cultural and linguistic resources. This finding echoes previous research, which indicates that teachers of color view themselves as agents of change because they experienced injustice in their own earlier schooling (Beauboeuf-Lafontant, 1999; Gordon, 1993; Michie, 2005; Murrell, 1991; Nieto, 1999; Quiocho & Rios, 2000; Toppin & Levine, 1992). Second, while many of the new teachers of color identified teachers who had held low expectations for the academic performance of students of color, several recalled teachers who had contributed to their academic success. Some explained that they had been supported and mentored by teachers who inspired them to become teachers who could make a positive difference in the lives of students who, like themselves, were members of culturally/linguistically non-dominant communities by serving as role models.

Influence of the education profession. The inspiration that several new teachers of color drew from their own teachers to improve educational opportunities for students of color foreshadowed the influence of the broader education profession on their cultural and professional commitments. Professions include individual practitioners as well as individuals and organizations that develop and disseminate the knowledge on which professional practice is based. Many elements of the teaching profession shaped and reinforced the commitments of the new teachers of color in this study, including their teacher education programs, professional sponsors and advocates, educational programs outside the schools where the teachers worked, and educational research.

The commitment of the new teachers of color to enhancing educational opportunities for students from low-income and culturally/linguistically non-dominant communities and to changing the educational system toward that end were sustained and reinforced by their professional preparation. As we documented in Chapter 3, all of the teachers were prepared in one of two university-based credential- and master's-granting teacher preparation programs. Both programs were offered by prestigious universities, were committed to social justice agendas, and prepared students to be culturally/linguistically responsive teachers and agents of change in urban schools serving low-income and culturally/linguistically non-dominant communities. This is consistent with a substantial body of research documenting innovative teacher preparation that builds on the cultural resources of people of color to enable them to engage in culturally relevant and socially just practices (Bennett, Cole, & Thompson, 2000; Boyle-Baise, 2005; Darling-Hammond, French, & Garcia-Lopez, 2002; Hammerness, 2006; Irizarry, 2007; Ladson-Billings, 2001; Oakes, 1996; Oakes, Franke, Quartz, & Rogers, 2002; Quartz & TEP Research Group, 2003; Sleeter & Thao, 2007; Wong et al., 2007).

Some teachers in this study received the support of educators who served as sponsors and advocates. Sponsors sustain teachers by providing access to human, social, and/or multicultural capital that may not be abundant or even available in teachers' schools, enabling teachers to perform as role models, culturally/linguistically responsive teachers, and agents of change. For example, Alejandra continued to receive support from professors at the university where she received her teaching credential because that university sponsored the school where she worked. Carmen connected with her preservice colleagues to create a Latina educator group to raise funds for other Latina/os to attend college and become teachers. Advocates actively advance a new teacher's efforts in enacting cultural/professional roles to which they are committed by removing barriers, buffering the teacher from sources of resistance, or placing the teacher in a position in which the teacher could work to change his or her school. For example, Tanya was supported by advocates who were her former teachers and advocated for her appointment to a committee charged with revising the school district's history curriculum to reflect diverse cultural influences. Some new teachers of color were sponsored not by individual educators but by organizations, such as AVID or a nationally recognized math reform project serving non-dominant communities that sponsored educational programs in their schools.

Research that informs the practice of educators was the final source of support for the teachers' commitment to enhance educational opportunities for students from non-dominant cultural communities. This was linked to professional preparation programs, where teachers were introduced to research-based concepts to guide their thinking and practice. The new teachers of color often cited concepts drawn from the work of prominent educational scholars, including "culture of power" (Delpit, 1995), "funds of knowledge" (Moll, Amanti, Neff, & Gonzalez, 1992), "democratic communities" (Meier, 1995), and "liberatory education" (Freire, 1983), to support or explain their efforts to perform as role models, culturally/linguistically responsive teachers, and agents of change in the educational system.

Systemic Challenges to Teachers' Commitments

In Chapters 5 and 6, we documented systemic challenges that teachers faced in attempting to act on their commitments to improve educational opportunities for students from low-income and culturally/linguistically non-dominant communities and to change the education system. These challenges reveal the reproductive purpose of schooling and are reflected in the "subtractive" structures of schools and reinforced by schools' responses to state and federal accountability policies.

Subtractive schools. In Chapter 5 we documented the culturally subtractive conditions that prevailed in most of the schools where the new teachers of color worked. These schools provided little social, human, or multicultural capital and were characterized by power relations that emphasized control. These conditions contributed to three types of subtractive challenges that inhibited the ability of the new teachers of color to perform the cultural/professional roles to which they were committed. These challenges parallel the ones that previous research has documented as "culturally subtractive" for students of color (Valenzuela, 1999).

First, subtractive schools often concentrate students from culturally or linguistically non-dominant communities in particular academic tracks, such as tracks for students whose first language is not English. Because many of the new teachers of color were committed to working with students from these communities, they, too, found themselves "tracked," limiting their access to social capital, or connections with colleagues in other tracks. This, in turn, can limit teachers' access to their colleagues' knowledge and skills, or human and multicultural capital, for performing as role models, culturally responsive teachers, and agents of change.

Second, the new teachers of color faced curriculum challenges in subtractive schools, where instructional materials and curriculum frameworks largely ignored the linguistic and cultural resources of students from non-dominant communities. In addition, the informal, or "hidden," curriculum of subtractive schools undermined the ability of new teachers of color to serve as role models for and build caring relations with students of color by limiting opportunities to connect with students outside of class and, in some cases, emphasizing a "culture of control."

Third, relations between subtractive schools and their students' families and communities were tenuous. This challenged new teachers of color by limiting their access to the social and multicultural resources that stronger links to families and communities could provide, consequently compromising their ability to perform as role models, culturally/linguistically responsive teachers, and agents of change for students from non-dominant cultural and linguistic communities.

In contrast, a few teachers of color worked in schools that invested in social, human, and multicultural capital and engaged in power relations that presented "culturally additive" conditions (Valenzuela, 1999). These schools supported the ability of teachers to perform as role models, culturally/linguistically responsive teachers, and agents of educational change. More culturally additive schools enacted norms and policies that did not categorize students from non-dominant communities in ways that rendered their educational experiences inferior. These schools valued cultural and linguistic diversity, which was reflected in curriculum and instructional practices. They also sought to build relations with parents and communities.

Although these more "additive" schools are exceptions to the "subtractive" pattern, they also presented challenges. While the schools included non-dominant cultures in the curriculum, they also emphasized the traditional goal of preparing students to attend college, which meant exposing students to traditional curriculum elements. Thus, while these schools tended to empower teachers to engage in culturally/linguistically responsive teaching, they also expected teachers to adhere to traditional norms of schooling in the United States. The schools also struggled to establish authentic and sustained relations with their students' parents and communities.

Schools' responses to accountability policies. Many teachers who participated in this study explained that two elements of state and federal accountability policies—curriculum standards and standardized testing—challenged their ability to engage in culturally responsive teaching because state standards and standardized tests do not reflect the cultural resources and historics of students from non-dominant cultural communities. In addition, these teachers explained that the standardized instructional programs and instructional pacing guides that were adopted by their districts and schools to improve test scores forced them to engage in transmission-oriented teaching instead of the collaborative and culturally responsive approaches to which they were committed and in which they were trained. Such constraints were reinforced by enforcement mechanisms adopted by schools and districts in response to accountability pressures, ultimately resulting in teachers' experiencing a fear of monitoring from administrators who closely scrutinized them for compliance with district-mandated practices.

A smaller group of teachers worked in schools with extensive curricular and instructional freedom and used this to support culturally responsive teaching. Others felt buffered from accountability pressures because they taught grade levels or advanced topics that were not covered by the state's standardized achievement test. Still others were supported by strong professional cultures, often in higher-performing schools, which experienced little pressure from the state's accountability system.

Systemic Origins of the Double Bind

The new teachers of color confronted a paradox pitting (1) their commitment to enhancing educational opportunities for students from low-income and culturally/linguistically non-dominant communities by performing as role models, culturally responsive teachers, and agents of change against (2) the challenges presented by the culturally subtractive schools and schools' responses to state and federal accountability policies. Consistent with the "double bind" metaphor, the contradiction reflected in this paradox has systemic origins.

At a fundamental level, the contradiction is rooted in the historic tension between the transformative and reproductive functions of schooling in the United States. More specifically, the contradiction is reflected in different approaches to improving the educational performance of students from historically underserved communities, which are supported by different stakeholders in the education system. The teachers' families and communities emphasize the potential for schooling to eradicate social, cultural, and economic inequities and the education profession supports and informs the teachers' efforts to contribute to the transformation. However, schools continue to be dominated by their reproductive functions, as reflected in culturally subtractive structures and reinforced by schools' responses to accountability policies. The new teachers of color thus found themselves caught in a systemic, not personal, double bind, which they could not opt out of, confront, or resolve without leaving the profession. As Bateson's ecological model reminds us, the existence of a double bind reveals more about the ecology or interactional system in which a person is involved than it reveals about the individual. Thus, the teachers' double bind reveals ills in the education system.

Changed Agents: Internalizing the Systemic Contradiction

While the paradox, or double bind, in which the new teachers of color were caught is systemic, they experienced it in deeply personal and sometimes quite troubling ways. They faced intensified expectations to serve the needs of students of color because, as people of color, these teachers expected to and their families, communities, and profession expected them to improve learning for students of color by acting as role models, culturally/linguistically responsive teachers, and agents of change. However, they were expected to accomplish this while working within the very system that they were supposed to change.

Consistent with the "double bind" metaphor, many of the teachers responded by internalizing the systemic contradiction. This is evident at three embedded levels: (1) the individual level in the shifting cultural identifications of the new teachers of color, (2) the classroom level in teachers' exchanges with students regarding the issue of cultural match, and (3) the institutional level in the participation of teachers in the reproductive functions of schooling. Taken together, these internalized manifestations of the double bind reveal that the new teachers of color became change(d) agents; the teachers were shaped by the very system they sought to change.

Shifting Cultural Identifications

Many of the new teachers of color revealed that their cultural identifications shifted as the result of their experiences in college and as beginning teachers. Generally, the shifts moved the teachers from identifying as members of a non-dominant cultural or linguistic community to meshing this identification with an accommodation of the dominant culture into which they were moving as college-educated professionals. For example, Alicia reported that she became aware of racial/ethnic and linguistic differences in college and felt alienated, which caused her to want to drop her accent. She explained: "Because I grew up in a Latino community, Latinos were all around me. Everyone spoke Spanish at home, and everyone spoke Spanish at school . . . that was something I never really thought about very often." She continued:

> I went to [a college] where I was definitely part of the minority. Race became a larger issue. And things like my accent, which I never even realized I had one up until I went to university and people pointed it out, [became an issue]. I think that all became an issue once I was completely put into a new setting.

Alicia described an incident in college when another student pointed out her accent. She had never previously thought of herself as having an accent but became self-conscious and tried to change her accent in school. While she did not try to speak without an accent at home, her family noticed a difference:

> I think more when I was in formal settings like a classroom, I was more conscious about not letting an accent come out. . . . But when it came to just informal conversation, I haven't . . . I don't think I've made a conscious effort to, not let my accent come out. . . . My family and friends had said . . . that when I was in college, they said every time I came home for vacation, they said, "Oh yeah, you're speaki ng differently. You're acting differently."

The emergence of hybrid cultural identifications reflects the systemic double bind confronting the new teachers of color. This crystallized when the teachers encountered students of color, reminding the teachers of the cultural distance they had covered in moving from being students of color themselves to becoming middle-class professionals in education, an institution of the dominant culture. For example, Alejandra acknowledged that going to college and becoming a teacher shifted her social and economic status, distancing her from her cultural and community roots. Like Alicia, Alejandra adopted dominant cultural and linguistic practices in college: "I didn't want people to judge me by my accent. I made a conscious effort to change the way I spoke and I learned to have mannerisms of the people who were surrounding me, most of whom were White." Alejandra explained how her shifting cultural identifications affected her relations with students from non-dominant cultural and linguistic communities: "I have a feeling of disconnect sometimes because the last time I really lived in the barrio, in the kind of place where [my students] live, I was 18 years old." Alejandra characterized the contrast between her life before college and her life as a middle-class professional as a "contradiction" that made her feel "disjointed" from her community and "culturally suspect" in the eyes of some Latina/o students.

The multifaceted and shifting identities of the teachers of color reflect the deeply personal impact of the paradox, or double bind, in which they found themselves. In attending and completing college, teachers' cultural identities underwent shifts, with changes in their cultural capital and social and economic status, as reflected in how they spoke. The "contradiction" that Alejandra identified is evident when teachers of color who have been successful in school and thus adapted to, if not assimilated into, the dominant culture talk to their students of color about what it takes to succeed educationally. Thus, the contradiction that teachers experience on a personal level is enacted in interactions with students in the classroom.

The Issue of Cultural Match

A critical rationale for increasing the numbers of teachers of color, and retaining them, is that they provide a cultural match for students of color, enabling teachers to bridge home and school, serve as cultural brokers and role models, and foster learning for students of color by seeing with a "cultural eye" (Irvine, 2003). This reflects one side of the paradox faced by teachers of color: transforming schools to embrace the cultural resources of and thereby enhancing opportunities to learn for students of color. All of the teachers in this study initially described themselves as having some form of cultural match with students, connecting with students' cultural identities in terms of race, ethnicity, culture, language, or class. Their students also identified benefits of having teachers of color, particularly their serving as role models who affirmed students' potential and held high expectations for their students' academic performance.

However, the teachers encountered the complexities of cultural match through their interactions with students. While students admired their teachers' cultural backgrounds, they also challenged them (for further discussion, see Achinstein & Aguirre, 2008). Through such exchanges, teachers recognized that their shifting social and cultural identifications, which arose in part from their educational success and emergence as middle-class professionals, complicated their relations with students along lines of language, culture, and social class. The teachers had been changed by the system that they had sought to change. This reflects the second side of the paradox confronting teachers of color by revealing that they had adopted norms of the culture of power and, as teachers, enacted these norms within the institutional context of schools.

Promises and benefits of cultural match. In their first year of preservice preparation, three-fourths of the new teachers of color believed that their racial, linguistic, class, cultural, and gender identities would support better relationships with students of color, while just one-fifth anticipated that conflicts might arise as a result of their cultural identities. When they first began teaching, all of the teachers reported having positive relationships with students based on shared sociocultural histories, and most described how this supported them in efforts to teach content that was relevant to their students' cultures and to act as role models.

Teachers and students identified several dimensions on which similarities in their backgrounds contributed to positive teacher–student relations, including growing up in similar neighborhoods and family structures, experiencing poverty, being people of color, and being English language learners (for further discussion see Johnson, 2008). Alejandra explained how she connected to the experiences of her Latina/o students: "Because I look like the students, [they] know immediately that in many ways I am one of them . . . [I connect to their] socioeconomic status simply because I know what they are going through." She also noted how she connected with her students linguistically: "When I'm talking to them one-on-one, I speak in Spanglish or all Spanish and I'll use more slang. I think that that shows them that they don't have to give up their identity to become a successful academic person." Another teacher, Carmen, similarly identified the many dimensions on which she related to the experiences of her students: "I connect with the experiences and backgrounds . . . of my students and their parents. I grew up in a surrounding neighborhood." She also explained, "I've noticed that a lot of the Latino kids . . . feel that connection because they're able to speak Spanish to someone in the school."

One of Jose's students explained that, having grown up in a similar neighborhood, Jose would understand the students' experiences and priorities:

> In our neighborhood we kinda hear cars speeding, gunshots, and stuff like that and [Jose's] gone through the same things, too . . . and it's a good thing to know that there's someone here with us that can help us out in almost every single thing that we're going through or we are going to go through. . . . Yeah it's different living in the White neighborhoods than living in the neighborhood where we live. . . . He understands you better, understands where you're coming from 'cause he's lived through it already.

A student in a Latina teacher's classroom expressed a sense of cultural and linguistic connection:

> I feel more confident, more calm around a teacher that understands us because it's something similar with her because we're both Latino. And I feel happy being in her class because I can express who I am, and in other classes I'm quieter because I can't say what I am thinking in an open manner, and with her, I do. It raises my interest to always be participating or doing things because if I don't understand it in English, she can say it to me in Spanish.

Complexities of cultural match. Despite the promises and benefits of the cultural match that the new teachers of color enjoyed with their students of color, the teachers recognized that such a cultural match was complicated by perceived differences between teachers and students. These differences were manifested in teacher–student interactions where students challenged teachers' cultural identifications. Tanya explained, "Minority teachers come from the same backgrounds that the students come from and . . . they still believe that they're like their students. [But] you are not the same anymore . . . and that's why [students] are standoffish and they say you 'act White' when you come in, because you don't act like them anymore." Similarly, Alejandra explained in her advice to novices of color:

> Be prepared to have your race be called in question. Be prepared to have your identity be called into question. . . . Be prepared to be criticized for that background and admired for it. . . . I think that's the hardest part about being a teacher of color at [my school] because I went in, and I know who I am, and I formed my identity. But just because you know who you are doesn't mean the students are going to accept it. They're going to play with it. They're going to tweak it.

Over the first few years of their careers, the shifts in cultural identifications that the teachers experienced contributed to a sense of distance between themselves and their students. In particular, the teachers described how language, gender, and social class complicated the meaning of cultural match. Indeed, Alejandra questioned assumptions about the importance of cultural match that are reflected in the media and expressed by proponents of matching teachers and students on the basis of race or culture. About media depictions, she incisively observed: "If your inspiration was *Stand and Deliver* . . . then you are choosing the wrong profession. It takes much more than what was projected on the movie; that notion that he can inspire the kids . . . because he looks like the kids." About the underlying assumptions of many educators, including colleagues, who promote hiring teachers of color to work with students of color, she keenly observed:

> In every place that I applied to [teach], they made a comment about how it would be great to have a Mexican teacher. . . . So that it's sort of thrust on you . . . because you come from the same background as the kids, because you look like the kids, then you're going to be able to reach them maybe in ways that we can't or be able to understand them maybe in ways that we can't. People make those assumptions about you, your colleagues or administrators.

Like Alejandra, all of the new teachers of color learned that cultural match was extremely complicated. They identified shifts in their cultural and social-class identifications, which often resulted from their "success" in school and emergence as middle-class professionals. These shifts resulted in cultural and class differences that often separated the teachers of color from their low-income students of color. On the issue of language, Gabriel's students commented, "Your words are real White." Linh's students said her reading of Shakespeare, "You sound like a White girl." Alejandra, who code-switched among

English, Spanish, and Spanglish, reported that her students at times "called me out on talking White."

Alejandra explained the challenge presented by differences in social class:

> I have been forced to recognize more than ever the privilege I've acquired in the past few years. I have two degrees from [a university] and that has strongly shaped my identity. Five years there changed the way I speak and the way I dress, among other things, but those two in particular really set me apart. My students notice that and latch onto it and this can create what sometimes seems like an insurmountable distance between us.

Linh concurred: "Culture and race issues within the same race seem to be tied around the class issues within that race. I know I am so far from my students' reality, yet we share so much, too. 'What do we really share?' is something I've been digging into." Tanya reported, "I don't think I can connect with my students in terms of class. . . . You're not the same anymore [since going to college and becoming a teacher]. You've gone on and experienced things that your kids haven't experienced yet."

The new teachers of color experienced and recognized the complexities of the cultural match between themselves and their students of color. They described how shifts in their own cultural and class identifications, which often occurred in college, presented barriers in their relations with students from low-income, culturally non-dominant communities. This sense of separation, which deeply complicated the cultural match between teachers and students of color, was also apparent in the role of the new teachers of color in pursuing the mainstream institutional purposes of schooling: preparing students for college.

Institutional Manifestations of the Paradox: "Go to College and Be Brown"

Teachers of color play a role in schools, which, coupled with their often-emergent middle-class status, embodies the paradox of their commitment to changing schools *and* working within the institutional frame of schools. Many of the teachers recognized that, just as they personally struggled to balance the maintenance of their home cultures with their adherence to the dominant culture, they professionally struggled to strike an appropriate balance between engaging the cultural experiences and resources of students from non-dominant cultural communities and helping these students access the dominant social values they needed to succeed in school. In striking this balance, teachers expressed the internalized contradiction: seeking to change schooling to improve opportunities for students from non-dominant cultural communities *and* contributing to the institutional purposes of schooling.

This "balance" was apparent in Chapter 6, where we described how the new teachers of color internalized the contradiction of engaging the cultural and linguistic resources of their students of color, while preparing them for the standardized tests required by accountability policies. Teachers squared themselves with the latter by adopting the pragmatic approach that their students of color would have to learn to "play the game" of taking standardized tests in order to graduate from high school and gain admission to college. We pursue this analysis more deeply by examining the role that the new teachers of color played in preparing their students of color to pursue a college education.

Teachers revealed a manifestation of the paradox when they described their students' fears that success in school would mean losing contact with their home cultures and, thus, their families. For example, Jose explained, "It is not just helping students stay in school, it is realizing that staying in school is very different from what is familiar to them." He characterized it as "scary" for students: "It's almost like I'm asking them to give up their culture or to leave, abandon their parents, or to be different from their parents and I know that that tension exists. . . . They can't fathom it or they worry that maybe they'll forget their Spanish and their culture." Jose directly linked this tension to his efforts to encourage students to attend college:

> I'm trying to sell them something—the idea of college, of going for it. . . .
> I'm proposing being a member of society and studying what you want and teaching, doing. But theirs, it's a little harder reality. . . . I think they experience racism more on a day-to-day level and I don't have the same obstacles. I feel very privileged and I'm very conscious of that and I'm also conscious of the courage it takes them to even entertain the idea of going for it.

The potential conflict that students experience in aspiring to educational success while maintaining their home cultures was evident in an exchange between Liz and her students about the mission of her school, which is to enable low-income, Latino students to be the first generation from their families to attend college:

> *Teacher:* What's the message of our school?
> *Saul:* Go to college and be Brown.
> *Elena:* Like, being proud of being Brown and going to college, 'cause they say that a lot of other schools can't really help minorities or "Browns" or whatever. So our school is saying that we can take you and get you to college.
> *Diego:* Basically, being Brown and proud.

Dolores: Latinos going off to college, because—

Teacher: [To challenge] the status quo.

Dolores: The school was created because the research showed one out of a hundred only [students of color make it to college], so they wanted to change that and that was specifically Latinos and people that were not White.

Other teachers who participated in this study reviewed the transcript of Liz's exchange with her students. They noted that the students seemed to recognize that attending college as a person of color meant having to balance the maintenance of one's home culture with the use of the culture of power. For example, Jose described the importance of students using both their primary language and the language of power in navigating the education system:

I think it was Aida Walqui maybe who talked about in relation to language, of having a primary language and the language of power as two wings— one that kind of keeps you, guides you and the other one that helps you elevate to the height where you need to go to achieve power. I think that's one conversation with the students that merits [addressing, that] when you are a person of color, how to succeed, how to enter these institutions of higher learning and how to deal, how to stay true to who you are.

Liz cited a colleague's assignment of *Nickel and Dimed,* a book documenting the impact of the 1996 federal welfare reform on the working poor, to an Advanced Placement English class. Liz thought that this assignment pushed students of color from low-income backgrounds to question what might be lost or gained by succeeding educationally and thus having different career options:

What would it mean to you to be beyond this, [to use] education to work, to have a different career, having the possibilities? So it starts to really raise questions about . . . do you have a responsibility to your community? Do you think you'll be a different person? Have you got a different SES [socioeconomic status] after college?

Teachers expressed how students of color would have to engage in the practices of the dominant culture to be accepted and succeed in college. For example, Alejandra, cited the importance of language:

We talk about how when they grow up, and they go to college, if they bust out with some of the language that they are using [now] in a college classroom, they will be looked down upon. It doesn't mean that it is wrong, but it just means that that is the way society works. If they want to be able to advance in society, there are certain rules that they need to play by. Whether or not that is fair is a different question. That is the way it is right now, and some of them are sort of starting to understand.

Liz similarly explained how she worked with students of color to dress appropriately as professionals:

We put a conference on for the sophomores and in the previous lesson before the class I had specifically gone over professional dress guidelines that I found online. . . . I always preface it: "This is one of my favorite topics to talk about with you guys," and they're all like, "Why, Ms. [teacher's last name]?" "Well because one, I like to get dressed up but two, who's gonna tell you . . . when are you gonna show up for your first interview wearing the wrong thing and then you're off on the wrong start because someone has a first impression of you. It's important; you should know these sort of unwritten rules of our society."

The teachers of color in this study described how they worked with students of color to maintain their home cultures while learning how to engage in behaviors that conformed to the norms of the dominant culture in order to succeed in school, in some instances having to overcome students' fears of cultural loss. In so doing, the teachers introduced students to the very tensions that they, the teachers, encountered in their shifting identities from members of low-income and culturally non-dominant communities to becoming college graduates, professionals, and members of the middle class. The teachers of color enacted the paradox of changing schools while working within the institutional constraints that schools present by affording students of color educational opportunities previously unavailable to members of their families and communities. These opportunities would enable students to succeed in school and even attend college, where they, like many of their teachers of color, would confront the personal paradox of struggling to maintain ties to their home cultures while establishing new identities in the dominant culture.

Products of a Double Bind:
New Teachers of Color as Change(d) Agents

Together, the shifting cultural identifications of the new teachers of color, the issue of cultural match between themselves and their students of color, and their role in affording students of color opportunities to attend college, where their students, too, might experience cultural shifts, embody the internalization of the paradox, or double bind, confronting these teachers. They had entered the teaching profession to improve educational opportunities for students from culturally and linguistically non-dominant communities by performing as role models, culturally responsive teachers, and thus agents of change in the education system. They were confronted by an education system that historically emphasized its reproductive purpose, which was reflected in the culturally subtractive character of schools and reinforced by schools' responses to accountability policies. Thus, these prospective agents of change were themselves changed by the education system they endeavored to and may ultimately change. They became change(d) agents of change. Alejandra, who consistently and incisively captured the lived experience of the new teachers of color in this study, concluded:

> There's this feeling of disconnect [with students] sometimes because the last time I really lived in the barrio ... I was 18 years old and since then I've basically lived at [the university] and then very different places than [my students] did. So I need to get better at balancing those two things and being up front with my students that I have this other side of me that's very different from them and it doesn't necessarily need to be different forever 'cause hopefully they're gonna go to college and they're gonna acquire this other side of them, too.

CHANGE AGENTS
AND CHANGE(D) AGENTS

This chapter highlights how the new teachers of color were influenced by family, community, and their professional backgrounds to become change agents in schools to improve educational opportunities for students of color. However, many of these schools were culturally subtractive and thus confronted teachers with a double bind, which the teachers ultimately internalized and thus became changed. Our study's findings build on two related bodies of research by broadening and deepening the analysis to examine the nature of a systemic contradiction and how it results in teachers becoming change(d) agents. A groundbreaking body of work chronicled the missing stories of teachers of color and their unique contributions as change agents for students of color. More recently, studies have explored the complexities confronted by teachers of color who are attempting to act as agents of change, complexities that include systemic constraints.

Untold Stories: Teachers of Color as Change Agents

Researchers made an important breakthrough when they focused attention on the "power of the presence" of teachers of color who work to improve educational opportunities for students of color (Quiocho & Rios, 2000). This research was critical in focusing attention on the extent of the contributions of teachers of color, which was missing from the existing literature on teachers. In her study of the life histories of 20 Black teachers born between 1905 and 1973, Foster (1997) makes an observation about the invisibility of Blacks in research on teachers that generally applies to teachers of color:

> Black teachers' unique historical experiences are either completely
> overlooked or amalgamated with those of White teachers. In the few
> instances where Black teachers are visible, their cultural representations
> are biased by society's overarching racism. For the most part these cultural
> representations continue to render Black teachers invisible as teachers of
> students of their own or other ethnic backgrounds. (p. xxlix)

Several studies provide portraits and "counterstories" of teachers of color who act as change agents, reformers, or activists, utilizing their cultural assets and commitments to social change to improve educational opportunities for students of color. Villegas and Irvine's (2010) synthesis of research on the potential of teachers of color to improve the academic outcomes and school experiences of students of color identifies practices of effective teachers of color, including working for social reform and acting as advocates for students of color. Irvine's (1990, 2002) own research highlights how teachers of color play essential roles as cultural translators and advocates for culturally diverse students, helping students navigate school culture and, at times, questioning and defying regulations that are not in the best interest of students of color. Beauboeuf-LaFontant (1999) reports that some teachers of color view themselves as engaging in "politically relevant teaching" by confronting issues of racism in society. King (1991) notes that African American teachers enact an "emancipatory pedagogy" to advocate for students whose interests are threatened by schooling. Michie's (2005) portraits of five new teachers of color who are "working for change" highlight their political clarity and how their personal histories shaped their commitments and inspired their practices, which included building on their students' outside-of-school knowledge and creating spaces where students' voices were heard, debate ensued, and people questioned both historical and contemporary injustices. In these spaces, teachers developed strong relationships, which provided authentic caring and high expectations.

Stanton-Salazar (in press) identifies the importance of "empowerment agents," who seek to disrupt the status quo of social reproduction in institutions like schools and can act as advocate, cultural guide, decoder, and bridging agent for low-income minority youth. In characterizing the motivation of empowerment agents, Stanton-Salazar describes a willingness to identify as advocating on behalf of low-status students and providing them with institutional support in the form of social capital. In many ways, the new teachers of color in our study share these motivational characteristics of empowerment agents; in personal communication with Stanton-Salazar about our study he identified seeing this parallel. Nonetheless, we found that even those new teachers of color with strong commitment, preparation, and potential capacity to be empowerment agents were hemmed in by the institutions in which they were embedded.

Complicating the Concept of Change Agents

Building on research that makes visible the lives and contributions of teachers of color to the education of students of color, an emerging line of work renders a more complicated understanding of teachers of color as change agents by identifying constraints and uncovering complexities. Quiocho and Rios's (2000) review of research foreshadows our treatment of the systemic double bind by identifying conflicts that confront teachers of color:

> It is clear to us that many ethnic minority teachers come to the profession with social-cultural experiences that lead them to see society (and schools, by extension) as being unfair for large groups of students. It is equally clear to us that, while not autonomic or guaranteed, most of these teachers quickly embrace a social justice framework for schooling that would ameliorate some of the effects of these unjust practices. Unfortunately, what many ethnic minority teachers experience in preservice and inservice context is pressure to conform to traditional approaches to teaching and learning. This becomes a source of conflict/tension and professional disappointment. (p. 517)

Research has begun to reveal how teachers of color are constrained in their efforts to engage in culturally and linguistically responsive teaching. Tellez (1999) found that teachers of Mexican descent were unable to incorporate their cultural knowledge in schools with pre-established curricula. Foster (1994) and Feuerverger (1997) report that teachers of color found that schools did not recognize their cultural resources and thus experienced alienation from their schools' goals, particularly concerning issues of diversity, antiracism, and social justice. Bascia (1996) reports that teachers of color who were committed to students of color found themselves marginalized in formal or informal language and ethnic tracks, resulting in lower status and access to professional opportunities.

The findings of Ochoa's (2007) study of eight Latina/o teachers are consistent with our description of how teachers of color can be both change agents and changed agents. Ochoa describes how the accommodations that Latina/o teachers make to succeed in school and to become teachers contribute to their growing sense of distance between school and home cultures. Teachers noted that they had to balance, or even forgo, the values and primary language of their homes and communities with the dominant values and language of school in order to advance academically. They also recounted how the schools in which they taught confronted them with norms and structures, such as academic tracking and responses to accountability policies, that challenged their ability to enhance educational opportunities for their Latina/o students. Ochoa even employs the metaphor of the "double bind" to characterize the tension with which the Latina/o teachers were confronted: ". . . they are caught in a double bind: they find themselves working within an unequal system that hurts the very students with whom they often identify—working-class Latinas/os." (p. 155).

Change(d) Agents and Systems

Our study builds on previous research by deepening and broadening the analysis of both the systemic origins of the bind new teachers of color face and the implications of internalizing that bind in ways that result in these teachers becoming change(d) agents. We highlight how the influence of families, communities, and the teaching profession versus subtractive schools and responses to the broader policy environment create a double bind that is internalized by teachers as reflected in their shifting cultural identifications, in the challenges of cultural match with students of color, and in their self-conscious participation in certain reproductive aspects of schooling. These manifestations of the bind take a toll on new teachers of color and ultimately may undermine their commitments to practices that support students of color—the very commitments that attracted the teachers to and for which they were recruited into the profession.

CHAPTER 8

Supporting New Teachers of Color
A Call to Collective Action

LESSONS LEARNED

What lessons have we learned from the new teachers of color who participated in this study? To answer this question, we return to the two primary reasons that are given for increasing the number and thus the representation of people of color in the teacher workforce. The "demographic imperative" seeks to reduce, and someday eliminate, the disparity between the racial and cultural backgrounds of students and teachers in the United States, where 45% of students but just 17% of teachers are people of color (National Center for Education Statistics [NCES], 2010). The disparity is particularly dramatic in urban settings where schools have extremely high proportions of students from low-income and racially and culturally non-dominant communities but the majority of teachers are White. The new teachers of color in this study, who were motivated by their personal and professional commitments to improve educational opportunities for students of color, responded to the demographic imperative: They sought and for the most part remained in teaching positions in urban schools serving students from low-income and non-dominant cultural communities.

The "democratic imperative" seeks to enhance educational opportunities for and thus the academic performance of students of color. It is rooted in an assumption that teachers of color may be particularly suited to teaching students of color. An emerging body of research does suggest that teachers of color can produce more favorable academic results for students of color than White colleagues by engaging in culturally responsive practices, serving as role models, and transforming education to prepare all students to engage in a multicultural democracy. However, the experiences of the new teachers of color in this study reveal a critical challenge to moving beyond the demographic imperative's numerical goal of increasing the numbers of teachers of color to fulfilling the moral promise of the democratic imperative by having teachers of color improve educational opportunities for students of color. These teachers confronted a paradox: They were committed to changing schools to improve educational opportunities for students from low-income, culturally and linguistically non-dominant communities and thus advance the demographic imperative by working in schools with high concentrations of students of color. However, the new teachers were often kept from acting on their commitments by the culturally subtractive conditions of the schools in which they worked and by the schools' responses to state and federal accountability policies, thus blunting their efforts to advance the democratic imperative.

The paradox that compromised the ability of the new teachers of color to pursue the democratic imperative is not personal. Rather, it is rooted in a systemic "double bind" that the teachers as individuals therefore cannot address, let alone resolve. The contradiction stems from the historic tension between the transformational and reproductive purposes of schools in the United States. The two poles of the contemporary contradiction confronting the new teachers of color are supported by different sets of stakeholders in the education system. The commitment of the teachers to improve educational opportunities for students from low-income and culturally/linguistically non-dominant communities, which reflects the transformational view of schooling, was supported by teachers' families and cultural communities and by the education profession. The challenges the teachers faced in attempting to act on their commitments reflect the reproductive purpose of schooling, which is institutionalized in the "subtractive" structures of schools. It is reinforced by accountability policies to which schools respond by emphasizing the preparation of students for standardized tests. This narrows the curriculum and emphasizes teacher-centered, direct instruction, limiting opportunities for teachers to engage in culturally and linguistically responsive instruction.

The new teachers of color in this study internalized the systemic contradiction, or double bind. This is reflected in their shifting cultural identifications, the questioning by students of color of a "cultural match" between themselves and their teachers of color, and the self-conscious participation of teachers in reproductive aspects of schooling. Taken together, these internalized manifestations of the double bind reveal that the new teachers of color became change(d) agents; the teachers were reshaped by the education system they sought to change.

A CALL TO COLLECTIVE ACTION

These conclusions point to two clearly related problems. First, the public education system in the United States is marked by a contradiction that compromises its capacity to meet the educational needs of students from low-income and culturally and linguistically non-dominant communities. Second, this contradiction causes new teachers of color to suffer professionally as well as personally because the systemic contradiction positions them to improve educational opportunities for students of color but frustrates their efforts in culturally subtractive schools and through state and federal accountability measures. What can be done to address these problems?

The democratic imperative to which these teachers responded by committing to enhance educational opportunities for students from non-dominant cultural communities and the systemic nature of the contradiction that compromised the teachers' ability to act on their commitments suggest that a collective, democratic strategy will be required. The democratic imperative highlights the transformational potential of education; it reflects the historical purpose of public education in the United States to educate a literate polity to sustain a democratic republic (Tyack, 1974). Contemporary proponents of the democratic imperative build on this tradition to argue that a high-quality education is a civil right because it can provide historically marginalized groups, including culturally non-dominant communities, with the skills and knowledge to participate fully in the nation's political, social, and economic institutions. The pursuit of such democratic ideals will require the engagement of stakeholders with diverse and even conflicting interests; only through broad participation in democratic institutions and processes can the virtues of democratic equity and social justice be pursued through the education system.

The fundamental problem uncovered by this study is the systemic contradiction, or double bind, in which the new teachers of color were caught. On one side are stakeholders who emphasize the promise of teachers of color to transform schools into places that engage the cultural and linguistic resources of students of color and thus improve educational opportunities for and the academic performance of these students. These stakeholders include the teachers' families and communities, who see the transformative potential of education and encourage new teachers of color to become agents of change, and the teaching profession, which prepares the new teachers of color and provides research that informs their efforts to become role models, culturally responsive teachers, and agents of change. On the other side of the bind are schools that reflect the reproductive purpose of education in their culturally subtractive structures, which marginalize the cultural and social resources of both teachers and students of color, and policymakers who enact accountability measures that result in schools narrowing their curriculum to concentrate on the preparation of students for high-stakes, standardized tests, which reinforces the culturally subtractive bias of many schools with high proportions of students of color.

Despite these marked differences of perspective, stakeholders on both sides of the contradiction share a common goal: to improve educational opportunities for and thus the academic performance of students from low-income and culturally non-dominant communities. The families and communities of the new teachers of color in this study have an expressed and vested interest in attaining this goal. So, too, does the teaching profession, including the teacher education programs in which the new teachers of color were prepared to pursue equity and social justice in urban schools and researchers who report the advantages of culturally and linguistically responsive teaching. Similarly, officials in schools serving students from low-income and culturally non-dominant communities and state and federal policymakers seek to improve the academic performance of students and eliminate disparities in the achievement of students from different racial, cultural, and linguistic backgrounds. In fact, these are among the stated goals of accountability policies. They are also the often-unstated goals behind policies to recruit teachers of color into the workforce to serve in schools with students from non-dominant communities.

Building on this shared goal, policymakers, educators, and the communities and families they serve must find a middle ground and resolve the contradiction between accountability policies that reinforce the culturally subtractive structures of schools and the position taken by the education profession and non-dominant cultural communities that teachers of color can improve educational opportunities for students of color by drawing on their own cultural resources and those of their students to perform as role models, culturally responsive teachers, and agents of change. An overall strategy to accomplish this can be pieced together using a mix of elements recently proposed by scholars who reflect the entire spectrum of thinking about educational reform.

Policymakers provide the institutional frame within which educational change develops. A strong proponent of markets as the mechanism for nurturing educational innovation and change argues that policymakers should provide the environment for invention, not design and mandate the new system (Hess, 2010). This includes establishing multidimensional measures of the academic performance of schools, providing infrastructure and funding to spur innovation through research and development, and, we would add, making available adequate resources, financial and otherwise, to support high-quality education for students generally and for students from underserved communities particularly. Rather than rely on the policy-supported market to design schools, other analysts suggest a strategy that is more in keeping with the democratic imperative. This strategy calls for involving educators and communities as principal architects of educational reform.

A former proponent of accountability and market-based approaches to educational reform recently reversed direction, now arguing that "professional educators and scholars," not policymakers or market-wise entrepreneurs, must determine what is to be taught in schools and how it should be taught (Ravitch, 2010). A scholar who has long been a proponent of teacher professionalism and progressive educational reform shares this view of the role of educators. She takes issue with the detachment of teachers from educational reform and promotes their direct involvement in developing ways to make schools places where students, especially students from low-income and culturally non-dominant communities, will succeed (Cochran-Smith, 1991).

The scholar who turned away from market- and accountability-based reform also recognizes the important role that communities play in the performance of schools (Ravitch, 2010). Progressive educational scholars have long called for the grassroots involvement of parents and communities in developing and supporting schools that serve their children's educational needs. The participation of communities in educational reform clearly resonates with the democratic imperative. Recent research highlights how low-income, non-dominant cultural communities can work with educators to organize and exert local power in pursuing equity and justice in education (Oakes & Rogers, 2006).

Thus, to eliminate the systemic contradiction that bound the new teachers of color in this study and thereby enable these teachers to contribute to the democratic imperative, we must enact democratic principles. The goal of the imperative is to enhance learning opportunities for low-income students of color so that they can participate fully in the nation's political, economic, and social institutions. To accomplish this goal, schools must attract and support teachers of color who draw on their cultural resources and those of their students of color to enhance educational opportunities and performance. This also calls for recasting the policy logic to move beyond retention as the sole goal for teachers of color because it does not make sense to be concerned about the retention of teachers of color if they are not provided opportunities to develop and enact the very commitments and practices that are intended to promote academic success for students of color. To develop schools that are culturally additive and provide adequate physical, human, social, and multicultural capital and positive power relations, educators and communities must collaborate in designing and organizing innovative schools. To nurture innovation, policymakers must provide infrastructure and resources to support research and development by educators and the communities with which they work. Researchers need to investigate and shine the light on culturally additive school conditions that support teachers of color in performing the cultural/professional roles that are intended to advance educational opportunities of students of color. Communities must organize to build and exert their influence to shape the priorities of policymakers and educational professionals. Indeed, a small body of research indicates that when policymakers, educators, and interest groups work together, they can develop, spread, and sustain educational innovation (Rowan, 1982).

To identify conditions that support teachers of color to develop their cultural resources for students of color, we draw on some instances from our study. Alejandra's school engaged in a hiring process focused explicitly on recruiting teachers from diverse racial and cultural backgrounds with a social justice perspective; administrative mentoring, new teacher support, and collegiality focused on culturally/linguistically responsive teaching; an advisory program that connected teachers with students and families over 4 years; and a whole-school mission and structures affirming the multicultural capital of home and school cultures. Carmen described two sources of support: her preservice program's focus on social justice and a group formed by Latinas from her preservice program to raise funds for other Latina/os to attend college and become teachers. Inez experienced support from the local community where she was raised and where she chose to teach. She sought to link her school to her English language learners' (ELLs) families, who were the strongest advocates for her cultural/professional commitments. Tanya was supported by advocates and sponsors, her former principal and teachers, who promoted her appointment to a committee charged with districtwide curriculum reform to reflect diverse cultural influences. Sonya reported how being buffered from accountability pressures to teach to the test allowed her to be more culturally responsive in her practices. Gabriel and Manuel were sponsored by organizations, such as AVID and a national math reform effort targeting non-dominant communities that developed educational programs in their schools to support the teachers in acting on their commitment to students of color. Jose was influenced by educational research on creating schools as democratic communities in shaping his views of schooling. These multiple and varied supports reflect within- and beyond-school sources needed to access and develop the cultural resources of teachers of color working to change educational opportunities for students of color.

Even in our most optimistic moments, we recognize that the changes needed to remove the systemic contradiction that perplexed the new teachers of color in this study will require a complex and massive effort and thus will require time. However, teachers who are committed to improving educational opportunities for students of color continue to work in schools and a policy environment that challenge their abilities to act on their commitments. A recent review of research indicates that relatively high proportions of teachers of color work in low-performing, urban schools with high proportions of students from low-income and non-dominant cultural and linguistic communities (Achinstein, Ogawa, Sexton, & Freitas, 2010). These are the very schools that are underresourced and often face increased accountability pressures. These teachers will continue to encounter schools that are culturally subtractive and that have responded to accountability policies by narrowing curriculum and requiring teachers to prepare students to take high-stakes, standardized tests. Many will internalize the contradiction and thus experience shifting cultural identifications, have their cultural identifications challenged by students of color, and self-consciously and often self-critically participate in reproductive aspects of schooling. Who is responsible for supporting and caring for these teachers?

Our study reveals that the contradiction confronting the new teachers of color has systemic origins. Consequently, we believe that the educational stakeholders who occupy opposing poles of the contradiction are accountable to these teachers. The non-dominant cultural communities whose educational interests these teachers are committed to serving can provide spaces outside of schools where teachers of color can perform as role models and culturally responsive educators. These include educational and cultural programs offered by various community groups. These same community-based organizations could also provide forums where teachers of color can discuss the relationship between success in school and shifting cultural identifications, an issue that some teachers in our study reported to be problematic for some parents from culturally non-dominant communities. These discussions can also provide teachers with opportunities to openly share and work through the difficulties they encounter as they help their students "go to college and be Brown." Community-based organizations may also serve as a site for novices investigating the complexities of being change(d) agents, holding dialogues about navigating multiple terrains and sustaining commitments.

Individuals and organizations associated with the teaching profession can play a major role in supporting and caring for new teachers of color. While we know much about culturally responsive teaching, it is important to investigate what culturally responsive induction of new teachers of color might entail. A recent review of research on turnover among teachers of color indicates that teachers of color are more likely than White teachers to be motivated by a "humanistic orientation" to improve educational opportunities for students of color (Achinstein et al., 2010). However, research indicates that, if left on their own, new teachers of color may not cultivate the cultural resources needed to perform cultural/professional roles and may even leave the profession (Villegas & Lucas, 2004). It is unjust to hold teachers of color accountable for culturally responsive teaching without the professional cultures and school contexts that support this pedagogy and the help needed to negotiate a double bind. In the end, the very reason teachers of color come into the system to transform it, may be the reason they leave it or else risk losing their commitments. New teachers of color must be supported in navigating the systemic double bind; finding allies, sponsors, advocates, and communities of support; determining ways to cultivate and employ their own and their students' cultural/linguistic resources in the classroom; advocating on their own and students' behalf; and sustaining commitments to cultural/professional roles without burning out or being fired.

Within schools, new teachers of color can be supported by administrators and more veteran colleagues who buffer and support the enactment of cultural/ professional practices of teachers of color. Principals, department chairs, mentors, and senior teachers can be allies to new teachers of color by promoting professional development in teaching in culturally responsive ways, by responding to accountability measures in ways that support school and teacher agency in instructional decisionmaking, and in holding public discussions on managing equity goals and talking about culture. In this way, educators can support each other in holding the profession accountable for the success of under-served students, and for providing support to teacher development to meet such equity goals.

Teacher education and induction programs should provide opportunities for prospective teachers of color to identify and deal with personal and professional challenges that result from the double bind that the novices in our study faced. They must also support novices in navigating the bind while sustaining commitments in ways that do not result in teacher burnout or, alternatively, make novices vulnerable to being fired. Formal and informal mentors who are experienced colleagues might play a critical role here. What is unique about induction support for teachers of color is that their sources of support may need to act as what Carter (2005) described as "multicultural navigators," educators who draw from their own cultural resources and support people of color in negotiating both dominant and non-dominant cultures. While Carter wrote of the importance of multicultural navigators for youth of color, this study highlights the need of such support for teachers of color. This is not generic support from professional communities, but support focused on unique expectations and dilemmas faced by new teachers of color as they attempt to be role models, culturally/linguistically responsive teachers, and agents of change. It might mean that mentors support novices of color in unpacking cultural challenges they face from students and colleagues or negotiating/advocating with administrators and colleagues to sustain the novices' culturally responsive practices in the face of organizational constraints.

Research indicates that novice teachers can receive support from broader professional circles, particularly when such support is introduced by mentors (Achinstein & Ogawa, 2006; Chubbuck, Clift, Allard, & Quinlan, 2001). Professional organizations and their state and local affiliates could develop professional development opportunities that are designed to address the challenges confronting teachers who aspire to be agents of change, especially teachers of color who are committed to serving their cultural communities. Networks of educators who are dedicated to social justice concerns or antiracist education might also serve as sources of support for new teachers of color with similar commitments. Researchers can collaborate with teacher education programs and teachers' organizations to design programs to support and care for teachers of color who are committed to changing schools to better meet the educational needs of students of color and thus are drawn to working in urban schools with high proportions of students from low-income and culturally non-dominant communities.

Moreover, teacher education needs to revisit what the "overwhelming presence of Whiteness" (Sleeter, 2001) means for prospective teachers of color and seek to address ways for new teachers of color to negotiate some of the binds they might face being in teacher education programs and in their future schools. Preservice education, even those programs that explicitly focus on culturally responsive teaching and socially just practices, still may not take into account the cultural and linguistic resources of the teacher candidates and communities that reflect non-dominant cultures. This could result in undermining cultural/professional roles that novices of color seek to undertake. Even the most "culturally responsive" teacher education programs might still need to think further about preparing new teachers of color for a systemic bind they might face, providing ongoing support beyond the preservice experience. Furthermore, those teachers of color who enter teaching through pathways that do not include opportunities to student-teach, to engage with communities and schools prior to teaching, need to consider how this might leave them both unprepared for the challenges they may face and lacking the skills needed for effectively teaching diverse youth.

Finally, policymakers in the majority of states have enacted policies to increase the presence of people of color in the teacher workforce. Therefore, they, too, should be accountable to teachers who, like the new teachers of color in this study, are committed to improving educational opportunities for students from culturally non-dominant communities but often find themselves inhibited by their schools' responses to accountability measures adopted by these same policy makers. Policymakers must investigate unintended consequences of policies that pit teachers against approaches, such as culturally/linguistically responsive teaching, supported in the professional environment. The constraints that the teachers in this study reported call for policy makers to join educators at the policy-making table to eliminate the double bind they have created for new teachers of color. This may also call for including in policy decisions the very teachers of color and community members who reflect the populations of the schools hardest hit by accountability measures. School level groups, including teachers, that make policy decisions would need to collectively take up a number of specific measures that challenged the efforts of teachers of color to enact culturally responsive teaching and resulted in such perverse effects as: a climate of fear for new teachers of color, teaching to the test, or teaching only those students who will easily bring up the school's scores, leaving English learners behind, and compromising the cultural/ professional principles of the very teachers policy makers recruited to diversify the profession. Further, such collective policy making bodies would need to focus on providing needed supports and developing quality teaching, which may include responsiveness to the cultural and linguistic diversity of students, instead of punishing low-performing students and schools. They may need to address how uniform, standards based curriculum which has become a form of standardization limits culturally responsive teaching, and identify content standards that are more broadly culturally inclusive. They may revisit the limitations of responses to accountability that result in mandated pacing guides to cover materials for tests. Local policy making bodies will want to redress implementation of state and federal policies that put all the focus on test results, which resulted in leaving students behind. The local policy making bodies will have to consider the contradictory policies of recruiting new teachers of color who seek to teach in settings with students of color, only to face low classroom autonomy and exclusion from schoolwide decisionmaking, which are working conditions that increase minority teacher turnover (Ingersoll & May, 2010).

It makes little sense to employ strategies to culturally diversify the teacher workforce if new teachers of color are not provided opportunities to develop and enact the very commitments and practices for which policymakers and educators sought them out. While policymakers work with educators and communities to eliminate the systemic contradiction to which they contributed, they should allocate resources to nurture innovative programs developed and offered by educators and community groups to support and care for teachers, who serve on the frontlines of the campaign to secure the educational justice and equity that undergird our democracy.

Methodological Appendix

This methodological appendix provides further details about the data collection and analysis used in the study that informed this book.

DATA COLLECTION

Educator Interviews

We conducted audio-recorded semistructured interviews with 21 new teachers of color as well as 31 administrators and support providers (e.g., mentors). In each year of the 5-year study, we interviewed the novices three times (fall, winter, and spring); interviews ranged from 45 to 120 minutes in length. We also engaged the new teachers in summer retreats, where we reported emergent themes from the study and solicited their feedback in a focus group session.

In the 1st year of the study, the interviews focused on the teachers' professional and personal backgrounds; their reasons for becoming teachers; and their teaching beliefs and practices, sociocultural conceptualizations, relationships with students, preservice experiences, and supports and challenges in learning to teach. In the 2nd year, which was the teachers' 1st year of teaching, the interviews focused on school contexts, reflections on the lessons that researchers observed, and how—if at all—the teachers' own and their students' cultural identifications influenced their teaching; we also continued to ask teachers about the topics addressed in the 1st-year interviews. In the 3rd, 4th, and 5th years of the study, several questions were repeated from the 2nd-year protocols to check for consistency over time, while other questions pursued themes emerging from the first 2 years of data, including questions about professional beliefs, conceptions about culturally responsive teaching (those espoused in their preservice programs and their own beliefs about connecting teaching to students' cultures), school and district contexts, instructional control, and accountability climates. For example, teachers were asked to describe their conceptions about culturally responsive teaching and what challenges and supports they received in such practices. Because the issue of how schools responded to accountability policies emerged as a common theme among the respondents, we then asked how, if at all, accountability measures impacted their school and their own practices and experiences as a teacher.

Teacher Interviews

A sample of the kinds of teacher interview questions we asked over the 5 years is included below. While we cluster questions here by theme, you will note how some questions pick up on emergent themes drawn from the data and voices of the participating teachers, asking them to speak directly to the themes that emerged from earlier responses.

Teacher Background and Commitments

1. Please describe your personal background and education.
2. Why do you want to become a teacher? Why in your specific subject area?
3. In what kind of school are you planning to teach and why?
4. Please describe your earliest school experiences and compare and contrast them with your home experiences. What positive and negative school experiences have you had that may inform your own teaching?

School Context

5. Please describe your school context, your students, what it's like to work there, and why you took this job. (Follow-up on relationship and work with colleagues, principal, district, parents, larger community, and fit with school's teaching beliefs and practices.)
6. How much teacher control is there at your school in decisions about what and how to teach (e.g., curriculum and instruction)? What kind of role, power, or voice do teachers have in school decisionmaking in general? What are the governance arrangements at your school? What are relationships like between administrators and teachers?
7. In what ways, if at all, does your school encourage or discourage connections to the broader community that it serves, including parents and neighborhood?
8. What supports are you receiving in learning to teach (and how valuable do you find this support); and what challenges are you facing in learning to teach, giving examples of how it is influencing your practice

(e.g., district and school professional development, induction/new teacher support program, mentor, connection to preservice program, family/community)?

9. Please describe how, if at all, your school specifically supports teachers of color. In what ways, if at all, may it challenge you as a teacher of color?

Teaching Beliefs and Practices

10. Your preservice program promoted teaching for social justice and culturally responsive teaching. If you are trying to teach this way in your own practice, can you describe what these principles look like in your own teaching and subject area? Please give an example.

11. What are the supports and challenges related to culturally responsive and socially just teaching you've experienced?

12. Let's talk about the lessons we videotaped. Pick one lesson to talk about and please tell us about the following areas:

   - The lesson goals and how they connect to your curriculum
   - Your beliefs about teaching, learning, and subject matter reflected in your lesson
   - Any considerations of culture, race, and language in this class reflected in the lesson
   - With respect to your vision of social justice and equity
   - Overall, how do you think the lesson went?

13. Please describe your relationship with your students (e.g., in what ways are you similar/dissimilar to your students; how, if at all, is anything unique about your relationships you have with students of color; what, if any, challenges do you experience that may relate to your own and your students' cultural identifications; how, if at all, does language or dialect influence your work with students).

14. What do you see as the most significant issues for teachers of color in terms of sustaining and developing them as teachers? What will it take to support more teachers of color to stay in the profession?

15. How do you decide what to teach and how to teach it? Do you have a curriculum that you are expected to follow? If so, explain and identify how these approaches of what and how to teach align or do not align with your own vision of teaching.

16. How, if at all, have accountability measures impacted (a) your school and (b) your own practices, commitments, and experiences as a teacher?

17. In what ways, if any, do the curriculum and school support or inhibit culturally responsive and socially just teaching? In what ways, if any, do they not?
18. Do you feel sufficiently supported to teach in a way that aligns with your vision?
19. In thinking about your initial motivation for entering teaching, in what ways have you or have you not become the kind of teacher you wanted to be when you entered teaching? What changes would you identify? What are the causes of those changes?
20. How, if at all, has participating in this research project affected you?

Sociocultural Identifications and Teaching

21. How do you identify yourself culturally (e.g., race, ethnicity, class, and language)?
22. What aspects of your self-identifications do you feel inform your role as a teacher, and how (e.g., a person may identify by racial, linguistic, class, cultural, gender membership, or many other things)?
23. In what ways, if at all, do the cultural identifications of the students you teach impact what you are doing in the classroom? Please give an example.
24. How, if at all, have you changed as a result of this year's educational experiences (in regard to assumptions about teaching, students, or schools and ideas about issues of diversity; how your own identifications may inform your role as a teacher)?
25. How, if at all, have your conceptions of your cultural identifications changed over time? Who and what influenced those changes in conceptions about your cultures?
26. How, if at all, have your conceptions of your cultural identifications and being a teacher of color changed since you started teaching at your school(s)? Who and what influenced those changes since starting teaching?
27. Who/what have you turned to in the past or now to help you think or talk about issues of race, ethnicity, class, and language in your teaching?
28. We are developing some emerging themes from the study. Please describe your own ideas and experiences in relation to the themes (whether it is relevant to you, identify what this theme means to you, provide some examples, explain some challenges, identify who you talk to about those challenges, what support you would like related to this theme, and how conceptions/experiences about this theme changed since you started teaching): (a) being a role model for students of color;

(b) having special relationships and connections with students of color (e.g., cultural match); (c) connecting your teaching to your students' and your own cultures, and culturally responsive and socially just teaching); (d) being an agent of change.

29. Early on in this study, many teachers identified how their cultures would influence their teaching. For example, people described wanting to be culturally responsive teachers, role models, and change agents for students of color. How are you thinking about those issues now? How, if at all, have your views changed over time? If so, why?

30. Given your experience as a teacher of color, what advice would you give to educators, administrators, and policymakers about the kinds of support you wish that you had or did have that were important to you as a teacher of color? In reflecting on your own experience as a new teacher of color, what advice would you give to prospective teachers of color?

Career Plans

31. What are your future career plans, both short-term and long-term plans?
32. Will you be remaining at your school next year and why/why not?
33. How long do you plan to stay at the school and why?
34. How long do you plan to stay in the profession and why?
35. Why did you/didn't you remain at your school (and in education)?

Administrator/Support Provider Interviews

A sample of interview questions for administrators and support providers is included below, addressing issues of school culture, role and background, reflections on the beginning teacher and her or his teaching, and supporting new teachers of color. The support providers were primarily mentors or coaches. Administrators were predominantly principals, with some assistant principals included.

School Culture

1. How would you describe the professional culture at this teacher's school (e.g., quality of teachers, collaboration, professional development, relationship between administrators and teachers)?
2. What is the school culture like for new teachers?
3. What kinds of support do new teachers in your school receive?
4. How many new teachers are currently at your school? How many teachers are there in your total faculty?
5. What is the retention rate of new teachers at the school?

Role and Background

6. What is your current position/role [in the school]?
7. What kind of involvement do you have in terms of new teacher support? Please describe your role and your relationship with the beginning teacher in this study.
8. How do you support him or her?
9. How has this relationship changed over time (changed/developed?)?
10. Please tell me about your own family/cultural background and educational background. [Probe for demographics of where the person grew up, including SES.]
11. How, if at all, does your own background relate to how you mentor or support this beginning teacher?

Beginning Teacher

12. How is this [beginning teacher] doing? Share any insights from your work with this beginning teacher.
13. What do see as this teacher's strengths and challenges in teaching now as compared to the beginning of the year? (Be sure to probe on beginning of year and now; strengths and challenges.)
14. Using a scale of 1 to 4, with 1 = not at all effective, 2 = somewhat effective, 3 = effective, 4 = very effective, or 5 = Do not know, indicate the teacher's level of effectiveness in the following areas of teaching (at the beginning of the schoolyear and now close to the end of the schoolyear) AND briefly explain why you gave these ratings.

	Start of Year	End of Year	Why
a. The ability to engage all students in learning			
b. Making your classroom an effective learning environment			
c. Understanding and organizing subject matter for literacy instruction			
d. Planning instruction for all students			
e. Assessing student learning			
f. Establishing professional goals and pursuing professional development			
g. Working with colleagues, administrators, and parents			
h. Teaching in culturally relevant or responsive ways			
i. Teaching for social justice			

Supporting New Teachers of Color

15. What are the three most important things that educational leaders need to know, believe, and be able to do to support the needs of new teachers of color? What approaches do you use? Please describe your experiences.
16. Many argue that more should be done to recruit people of color into the profession of teaching. Do you think this is important? If so, why is that important?
17. Given your experience, what advice/insight would you give a person of color interested in a teaching career?
18. What do you see as the most significant issues or challenges facing teachers of color in terms of sustaining and developing them as teachers?
19. What will it take to support more teachers of color to stay in the profession?
20. What, if anything, are this new teacher's school and you doing to focus on recruiting and supporting teachers of color? (Be sure to probe on both school and you.)

Observations

To document classroom practice, we observed, took fieldnotes during, and digitally video-recorded eighteen 1- to 2-hour lessons in the first 3 years of each teacher's teaching. Each focal teacher had two focal classrooms that we observed 3 times in the fall and spring of the 2nd through 4th years of the study. For one of each teacher's focal classrooms, we observed 2 consecutive lessons in a week. For example, for one teacher we would visit her humanities period 2 class on Monday and Tuesday, and her ELL period 3 class on Monday. This allowed for capturing different groups of students and subject domains, while also capturing development of a curriculum unit beyond one lesson. We also revisited these same classes in the fall and spring. The researcher set up the digital video-recorder in the back of the room to get a view of the entire classroom, placed a lapel microphone on the teacher, and also had a boom microphone to pick up student responses. At times the boom microphone was moved to capture specific student group work. While the video-recorder was aimed to follow the teacher, there were times when the researcher panned the room or focused on student groups, and walls of the room were recorded.

Simultaneously, the researcher also compiled fieldnotes, using an open-ended protocol. The header of the protocol included: date, class, time, classroom physical description (layout, what's on walls, seating arrangements); lesson plan topic, activities, and resources; comments on student issues, teacher issues, other. The body of the protocol included pages to take notes on the lesson, including time (recorded at minimum of every 10 minutes), activity, teacher actions and words, and student actions and words. The protocol included an overall summary to be completed after the lesson. While the initial researcher summary noted the level of student engagement and included comments about cultural responsiveness in the lesson (pertaining to students or teacher), the overall summary developed over time as the themes of community of learners, cultural responsiveness, social justice, and student engagement emerged from the participants' descriptions of their practice. Thus, the full protocol came to address researcher summary remarks on the following:

1. Student engagement: Indicate evidence about the perceived level of student participation and involvement—mentally or physically—focusing on student voices contributing, hands raised, class disruption, engagement in the activity at hand, and percentage of students actively engaged as well as students disengaged. Also please describe any fluctuation and additional comments. At the end of your comments, give an overall score of low, moderate, or high for student engagement, with commentary.

2. Community of learners: Indicate evidence of involving students in the collaborative construction of knowledge and making the classroom environment inclusive of all students. Collaboration might include group work, active learning, inquiry, knowledge construction, and caring atmosphere. Opportunities for student talk might include dialogue, equity of participation, sustained student talk. At the end, give an overall score of low, moderate, or high for community of learners, with commentary.

3. Cultural responsiveness: Indicate evidence of connecting content to cultures of and differentiating instruction for diverse learners (cultures references ethnic, racial, linguistic, class identifications). Connecting instructional content to students' and teacher's cultures could include prior knowledge, funds of knowledge, tapping community resources, culturally relevant materials, multicultural curriculum, bridging or extending knowledge. Differentiating and adjusting instruction for diverse learners might include varied instructional activities for diverse learners, adapting curriculum resources, addressing language needs, cultural learning styles. At the end, give an overall score of low, moderate, or high for cultural responsiveness, with commentary.

4. Social justice perspective: Indicate evidence of fostering a critical perspective on curriculum, critical thinking, a sociopolitical/equity analysis, and a focus on change agenda. Critical perspective might

include critical thinking or interrogating curriculum, from multiple perspectives. Equity/antidiscrimination and social change agenda might include addressing sociocultural and sociopolitical contexts of unequal power relations and promoting education for social change. At the end, give an overall score of low, moderate, or high for social justice, with commentary.

5. Other cultural references: Indicate evidence of any other cultural references, including challenges related to issues of culture, any student–student cultural references, explicit reference to culture.

6. Extra notes or comments on lesson observed: For each of the focal classrooms, we asked the teachers to fill out a classroom profile that identified the following: class name and subject, grade level, number of total students, gender breakdown, race/ethnicity breakdown, number and home language of English learners, special education students, gifted students, and any additional comments that the teacher would like researchers to know about the class. We also collected any documents and classroom artifacts related to the lesson, such as lesson plans, handouts, reading materials, and assignments.

Student Focus Groups

Groups of students from ten teachers participated in focus groups, leading to a total of 61 students in grades 7 to 11. The ten teachers comprised a mix of ethnic/racial identifications (Latino, African American, Chinese American, Filipino American, and biracial); genders (6 male, 4 female); and cultures, including teachers from a variety of immigration generations, language proficiencies, and class backgrounds. The students were selected to participate in focus groups so as to assure race, gender, and language diversity. Students identified the following racial/ethnic identifications: Latino = 19, Mexican American = 13, Black or African American = 8, mixed race = 9, other = 5, White = 3, Tongan = 1, Chinese American = 1, Japanese American = 1, and Vietnamese American = 1. There were 27 males and 34 female students in our sample. When asked what language they primarily spoke at home, students reported the following categories: English = 19, Spanish/English = 18, Spanish = 17, English/Vietnamese = 2, Portuguese/English = 1; Japanese = 1, Tongan/English = 1, Chinese/English = 1, and Sinhala = 1.

Sample questions asked in student focus groups included:

1. What's it like to be a student in that teacher's class?
2. Describe a lesson from that class that was particularly relevant to the students.

3. In what ways do you see yourself as similar to or different from the teacher?
4. What is unique, if anything, about having a teacher of color?

DATA ANALYSIS

Based on Miles and Huberman (1994), the data were analyzed on three levels. The first level involved preliminary coding. This process aided in the development of descriptive as well as interpretive statements that supported identifying findings. These codes served as an organizing device to cluster segments of data related to particular concepts. Some codes were predetermined based on our initial conceptual framework, but we also generated new codes based on the data. We summarized segments of data for each teacher, creating a descriptive case study that entailed the following. (1) Teacher background: family/home background; own early and college schooling experiences; community background; and preservice experiences and entry into the profession. (2) Organizational context: teacher subject and grade level for teaching position; school context including norms, structures, and practices; teacher fit with school values; professional culture and colleagues; supports and challenges for learning to teach; new teacher support; administrator and department chair leadership; working conditions; student population; community and parent population and relation with school; and district and state policy environment. As new themes emerged, we also summarized organizational context factors associated with human, social, and multicultural capital and power structures as well as the broader environment. (3) Teacher cultural/ professional beliefs and activities: why they became a teacher; beliefs about teaching and learning; beliefs about students; beliefs about subject matter; beliefs about role of culture, race/ethnicity, language, and class in teaching; beliefs about social justice; teaching strengths and challenges; teacher change/development; critical incidents; descriptions of and reflections on lessons observed; student–teacher relationships; student engagement; student–student relationships; teacher cultural identifications and relation to teaching; and student cultural identifications. Subcodes under this code emerged from the data as teachers identified the significance of role model, culturally/linguistically responsive teacher, and agent of change. (4) Teacher retention and career paths: initial projections about how long teachers plan to remain in classroom, school, and profession; short- and long-term professional goals; teacher leadership roles; and rationale for staying, moving, leaving, or shifting.

We also documented evidence of elements of culturally and linguistically responsive teaching in practice from videotaped classroom practice. Here we sought to capture as much evidence as possible of teaching practices aligned with culturally and linguistically responsive teaching by using a rubric that captured enactment of the dimensions and writing vignettes of observed lessons and supplementing these with information from interviews with the teachers.

In further examining culturally/linguistically responsive teaching practices, we selected a sample of 11 (Latina/o) teachers to do in-depth analysis. A team of researchers on our project, with input from outside researchers and practitioners, developed an observation instrument and rubric to capture culturally/linguistically responsive teaching practice. The dimensions were adapted from common conceptualizations in the research literature on culturally responsive pedagogy and teaching, which all highlight these dimensions (Ladson-Billings, 1994, 1995, 2001; Villegas & Lucas, 2004). The rubric was developed based on other research capturing teaching practice related to issues of cultural relevance, linguistic relevance, and social justice (Doherty, Hilberg, Epaloose, & Tharp, 2002; Foster, 1997; Ladson-Billings, 1994, 1995, 2001; Moll, Amanti, Neff, & Gonzalez, 1992; Quiocho & Rios, 2000; Sheets, 2005; Villegas & Lucas, 2004; Zeichner, 1996). We piloted the observation instrument and rubric on videotaped lessons as a team. A subgroup of researchers calibrated to reach 90% inter-rater reliability. We analyzed videotapes of the teachers' instructional practices, fieldnotes, and interview data. Two researchers came to agreement on assessing the dimensions of culturally responsive teaching practice based on the following data: (1) observations of videotapes of two target lessons and analysis of interviews in the fall and spring of the 2nd year of teaching; (2) fieldnotes from observations of four other lessons during the 2nd year of teaching (also videotaped); and (3) case study information, including interview data with descriptions of other lessons that highlight culturally responsive or socially just teaching and examples of how the teachers are practicing culturally responsive and socially just teaching in their classroom.

We clustered teachers by lower, moderate, and higher enactment of practice using a rubric identifying evidence in three dimensions. The first dimension was "community of learners," or involving students in the collaborative construction of knowledge and making the classroom environment inclusive of all students. The second dimension related to "cultural/linguistic relevance," or connecting content and instruction to diverse cultures/languages and differentiating instruction for diverse learners. The third dimension was "social justice perspective," or fostering a critical perspective on curriculum, critical thinking, a sociopolitical/equity analysis, and a focus on change agenda.

The second level of analysis involved generating teacher case vignettes and pattern codes, using the constant comparative method (Strauss & Corbin, 1990) in an iterative process to generate, revise, and regenerate categories and codes (Miles & Huberman, 1994). Pattern codes "identify an emergent theme, configuration, or explanation. . . . They are a sort of meta-code" (Miles & Huberman, 1994, p. 69). This level facilitates data reduction, surfacing common themes and laying the groundwork for cross-case analysis. For example, we came to identify a common pattern of the significance of the influence of school organizational factors on each teacher's enactment of cultural/professional roles. Another pattern code that emerged was the level of organizational support for culturally and linguistically responsive teaching. For example, some teachers experienced tensions in enacting culturally/linguistically responsive teaching in the face of school responses to accountability pressures.

In this level of analysis, we began by examining the commitment to, and nature and level of, role performance of each of the three cultural/professional roles of role model, culturally/linguistically responsive teacher, and agent of change and then identifying representative examples. We next analyzed the kinds of challenges to and supports for engaging in the cultural/professional roles. We then examined the influences of both teacher background and school level on enactment of the roles. Finally, we analyzed the impact on retention decisions.

The third level of analysis involved conducting a cross-case analysis. We developed matrices and other displays to further condense data and draw comparisons (Miles & Huberman, 1994). We compared teacher background, preparation, teacher beliefs and practice, and school context factors to understand the differences in enactment of the roles and retention. We adopted a "mixed strategy" approach to cross-case analysis, whereby we drew on teacher case studies and vignettes and used matrices and other displays to analyze them. These displays were combined to form a "meta-matrix" that we further condensed and compared. An example of a meta-matrix analyzed the teacher background and school-level sources of challenges to and support for culturally/linguistically responsive teaching using data from each teacher's case study and vignettes. In this way, "subtractive schooling" and "additive schooling" as school contexts associated with inhibiting or supporting teachers' cultural/professional roles emerged as contrasting patterns across cases.

Finally, throughout the data collection and analysis process, we collaborated with a research team that reflected diverse cultural and linguistic backgrounds. This team fostered dialogue about the complexities of how our own positions and backgrounds informed the research process and understanding of data. We also solicited feedback from mentors, other scholars of color, and scholars on teachers of color on emergent themes and on drafts of writing. They provided new perspectives and critique, which we wove back into research analysis. Most importantly, we sought to incorporate feedback from the participants in the study. As Miles and Huberman (1994) state, "One of the most logical sources of corroboration is the people you have talked with and watched" (p. 275). We sought feedback through member checks conducted in the form of feedback during summer retreats. We shared emerging themes with participants and solicited their response and critique, which we then wove back into the analysis. We finally shared draft writing on key elements of the work with particular focal teachers for their further feedback.

Notes

Chapter 1

1. All names and school names are pseudonyms to protect confidentiality of participants.

Chapter 2

1. At times throughout this manuscript, we reference culturally and linguistically responsive teaching as culturally/linguistically responsive teaching, and at times, we shorten this to culturally responsive teaching.

2. We wish to acknowledge the significant contributions of Dena Sexton and Casia Freitas for their invaluable work in developing a literature review on the socialization of new teachers of color.

3. We distinguish our use of multicultural capital from Bryson's (1996) conceptualizations. Bryson, extending the work of Bourdieu (1984), focuses on cultural tastes (e.g., music) and finds that the primary form of status distinction among the more advantaged class in modern societies is an openness to a wide variety of cultural forms and expressions of cultural tastes (e.g., high- and low-status musical activities). Bryson (1996) identifies how this new cultural currency may be a type of "multicultural capital."

Chapter 5

Portions of this chapter are adapted from Achinstein, B. & Ogawa, R. T. (2011). Change(d) agents: School contexts and the cultural/professional roles of new teachers of Mexican descent. *Teachers College Record, 113*(11).

References

Achinstein, B. (2006). New teacher and mentor political literacy: Reading, navigating and transforming induction contexts. *Teachers and Teaching: Theory and Practice, 12*(2), 123–138.

Achinstein, B., & Aguirre, J. A. (2008). Cultural match or cultural suspect: How new teachers of color negotiate socio-cultural challenges in the classroom. *Teachers College Record, 110*(8), 1505–1540.

Achinstein, B., & Ogawa, R. T. (2006). (In)fidelity: What new teacher resistance reveals about professional principles and prescriptive educational policies. *Harvard Educational Review, 27*(1), 30–63.

Achinstein, B., & Ogawa, R. T. (2011). Change(d) agents: School contexts and the cultural/professional roles of new teachers of Mexican descent. *Teachers College Record, 113*(11).

Achinstein, B., Ogawa, R. T., & Speiglman, A. (2004). Are we creating separate and unequal tracks of teachers? The impact of state policy, local conditions, and teacher background on new teacher socialization. *American Educational Research Journal, 41*(3), 557–603.

Achinstein, B., Ogawa, R. T., Sexton, D., & Freitas, C. (2010). Retaining teachers of color: A pressing problem and a potential strategy for "hard-to-staff schools." *Review of Educational Research, 80*(1), 71–107.

Adams, G. J., & Dial, M. (1993). Teacher survival: A Cox regression model. *Education and Urban Society, 29*(1), 90–99.

American Association of Colleges of Teacher Education (AACTE). (1999). *Teacher education pipeline IV: Schools and departments of education enrollments by race, ethnicity, and gender.* Washington, DC: Author.

Anyon, J. (1994). Social class and the hidden curriculum of work. In J. Kretovics & E. J. Nussel (Eds.), *Transforming urban education* (pp. 253–275). Boston: Allyn & Bacon.

Apple, M. W. (1990). *Ideology and curriculum* (2nd ed.). New York: Routledge.

Arce, J. (2004). Latino bilingual teachers: The struggle to sustain an emancipatory pedagogy in public schools, *International Journal of Qualitative Studies in Education, 17*(2), 227–246.

Au, K. H. (1980). Participation structures in a reading lesson with Hawaiian children: An analysis of a culturally appropriate instructional event. *Anthropology and Education Quarterly, 11*(2), 91–115.

Bacharach, S. B., & Conley, S. C. (1989). Uncertainty and decision making in teaching: Implications for managing line professionals. In T. J. Sergiovanni & J. H. Moore (Eds.), *Schooling for tomorrow: Directing reforms to issues that count* (pp. 311–329). Boston: Allyn & Bacon.

Banks, J. (1991). Teaching multicultural literacy to teachers. *Teaching Education, 4*(1), 135–144.

Banks, J. (1995). Multicultural education: Historical development, dimensions, and practice. In J. Banks & C. Banks (Eds.), *Handbook of research on multicultural education* (pp. 3–24). New York: Macmillan.

Banks, J. (2003). *Teaching strategies for ethnic studies* (7th ed.). Boston: Allyn & Bacon.

Banks, J., Cochran-Smith, M., Moll, L., Richert, A., Zeichner, K., LePage, P., Darling-Hammond, L., Duffy, H., & McDonald, M. (2005). Teaching diverse learners. In L. Darling-Hammond & J. Bransford (Eds.), *Preparing teachers for a changing world: What teachers should learn and be able to do* (pp. 232–274). San Francisco: Jossey-Bass.

Bascia, N. (1996). Inside and outside: Minority immigrant teachers in Canadian schools. *International Journal of Qualitative Studies in Education, 9*(2), 151–165.

Basit, T. N., & McNamara, O. (2004). Equal opportunities or affirmative action? The induction of minority ethnic teachers. *Journal of Education for Teaching, 30*(2), 97–115.

Bateson, G. (1972). *Steps to an ecology of mind: Collected essays in anthropology, psychiatry, evolution, and epistemology.* Chicago: University of Chicago Press.

Beauboeuf-Lafontant, T. (1999). A movement against and beyond boundaries: Politically relevant teaching among African American teachers. *Teachers College Record, 100*(4), 702–724.

Belcher, R. N. (2001 March). *Predictive factors for the enrollment of African American students in special education preservice programs.* Paper presented at the annual meeting of American Council on Rural Special Education, San Diego.

Bennett, C., Cole, D., & Thompson, J. (2000). Preparing teachers of color at a predominantly White university: A case study of project TEAM. *Teaching and Teacher Education, 16,* 445–464.

Berger, J. (2000). Does top-down, standards-based reform work? A review of the status of statewide standards-based reform. *NASSP Bulletin, 84,* 57–65.

Berger, P. L., & Luckmann, T. (1966). *The social construction of reality: A treatise in the sociology of knowledge.* Garden City, NY: Anchor Books.

Blasi, M. W. (2001). *Returning to the reservation: Experience of a first year Native American teacher.* Unpublished manuscript.

Borman, G. D., & Dowling, N. M. (2008). Teacher attrition and retention: A meta-analytic and narrative review of the research. *Review of Educational Research, 78*(3), 367–409.

Bourdieu, P. (1977). Cultural reproduction and social reproduction. In J. Karabel & A. H. Halsey (Eds.), *Power and ideology in education* (pp. 137–153). New York: Oxford University Press.

Bourdieu, P. (1984). *Distinction: A social critique of the stratification of taste.* Cambridge, MA: Harvard University Press.

Boyle-Baise, M. (2005). Preparing community-oriented teachers: Reflections from a multicultural service-learning project. *Journal of Teacher Education, 56*(5), 446–458.

Bryson, B. (1996). "Anything but heavy metal": Symbolic exclusion and musical dislikes. *American Sociological Review, 61*(5), 884–899.

Bushnell, M. (2003). Teachers in the schoolhouse panopticon: Complicity and resistance. *Education and Urban Society, 35*(3), 251–272.

Cabello, B., Eckmier, J., & Baghieri, H. (1995). The comprehensive teacher institution: Successes and pitfalls of an innovative teacher preparation program. *Teacher Educator, 31,* 43–55.

California Department of Education (CDE). (2010a). *State of California education profile fiscal year 2009–2010 students by ethnicity.* Retrieved March 12, 2011, from http://www.ed-data.k12.ca.us/profile.asp?reportNumber=16&tab=1

California Department of Education (CDE). (2010b). S*tate of California education profile fiscal year 2009–2010 teachers by ethnicity.* Retrieved March 12, 2011, from http://www.ed-data.k12.ca.us/profile.asp?tab=2&level=04&reportNumber=16

Carnegie Forum on Education, the Economy, Task Force on Teaching as a Profession. (1986). *A nation prepared: Teachers for the 21st century.* Washington, DC: Carnegie Forum.

Carr, P. R., & Klassen, T. R. (1997a). Institutional barriers to the implementation of anti-racist education: A case study of the secondary system in a large, urban school board. *Journal of Educational Administration and Foundations, 19*(1), 46–68.

Carr, P. R., & Klassen, T. R. (1997b). Different perceptions of race in education: Racial minority and White teachers. *Canadian Journal of Education, 22(1),* 67–81.

Carter, P. (2005). *Keepin' it real: School success beyond Black and White.* New York: Oxford University Press.

Case, K. I. (1997). African American othermothering in the urban elementary school. *The Urban Review, 29*(1), 25–39.

Chavers, D. (1998). *Indian teachers and Indian control.* Report from the Native American Scholarship Fund. Albuquerque, NM: Native American Scholarship Fund.

Chubbuck, S. M., Clift, R. T., Allard, J., & Quinlan, J. (2001). Playing it safe as a novice teacher: Implications for programs for new teachers. *Journal of Teacher Education, 52*(5), 365–376.

Clark, E. R., & Flores, B. B. (2001). Who am I? The social construction of ethnic identity and self-perceptions in Latino preservice teachers. *The Urban Review, 33*(2), 69–86.

Clewell, B. C., Puma, M. J, & McKay, S. A. (2005, April). *Does it matter if my teacher looks like me? The impact of teacher race and ethnicity on student academic achievement.* Paper presented at the annual meeting of the American Educational Research Association, Montreal.

Clewell, B. C., & Villegas, A. M. (1998). Diversifying schools. *Education and Urban Society, 31*(1), 3–17.

Clewell, B. C., & Villegas, A. M. (2001). *Ahead of the class: A handbook of preparing new teachers.* Washington, DC: Urban Institute.

Cochran-Smith, M. (1991). Learning to teach against the grain. *Harvard Educational Review, 61*(3), 279–310.

Cochran-Smith, M. (1997). Knowledge, skills, and experiences for teaching culturally diverse learners: A perspective for practicing teachers. In J. Irvine (Ed.), *Critical knowledge for diverse learners and teachers* (pp. 27–88). Washington, DC: American Association of Colleges for Teacher Education.

Cochran-Smith, M. (2004a). *Walking the road: Race, diversity, and social justice in teacher education.* New York: Teachers College Press.

Cochran-Smith, M. (2004b). Stayers, leavers, lovers and dreamers: Insights about teacher retention. *Journal of Teacher Education, 55*(5), 387–392.

Coleman, J. S. (1988). Social capital in the creation of human capital. *American Journal of Sociology, 94,* 95–120.

Connor, R. (2008, April). *Factors that impact satisfaction and retention of teachers of color: A national profile.* Paper presented at that annual meeting of the American Educational Research Association, New York.

Cox, B. (1993). *Resolving a crisis in education: Latino teachers for tomorrow's classrooms.* Claremont, CA: Tomás Rivera Center.

Crosco, M. S., & Costigan, A. (2007). The narrowing of curriculum and pedagogy in the age of accountability: Urban educators speak out. *Urban Education, 42*(6), 512–535.

Cummins, J. (1984). *Bilingualism and special education: Issues in assessment and pedagogy.* Clevedon, Canada: Multilingual Matters

Darling-Hammond, L. (2000). *Studies of excellence in teacher education: Preparation at the graduate level.* Washington, DC: National Committee on Teaching and America's Future, American Association for Colleges of Teacher Education.

Darling-Hammond, L. (2004). Standards, accountability, and school reform. *Teachers College Record, 106*(6), 1047–1085.

Darling-Hammond, L., Dilworth, M. E., & Bullmaster, M. (1996). *Educators of color* [A background paper for the invitational conference "Recruiting, Preparing and Retaining Persons of Color in the Teaching Profession"]. National Alliance of Black School Educators, Inc., Washington, DC; Phi Delta Kappa Educational Foundation, Bloomington, IN; Recruiting New Teachers, Inc., Belmont MA; Office of Educational Research and Improvement, Washington, DC.

Darling-Hammond, L., French, J., & Garcia-Lopez, S. P. (Eds.). (2002). *Learning to teach for social justice.* New York: Teachers College Press.

Dee, T. (2004). Teachers, race, and student achievement in a randomized experiment. *The Review of Economics and Statistics, 86*(1), 195–210.

Delpit, L. (1995). *Other people's children: Cultural conflict in the classroom.* New York: The New Press.

Diamond, J. B., & Spillane, J. P. (2004). High stakes accountability in urban elementary schools: Challenging or reproducing inequality? *Teachers College Record, 106*(6), 1140–1171.

Dilworth, M. (1992). *Diversity in teacher education.* San Francisco, CA: Jossey-Bass.

Dixson, A. D. (2003). "Let's do this!" Black women teachers' politics and pedagogy. *Urban Education, 38*(2), 217-235.

Dixson, A. D., & Dingus, A. D. (2008). In search of our mothers' gardens: Black women teachers and professional socialization. *Teachers College Record, 110*(40), 805–837.

Doherty, K. M. (2001). Poll: Teachers support standards—with hesitation. *Education Week, 20*(17), 20.

Doherty, R. W., Hilberg, R. S., Epaloose, G., & Tharp, R. G. (2002). Standards performance continuum: Development and validation of a measure of effective pedagogy. *Journal of Educational Research, 96*(2), 78–89.

Driscoll, M. E., & Kerchner, C. T. (1999). The implications of social capital for schools, communities and cities. In J. Murphy & K. S. Louis (Eds.), *Handbook of research on educational administration* (2nd ed, pp. 385–404). San Francisco: Jossey-Bass.

Dworkin, A. (1980). The changing demography of public school teachers: Some implications for faculty turnover in urban areas. *Sociology of Education, 53*(2), 65–73.

Education Commission of the States. (2003). *Recruiting teachers of color: A 50-state survey of state policies.* Denver, CO: Author.

Ehrenberg, R. G., & Brewer, D. J. (1995). Did teacher's verbal ability and race matter in the 1960s? Coleman revisited. *Economics of Education Review, 14*(1), 1–21.

Ehrenberg, R. G., Goldhaber, D. D., & Brewer, D. J. (1995). Do teachers' race, gender, and ethnicity matter? Evidence from the National Educational Longitudinal Study of 1988. *Industrial and Labor Relations Review, 48*(3), 547–561.

England, R. E., & Meier, K. J. (1986). From desegregation to integration: Second generation school discrimination as an institutional impediment. *American Politics Quarterly,* *13*(2), 227–247.

Epstein, K. K. (2005). The Whitening of the American teaching force: A problem of recruitment or a problem of racism? *Social Justice, 32*(3), 89–102.

Evans, M. (1992). An estimate of race and gender role-model effects in teaching high school. *Journal of Economic Education, 23*(3), 209–217.

Farkas, G., Grobe, R. P. L., Sheehan, D., & Shuan, Y. (1990). Cultural resources and school success: Gender, ethnicity, and poverty groups within an urban school district. *American Sociological Review, 55,* 127–142.

Ferguson, R. F. (2003). Teachers' perceptions and expectations and the Black-White test score gap. *Urban Education, 38*(4), 460–507.

Feuerverger, G. (1997). "On the edges of the map": A study of heritage language teachers in Toronto. *Teaching and Teacher Education, 13,* 39–53.

Finley, M. (1984). Teachers and tracking in a comprehensive high school. *Sociology of Education, 57*(4), 233–243.

Flyvbjerg, B. (2001). *Making social science matter: Why social inquiry fails and how it can succeed again.* Cambridge, England: Cambridge University Press.

Foster, M. (1990). The politics of race: Through the eyes of African-American teachers. *Journal of Education, 172,* 123–143.

Foster, M. (1991). "Just got to find a way": Case studies of the lives and practice of exemplary Black high school teachers. In M. Foster (Ed.), *Readings on equal education: Vol. 11. Qualitative investigations into schools and schooling* (pp. 273–309). New York: AMS Press.

Foster, M. (1993a). Urban African American teachers' views of organizational change: Speculations on the experiences of exemplary teachers. *Equity & Excellence in Education, 26*(3), 16–24.

Foster, M. (1993b). Educating for competence: Exploring the views of exemplary African-American teachers. *Urban Education, 27*(4), 370–394.

Foster, M. (1993c). Recruiting teachers of color: Problems, programs, and possibilities. In J. James (Ed.), *Recruiting people of color for teacher education* (pp. 5–42). Bloomington, IN: Phi Delta Kappa.

Foster, M. (1994). Effective Black teachers: A literature review. In E. R. Hollins, J. E. King, & W. C. Hayman (Eds.), *Teaching diverse populations: Formulating a knowledge base* (pp. 225–241). Albany: State University of New York Press.

Foster, M. (1997). *Black teachers on teaching.* New York: New Press.

Fraga, L. R., Meier, K. J., & England, R. E. (1986). Hispanic Americans and educational policy: Limits to equal access. *The Journal of Politics, 48*(4), 850–876.

Friere, P. (1983). *Pedagogy of the oppressed* (M. B. Ramos, Trans.). New York: Continuum.

Galindo, R. (1996). Reframing the past in the present: Chicana teacher role identity as a bridging identity. *Education and Urban Society, 29*(1), 85–102.

Galindo, R., Aragon, M., & Underhill, R. (1996). The competence to act: Chicana teacher role identity in life and career narratives. *The Urban Review, 28*(4), 279–308.

Galindo, R., & Olguin, M. (1996). Reclaiming bilingual educators' cultural resources: An autobiographical approach. *Urban Education, 31*(1), 29–56.

Gándara, P., & Maxwell-Jolley, J. (2000). *Preparing teachers for diversity: A dilemma of quality and quantity.* Santa Cruz, CA: The Center for the Future of Teaching & Learning.

Garcia, E. (2004). Educating Mexican American students: Past treatment and recent developments in theory, research, policy, and practice. In J. A. Banks & C. A. M. Banks (Eds.), *Handbook of research on multicultural education* (2nd ed., pp. 491–514). San Francisco: Jossey-Bass.

Garcia-Nevarez, A. G., Stafford, M. E., & Arias, B. (2005). Arizona elementary teachers' attitudes toward English Language Learners and the use of Spanish in classroom instruction. *Bilingual Research Journal, 29*(2), 295–318.

Gay, G. (2000). *Culturally responsive teaching: Theory, research, and practice.* New York: Teachers College Press.

Gibson, M. A. (1993). The school performance of immigrant minorities: A comparative view. In E. Jacob & C. Jordan (Eds.), *Minority education: Anthropological perspectives* (pp. 56–87). Norwood, NJ: Ablex.

Giroux, H. A. (1983). *Theory and resistance in education: A pedagogy for the opposition.* South Hadley, MA: Bergin & Garvey.

Giroux, H. A. (1988). *Teachers as intellectuals: Toward a critical pedagogy of learning.* New York: Bergin & Garvey.

Giroux, H. A., & Purpel, P. (1983). *The hidden curriculum and moral education.* Berkeley, CA: McCutchan.

Gordon, B. (1992). The marginalized discourse of minority intellectual thought in traditional writings on teaching. In C. Grant (Ed.), *Research and multicultural education* (pp. 19–31). Washington, DC: Falmer.

Gordon, B. (1993). African-American cultural knowledge and liberatory education: Dilemmas, problems, and potentials in a postmodern American society. *Urban Education, 27,* 448–470.

Grossman, P., & McDonald, M. (2008). Back to the future: Directions for research in teaching and teacher education. *American Educational Research Journal, 45*(1), 184–205.

Guitiérrez, K. D., Asato, J., Santos, M., & Gotanda, N. (2002). Backlash pedagogy: Language and culture and the politics of reform. *The Review of Education, Pedagogy, and Cultural Studies, 24*(4), 335–351.

Guitiérrez, K. D., & Rogoff, B. (2003). Cultural ways of learning: Individual traits or repertoires of practice. *Educational Researcher, 32*(5), 19–25.

Hammerness, K. (2006). From coherence in theory to coherence in practice. *Teachers College Record, 108*(7), 1241–1265.

Hanushek, E. A. (1992). The trade-off between child quantity and quality. *Journal of Political Economy, 100*(1), 84–117.

Hanushek, E. A., Kain, J. F., O'Brien, D. M., & Rivkin, S. G. (2005). *The market for teacher quality* (Working Paper No. 11154). Cambridge, MA: National Bureau of Economic Research.

Hanushek, E. A., Kain, J. F., & Rivkin, S. G. (2004). Why public schools lose teachers. *The Journal of Human Resources, 39*(2), 326–354.

Harris & Associates. (1998). *The Metropolitan Life survey. The American Teacher 1988: Strengthening the relationship between teachers and students.* New York: Metropolitan Life Insurance Co. (ERIC Document reproduction service # ED30537)

Hartley, J. (1994). Case studies in organizational research. In C. Casell & G. Symon (Eds.), *Qualitative methods in organizational research: A practical guide* (pp. 208–229). London: Sage.

Haycock, K. (2001). Closing the achievement gap. *Educational Leadership, 58*(6), 6–11.

Haycock, K. (2006). No more invisible kids. *Educational Leadership, 64*(3), 38–42.

Heath, S. (1983). *Ways with words: Language, life, and work in communities and classrooms.* London: Cambridge.

Henke, R. R., Chen, X., & Geis, S. (2000). *Progress through the teacher pipeline: 1992–93 college graduates and elementary/secondary school teaching as of 1997.* Washington, DC: National Center for Educational Statistics, U.S. Department of Education.

Henke, R. R., Choy, S. P., Geis, S., & Broughman, S. P. (1997). *School and staffing in the U.S.: A statistical profile, 1993–94.* Washington, DC: National Center for Education Statistics, U.S. Department of Education.

Hess, F. M. (2010). *Education unbound: The promise and practice of greenfield schooling.* Alexandria, VA: Association for Supervision and Curriculum Development.

Hess, F. M., & Leal, D. L. (1997). Minority teachers, minority students, and college matriculation. *Policy Studies Journal, 25,* 235–248.

Horng, E. L. (2005, April). *Teacher tradeoffs: Poor working conditions make urban schools hard-to-staff.* Paper presented at the annual meeting of the American Educational Research Association, Montreal, Canada.

Hull, D. & Noguchi, S. (July 17, 2008). New California data show rate worse for Latinos, Blacks. *San Jose Mercury News.*

Ingersoll, R. M. (2003). *Who controls teachers' work: Power and accountability in America's schools.* Cambridge, MA: Harvard University Press.

Ingersoll, R. M., & Connor, R. (2009, April). *What the national data tell us about minority and Black teacher turnover.* Paper presented at the annual meeting of the American Educational Research Association, San Diego.

Ingersoll, R. & May, H. (2010). *Recruitment, retention, and the minority teacher shortage.* Philadephia, Pennsylvania: Consortium for Policy Research in Education, University of Pennsylvania and the Center for Research in the Interest of Underserved Students, University of California, Santa Cruz.

Irizarry, J. (2007). "Home-growing" teachers of color: Lessons learned from a town-gown partnership. *Teacher Education Quarterly, 34*(4), 87–102.

Irvine, J. J. (1988). An analysis of the problem of the disappearing Black educator. *Elementary School Journal, 88*(5), 503–514.

Irvine, J. J. (1989). Beyond role models: An examination of cultural influences on the pedagogical perspectives of Black teachers. *Peabody Journal of Education, 66*(4), 51–63.

Irvine, J. J. (1990). *Black students and school failure.* Westport, CT: Praeger.

Irvine, J. J. (2002). *In search of wholeness: African American teachers and their culturally specific classroom practices.* New York: Palgrave.

Irvine, J. J. (2003). *Educating teachers for a diverse society: Seeing with the cultural eye.* New York: Teachers College Press.

Jacullo-Noto, J. (1994, April). *Minority teachers in the induction phase: Further lessons for teacher educators.* Paper presented at the annual meeting of the American Educational Research Association, New Orleans.

Johnson, L. (2008, April). *What it takes to be a role model: Perspectives from new teachers of color and their students.* Paper presented at the annual meeting of the American Educational Research Association, New York.

Johnson, S. M., Berg, J. H., & Donaldson, M. L. (2005). *Who stays in teaching and why: A review of the literature in teacher retention.* Cambridge, MA: The Project on the Next Generation of Teachers, Harvard Graduate School of Education.

Jones, E. B., Young, R., & Rodriguez, J. L. (1999). Identity and career choice among Mexican American and Euro-American preservice bilingual teachers. *Hispanic Journal of Behavioral Sciences, 21*(4), 431–446.

Kauchak, D., & Burback, M. D. (2003). Voices in the classroom: Case studies of minority teacher candidates. *Action in Teacher Education, 25*(1), 63–75.

Kelchtermans, G., & Ballet, K. (2002). The micropolitics of teacher induction. A narrative-biographical study on teacher socialisation. *Teaching and Teacher Education, 18*(1), 105–120.

Kennedy, M. (1999). The role of preservice teacher education. In L. Darling-Hammond & G. Sykes (Eds.), *Teaching as the learning profession: Handbook of policy and practice* (pp. 54–85). San Francisco: Jossey-Bass.

King, J. E. (1991). Unfinished business: Black student alienation and Black teachers' emancipatory pedagogy. In M. Foster (Ed.), *Readings on equal education: Vol. 11. Qualitative investigations into schools and schooling* (pp. 245–271). New York: AMS Press.

King, S. H. (1993). Why did we choose teaching careers and what will enable us to stay? Insights from one cohort of the African American teaching pool. *The Journal of Negro Education, 62*(4), 475–492.

Kirby, S. N., Berends, M., & Naftel, S. (1999). Supply and demand of minority teachers in Texas: Problems and prospects. *Educational Evaluation and Policy Analysis, 21*(1), 47–66.

Klopfenstein, K. (2005). Beyond test scores: The impact of Black teacher role models on rigorous math taking. *Contemporary Economic Policy, 23*(3), 416–428.

Knight, M. G. (2002). The intersections of race, class, and gender in the teacher preparation of an African American social justice educator. *Equity & Excellence in Education, 35*(3), 212–224.

Koerner, M., & Hulsebosch, P. (1995 February). *Teaching to give students voice in the college classroom.* Paper presented at the annual meeting of the Association of Teacher Educators, Detroit.

Kottkamp, R. B., Cohn, M. M., McCloskey, G. N., & Provenzo, E. F. (1987). Teacher ethnicity: Relationships with teaching rewards and incentives. Washington, DC: Office of Educational Research and Improvement.

Lacey, C. (1977). *The socialization of teachers.* London: Methuen.

Ladson-Billings, G. (1994). *The dreamkeepers: Successful teachers of African American children.* San Francisco: Jossey-Bass.

Ladson-Billings, G. (1995). Toward a theory of culturally relevant pedagogy. *American Educational Research Journal, 32*(3), 465–491.

Ladson-Billing, G. (2001). *Crossing over to Canaan: The journey of new teachers in diverse classrooms.* San Francisco: Jossey-Bass.

Ladson-Billings, G., & Tate, W. F. (1995). Toward a critical race theory of education. *Teachers College Record, 97*(1), 47–68.

Lankford, H., Loeb, S., & Wyckoff, J. (2002). Teacher sorting and the plight of urban schools: A descriptive analysis. *Educational Evaluation and Policy Analysis, 24*(1), 37-62.

Lawson, H. (1992). Beyond the new conception of teacher induction. *Journal of Teacher Education, 43*(3), 163–172.

Lewis, C. W. (2006). African American male teachers in public schools: An examination of three urban school districts. *Teachers College Record, 108*(2), 224–245.

Lipka, J. (1991). Toward a culturally based pedagogy: A case study of one Yup'ik Eskimo teacher. *Anthropology and Education Quarterly, 22*, 203–223.

Lipka, J. (1994, Spring). Schools failing minority teachers: Problems and suggestions. *Educational Foundations*, 8(2) 57–80.

Loeb, S., Darling-Hammond, L., & Luczak, J. (2005). How teacher conditions predict teacher turnover in California schools. *Peabody Journal of Education, 80*(3), 44–70.

Lynn, M. (2006). Education for the community: Exploring the culturally relevant practices of Black male teachers. *Teachers College Record, 108*(12), 2497–2522.

Lynn, M., Johnson, C., & Hassan, K. (1999). Raising the critical consciousness of African American students in Baldwin Hills: A portrait of an exemplary African American male teacher. *The Journal of Negro Education, 68*(1), 42–53.

Marsh, J. A. (2002). How districts relate to states, schools, and communities: A review of emerging literature. In A. M. Hightower, M. S. Knapp, J. A. Marsh, & M. W. McLaughlin (Eds.), *School districts and instructional renewal* (pp. 25–40). New York: Teachers College Press.

Marvel, J., Lyter, D. M., Peltola, P., Strizek, G. A., & Morton, B. A. (2007). *Teacher attrition and mobility: Results from the teacher follow-up survey, 2004–05, first look.* Washington, DC: National Center for Educational Statistics.

McCray, A. D., Sindelar, P. T., Kilgore, K. K., & Neal, L. I. (2002). African-American women's decisions to become teachers: Sociocultural perspectives. *International Journal of Qualitative Studies in Education, 15*(3), 269–290.

McDonald, J. (1992). *Teaching: Making sense of an uncertain craft.* New York: Teachers College Press.

McEneaney, E. H., & Meyer, J. W. (2000). The content of the curriculum: An institutionalist perspective. In M. T. Hallinan (Ed.), *Handbook of the sociology of education* (pp. 189–211). New York: Kluwer Academic/Plenum.

McIntyre, L. D., & Pernell, E. (1983). The impact of race on teacher recommendation for special education placement. *Journal of Multicultural Counseling and Development, 13*(3), 112–120.

McLaughlin, D. (1993). Personal narratives for school change in Navajo settings. In D. McLaughlin & W. Tierney (Eds.), *Naming silenced lives* (pp. 95–117). New York: Routledge.

McLaughlin, M. W. & Talbert, J. E. (1993). *Context that matter for teaching and learning: Strategic opportunities for meeting the nation's educational goals.* Stanford, CA: Center for Research on the Context of Secondary School Teaching: Stanford University.

McLaughlin, M. W., & Talbert, J. E. (2001). *Professional communities and the work of high school teaching.* Chicago: University of Chicago Press.

McNeil, L. M. (2000). *Contradictions of school reform: Educational costs of standardized testing.* New York: Routledge.

Meier, D. (1995). *The power of their ideas: Lessons for America from a small school in Harlem.* Boston: Beacon.

Meier, K. J., Stewart, J., & England, R. E. (1989). *Race, class, and education: The politics of second generation discrimination.* Madison: University of Wisconsin Press.

Mercer, W. A., & Mercer, M. M. (1986). Standardized testing: Its impact on Blacks in Florida's education system. *Urban Educator, 8*(1), 105–113.

Merriam, S. B. (1988). *Case study research in education: A qualitative approach.* San Francisco: Jossey-Bass.

Metz, M. H. (1990). How social class differences shape teachers' work. In M. McLaughlin, J. Talbert, & N. Bascia (Eds.), *The contexts of teaching in secondary schools: Teachers' realities* (pp. 40–107). New York: Teachers College Press.

Michie, G. (2005). *See you when we get there: Teaching for change in urban schools.* New York: Teachers College Press.

Miles, M. B., & Huberman, A. M. (1994). *Qualitative data analysis: An expanded sourcebook* (2nd ed.). Thousand Oaks, CA: Sage.

Milner, H. R. & Hoy, A.W. (2003). A case study of an African American teacher's self-efficacy, stereotype threat, and persistence. *Teaching and Teacher Education, 19,* 263–276.

Mintrop, H. (2004). *Schools on probation: How accountability works (and doesn't work).* New York: Teachers College Press.

Moll, L., Amanti, C., Neff, D., & Gonzalez, N. (1992). Funds of knowledge for teaching: Using a qualitative approach to connect homes and classrooms. *Theory into Practice, 31*(2), 132–141.

Monsivais, G. I. (1990, Fall). *Policy issue: The attrition of Latino teachers.* Claremont, CA: Tomas Rivera Center.

Montecinos, C. (1994). Teachers of color and multiculturalism. *Equity & Excellence in Education, 27*(3), 34–42.

Montecinos, C. (2004). Paradoxes in multicultural teacher education research: Students of color positioned as objects while ignored as subjects. *International Journal of Qualitative Studies in Education, 17*(2), 167–181

Murnane, R. J., Singer, J. D., Willett, J. B., Kemple, J. J., & Olsen, R. J. (1991). *Who will teach? Policies that matter.* Cambridge, MA: Harvard University Press.

Murrell, P. C. (1991). Cultural politics in teacher education: What is missing in the preparation of minority teachers? In M. Foster (Ed.), *Readings on equal education: Vol. 11. Qualitative investigations into schools a nd schooling* (pp. 205–225). New York: AMS Press.

National Center for Education Statistics (NCES). (2010). The condition of education 2010. Retrieved March 12, 2011, from http://nces.ed.gov/pubs2010/2010028.pdf

National Collaborative on Diversity in the Teaching Force (NCDTF). (2004). *Assessment of diversity in America's teaching force: A call to action.* Washington, DC: National Educational Association.

Nieto, S. (1999). *The light in their eyes: Creating multicultural learning communities.* New York: Teachers College Press.

Nieto, S. (2000). *Affirming diversity: The sociopolitical context of multicultural education* (3rd ed.). New York: Longman.

Nieto, S. (2002). *Language, culture and teaching: Critical perspectives for a new century.* Mahwah, NJ: Erlbaum.

Oakes, J. (1989). What educational indicators? The case for assessing the school context. *Educational Evaluation and Policy Analysis, 11(2),* 181–199.

Oakes, J. (1996). Making the rhetoric real: UCLA's struggle for teacher education that is multicultural and social reconstructionist. *Multicultural Education, 4*(2), 4–10.

Oakes, J., Franke, M. L., Quartz, K. H., & Rogers, J. (2002). Research for high quality urban teaching: Defining it, developing it, assessing it. *Journal of Teacher Education, 53*(3), 228–234.

Oakes, J., & Rogers, J. (2006). *Learning power: Organizing for education and justice.* New York: Teachers College Press.

Ochoa, G. (2007). *Learning from Latino teachers.* San Francisco: Jossey-Bass.

Pew Hispanic Center (2010). *Demographic profile of Hispanics in California, 2008.* Retrieved December 14, 2010, from http://pewhispanic.org.states/?stateid=CA.

Quartz, K., & TEP Research Group. (2003). Too angry to leave: Supporting new teachers' commitment to transform urban schools. *Journal of Teacher Education, 54*(2), 99–111.

Quiocho, A., & Rios, F. (2000). The power of their presence: Minority group teachers and schooling. *Review of Educational Research, 70*(4), 485–528.

Ravitch, D. (2010). *The death and life of the great American school system: How testing and choice are undermining education.* New York: Basic Books.

Richards, C. E. (1982). *Employment reform or pupil control? Desegregation, bilingualism and Hispanic employment in the California public schools.* Stanford: California Institute for Research on Educational Finance and Governance, Stanford University.

Richards, C. E. (1986). Race and demographic trends: The employment of minority teachers in California public schools. *Economics of Education Review, 5*(1), 57–64.

Rios, F., & Montecinos, C. (1999). Advocating social justice and cultural affirmation: Ethnically diverse preservice teachers' perspectives on multicultural education. *Equity & Excellence in Education, 32*(3), 66–76.

Rowan, B. (1982). Organizational structure and the institutional environment: The case of public schools. *Administrative Science Quarterly, 27,* 259–279.

Scafidi, B., Sjoquist, D. L., & Stinebrickner, T. R. (2007). Race, poverty, and teacher mobility. *Economics of Education Review, 26,* 145–159

Sheets, R. H. (2002). Ethnic identity development through social studies instruction. *Multicultural Education, 9*(3), 45–46.

Sheets, R. H. (2004). Preparation and development of teachers of color. *International Journal of Qualitative Studies in Education, 17*(2), 163–166.

Sheets, R. H. (2005). *Diversity pedagogy: Examining the role of culture in the teaching-learning process.* Boston: Allyn & Bacon.

Sheets, R. H., & Chew, L. (2002) Absent from the research, present in our classrooms. *Journal of Teacher Education, 53*(2), 127–141.

Shen, J. (1998). Alternative certification, minority teachers, and urban education. *Education and Urban Society, 31*(1), 30–41.

Sleeter, C. (2001). Preparing teachers for culturally diverse schools: Research and the overwhelming presence of Whiteness. *Journal of Teacher Education, 52*(2), 94–106.

Sleeter, C., & Grant, C. A. (1999). *Making choices for multicultural education: Five approaches to race, class, and gender* (3rd ed.). Upper Saddle River, NJ: Prentice-Hall.

Sleeter, C., & Thao, Y. (2007). Guest editors' introduction: Diversifying the teaching force. *Teacher Education Quarterly, 34*(4), 3–8

Solomon, R. P. (1997). Race, role modeling, and representation in teacher education and teaching. *Canadian Journal of Education, 22*(4), 395–410.

Spillane, J. P., & Thompson, C. L. (1997). Reconstructing conceptions of local capacity: The local education agency's capacity for ambitious instructional reform. *Educational Evaluation and Policy Analysis, 19*(2), 185–293.

Spring, J. (2007). *Deculturalization and the struggle for equality* (5th ed.). Boston: McGraw-Hill.

Stanton-Salazar, R. D. (in press). A social capital framework for the study of institutional agents and their role in the empowerment of low-status students and youth. *Youth and Society.*

Steele, C. M. (1997). A threat in the air: How stereotypes shape intellectual identity and performance. *American Psychologist, 52,* 613–629.

Strauss, A., & Corbin, J. (1990). *Basics of qualitative research: Grounded theory procedures and techniques.* Newbury Park, CA: Sage.

Su, Z. (1997). Teaching as a profession and as a career: Minority candidates' perspectives. *Teaching and Teacher Education, 13*(3), 325–340.

Suárez-Orozco, C., & Suárez-Orozco, M. M. (1997). *Transformation: Immigration, family life and achievement motivation among Latino adolescents.* Stanford, CA: Stanford University Press.

Tabachnick, B. R., & Bloch, M. N. (1995). Learning in and out of school: Critical perspectives on the theory of cultural compatibility. In B. B. Swadener & S. Lubeck (Eds.), *Children and families "at promise": Deconstructing the discourse of risk* (pp. 187–209). Albany: State University of New York Press.

Talbert, J. E., & Ennis, M. (1990, April). *Teacher tracking: Exacerbating inequalities in the high school.* Paper presented at the annual meeting of the American Educational Research Association, Boston.

Tellez, K. (1999). Mexican-American preservice teachers and the intransigency of the elementary school curriculum. *Teaching and Teacher Education, 15*(5), 555–570.

Texas Education Agency. (1995). Texas teacher retention, mobility, and attrition: Teacher supply, demand, and quality policy research project [Report no. 6]. Austin, TX: Author.

Tharp, R., & Gallimore, R. (1988). *Rousing minds to life: Teaching, learning, and schooling in social context.* Cambridge, England: Cambridge University Press.

Thompson, A. (2004). Caring and colortalk. In V. Siddle Walker & J. Snarey (Eds.), *Race-ing moral formation African American perspectives on care and justice* (pp. 23–37). New York: Teachers College Press.

Thompson, K. (1980). Organizations as constructors of social reality. In G. Salaman & K. Thomson (Eds.), *Control and ideology in organizations* (pp. 216–236). Cambridge, MA: MIT Press.

Thompson, S. (2001). The authentic standards movement and its evil twin. *Phi Delta Kappan, 82*(5), 358–365.

Toppin, R. T., & Levine, L. (1992, April). *"Stronger in their presence": Being and becoming a teacher of color.* Paper presented at the annual meeting of the American Educational Research Association, San Francisco.

Tyack, D. B. (1974). *The one best system: A history of American urban education.* Cambridge, MA: Harvard University Press.

Valencia, R. R. (2002). The plight of Chicano students: An overview of schooling conditions and outcomes. In R. R. Valencia (Ed.), *Chicano school failure and success* (2nd ed., pp. 3–51). New York: Routledge-Falmer.

Valenzuela, A. (1999). *Subtractive schooling: U.S.-Mexican youth and the politics of caring.* Albany: State University of New York Press.

Villegas, A. M., & Davis, D. E. (2008). Preparing teachers of color to confront racial/ethnic disparities in educational outcomes. In M. Cochran-Smith, S. Feiman-Nemser, D. J. McIntyre, & K. E. Demers (Eds.), *Handbook on research in teacher education* (pp. 583–605). New York: Routledge.

Villegas, A. M., & Geist, K. (2008, April). *Profile of new teachers of color in U.S. public schools: A look at issues of quantity and quality.* Paper presented at the annual meeting of the American Educational Research Association, New York.

Villegas, A. M., & Irvine, J. J. (2010). Diversifying the teaching force: An examination of major arguments. *Urban Review, 42*(3), 175–192.

Villegas, A. M., & Lucas, T. (2002). *Educating culturally responsive teachers: A coherent approach.* Albany: State University of New York Press.

Villegas, A. M., & Lucas, T. (2004). Diversifying the teacher workforce: A retrospective and prospective analysis. In M. A. Smylie & D. Miretky (Eds.), *Developing the teacher workforce: 103rd yearbook of the National Society for the Study of Education, Part 1* (pp. 70–104). Chicago: University of Chicago Press.

Ware, F. (2006). Warm demander pedagogy: Culturally responsive teaching that supports a culture of achievement for African American students. *Urban Education, 41*(4), 427–456.

Weick, K. (1995). *Sensemaking in organizations.* Thousand Oaks, CA: Sage.

Weisman, E. M. (2001). Bicultural identity and language attitudes: Perspectives of four Latina teachers. *Urban Education, 36*(2), 203–225.

Wong, P. L., Murai, H., Berta-Avila, M., William-White, L., Baker, S., Arellano, A., & Enchandia, A. (2007). The M/M Center: Meeting the demand for multicultural, multilingual teacher preparation. *Teacher Education Quarterly, 34*(4), 9–26.

Yin, R. K. (1989). *Case study research: Design and methods.* Newbury Park, CA: Sage.

Yosso, T. (2005). Whose culture has capital? A critical race theory discussion of community cultural wealth. *Race Ethnicity and Education, 8*(1), 69–91.

Yosso, T. (2006). *Critical race counterstories along the Chicana/Chicano educational pipeline.* New York: Routledge.

Zeichner, K. (1996). Educating teachers for cultural diversity. In K. Zeichner, S. Melnick, & M. L. Gomez (Eds.), *Currents of reform in preservice teacher education* (pp. 133–175). New York: Teachers College Press.

Zeichner, K., & Gore, J. (1990). Teacher socialization. In W. R. Houston, M. Haberman, & J. Sikula (Eds.), *Handbook of research on teacher education* (pp. 329–348). New York: Macmillan.

Zitlow, C., & DeCoker, G. (1994). Drawing on personal histories in teacher education: Stories of three African American preservice teachers. *Teacher Education Quarterly, 21*(1), 67–84.

Zumwalt, K., & Craig, E. (2005). Teachers' characteristics: Research on the demographic profile. In M. Cochran-Smith & K. M. Zeichner (Eds.), *Studying teacher education: The report of the AERA panel on research and teacher education* (pp. 111–156). Mahwah, NJ: Erlbaum.

Index

About the Authors

Betty Achinstein is a researcher at the Center for Educational Research in the Interest of Underserved Students (CERIUS) at the University of California, Santa Cruz. Betty is responsible for designing and conducting research on new teacher socialization; supporting teachers of color in urban schools; professional and organizational contexts for teacher learning; organizational contexts that support Latina/o students; coaching, mentoring, and teacher professional development; diversity and equity for teachers and students; urban schooling; and teacher professional communities. She was a recipient of the 2006 Association of Teacher Educators' Distinguished Research Award. Her recent books include *Mentors in the Making: Developing New Leaders for New Teachers* (2006, Teachers College Press) and *Community, Diversity, and Conflict Among Schoolteachers: The Ties That Blind* (2002, Teachers College Press). Betty's most recent articles have been published in *American Educational Research Journal, Harvard Education Review, Review of Educational Research, Teaching and Teacher Education,* and *Teachers College Record.* She has taught on issues of diversity and education at UC Santa Cruz. Prior to her work with CERIUS, Betty was a senior researcher with The New Teacher Center at the University of California, Santa Cruz. She conducted research on new teacher socialization, mentoring, and induction in organizational contexts. She also co-facilitated the Leadership Network for Teacher Induction, a reform network of induction leaders in northern California. Before coming to the University of California, Santa Cruz, Betty Achinstein was Director of Member Schools at the Bay Area School Reform Collaborative. She also taught middle and high school students in Chicago, Boston, and New Jersey.

Rodney T. Ogawa is Professor of Education and Director of the Center for Educational Research in the Interest of Underserved Students (CERIUS) at the University of California, Santa Cruz. Rodney's research has focused on how and with what consequences school organizations adapt to educational policies. Currently, his research examines how and with what consequences the social structures of educational organizations are associated with the learning contexts they present and thus instructional interactions and educational outcomes. This work seeks to combine research and theory from the learning sciences and organization sciences to understand how educational organizations, such as schools and interactive science centers, can foster student learning with a particular focus on students from low-income and culturally non-dominant communities. Rodney's most recent work has been published in *Educational Researcher, American Educational Research Journal, Review of Educational Research, Harvard Education Review, Science Education,* and *Teachers College Record.* Rodney served as Vice President of Division A of the American Educational Research Association and currently serves on the editorial boards of the *American Educational Research Journal* and *Educational Evaluation and Policy Analysis.* Rodney has been selected as the 2010 recipient of the Roald Campbell Award for Lifetime Achievement in the academic field of educational leadership by the University Council for Educational Administration.